T0229811

Total Quality Management for Project Management

Kim H. Pries
Jon M. Quigley

CRC Press
Taylor & Francis Group
Boca Raton London New York

CRC Press is an imprint of the
Taylor & Francis Group, an **Informa** business
AN AUERBACH BOOK

CRC Press
Taylor & Francis Group
6000 Broken Sound Parkway NW, Suite 300
Boca Raton, FL 33487-2742

© 2013 by Taylor & Francis Group, LLC
CRC Press is an imprint of Taylor & Francis Group, an Informa business

No claim to original U.S. Government works

Printed in the United States of America on acid-free paper
Version Date: 20120518

International Standard Book Number: 978-1-4398-8505-5 (Hardback)

Library of Congress Cataloging-in-Publication Data

Pries, Kim H., 1955-
    Total quality management for project management / Kim H. Pries, Jon M. Quigley.
      p. cm.
    Summary: "Total Quality Management (TQM) tools alone are insufficient to guarantee successful endeavors. Project management expertise is also required to make the most of the information gleaned from TQM activities. This book shows you how to apply project management tools in conjunction with TQM activities and projects. It covers the application of TQM tools to the project management discipline by treating it as a process with deliverables. For the section of the book that covers the application of TQM to scrum, the authors demonstrate how these analytical methods can be used on the data produced within a scrum project"-- Provided by publisher.
    Includes bibliographical references and index.
    ISBN 978-1-4398-8505-5 (hardback)
    1. Total quality management. I. Quigley, Jon M. II. Title.

HD62.15.P7524 2012
658.4'013--dc23
    2012015719

Visit the Taylor & Francis Web site at
http://www.taylorandfrancis.com

and the CRC Press Web site at
http://www.crcpress.com

Contents

I.	Acknowledgments	xix
II.	About the Authors	xix
III.	Preface	xxi
IV.	The State of the Art?	xxiii

CHAPTER 1 – INTRODUCTION — 1

I.	Rubric	1
II.	Questions to Ponder	1
III.	Why TQM Is Important to the Project Manager	2
IV.	TQM Project Manager Scenario	2
V.	Total Quality Management Prerequisites	3
VI.	Organizational Attributes	5
VII.	PDCA—Shewhart Cycle	6
VIII.	Project Management	7
IX.	What Is Program Management?	8
X.	Why TQM Is Not Another Management Fix	10
XI.	How to Change the Culture	10
XII.	Eliminating Junk Activities	12
XIII.	Exercises	14

CHAPTER 2 – METRICS AND REQUIREMENTS   **15**

    I.   **Rubric**   **15**

    II.   **Questions to Ponder**   **15**

    III. **Why Metrics and Requirements Are Important to the Project Manager**   **16**

    IV. **TQM Project Manager Scenario**   **16**

    V.   **Product Requirements**   **17**

    VI. **Project Requirements**   **31**

    VII. **Derived Requirements**   **34**

    VIII. **Internal Requirements**   **34**

    IX. **Regulatory Requirements**   **34**

    X.   **Standards**   **35**

    XI. **Exercises**   **40**

CHAPTER 3 – TQM TOOLS   **41**

    I.   **Rubric**   **41**

    II.   **Questions to Ponder**   **41**

    III. **Why TQM Tools Are Important to the Project Manager**   **42**

    IV. **TQM Project Manager Scenario**   **42**

    V.   **Benefits to the TQM Project Manager**   **43**

VI.   **Pareto Chart**   44

VII.   **Scatter Plots**   46

VIII.   **Control Charts**   54

IX.   **Selection of Variable**   55

X.   **Flow Charts**   56

XI.   **Ishikawa Diagram (Fish Bone Diagram, Cause and
Effect Diagram)**   58

XII.   **Histogram/Bar Graphs**   58

XIII.   **Checklists/Check Sheets**   59

XIV.   **Exercises**   61

CHAPTER 4 – PROJECT MANAGEMENT TOOLS   63

I.   **Rubric**   63

II.   **Questions to Ponder**   63

III.   **Why Project Management Tools Are Important to the
Project Manager**   64

IV.   **TQM Project Manager Scenario**   64

V.   **Scope**   65

VI.   **Project Estimating Techniques**   66

VII.   **Project Budgeting**   75

VIII.   **Cost Estimating**   76

IX.   **Project Scheduling Fundamentals**   79

X.   **Communications Basics**   82

XI.   **Project Metrics and Control**   85

XII. **Risk Management Fundamentals**   96

XIII. **Project Termination Techniques**   100

XIV. **Exercises**   107

CHAPTER 5 – STATISTICS AND CONTROL   109

I.   **Rubric**   109

II.   **Questions to Ponder**   109

III. **Why Statistics and Control Are Important to the
      Project Manager**   110

IV.   **TQM Project Manager Scenario**   110

V.   **What Does Control Mean?**   111

VI.   **Project Risk and Management**   111

VII. **Attributes Data**   113

VIII. **Variables Data**   116

IX.   **Statistical Process Control (SPC) in Use**   116

X.   **Exercises**   120

CHAPTER 6 – PROCESS ANALYSIS AND IMPROVEMENT   **121**

    I.   **Rubric**   121

    II.   **Questions to Ponder**   121

    III.   **Why Process Analysis and Improvement Are Important to the Project Manager**   122

    IV.   **TQM Project Manager Scenario**   122

    V.   **Functional Decomposition**   123

    VI.   **Work Breakdown Structures**   123

    VII. **Scope of Work**   130

    VIII. **Exercises**   143

CHAPTER 7 – PROCESS CONTROL AND METRICS   **145**

    I.   **Rubric**   145

    II.   **Questions to Ponder**   145

    III.   **Why Process Controls and Metrics Are Important to the Project Manager**   146

    IV.   **TQM Project Manager Scenario**   146

    V.   **Risk Management**   147

    VI.   **Hazard Analysis and Critical Control Point Method**   155

    VII. **Scope**   156

    VIII. **Communication**   159

IX.   **Change Management**   160

X.   **Exercises**   174

CHAPTER 8 - INSPECTION AND QUALITY ASSURANCE   177

I.   **Rubric**   177

II.   **Questions to Ponder**   177

III.   **Why Inspection and QA Are Important to the Project Manager** 177

IV.   **TQM Project Manager Scenario**   178

V.   **Inspection with Attributes**   179

VI.   **Inspection with Variables**   181

VII.   **Skip Lot Inspection**   182

VIII.   **Continuous Sampling Plans**   182

IX.   **Dodge-Romig**   183

X.   **First Article Inspection**   183

XI.   **What Is a Meaningful Sample?**   183

XII.   **Failure Types**   184

XIII.   **Inspections and Project Management**   184

XIV.   **Exercises**   184

CHAPTER 9 – TRACKING METRICS   187

    I.   **Rubric**   187

    II.   **Questions to Ponder**   187

    III.   **Why Statistics and Control Are Important to the**
          Project Manager   188

    IV.   **TQM Project Manager Scenario**   188

    V.   **Tracking Metrics**   189

    VI.   **Product Quality over Time**   195

    VII. **Project Quality over Time**   196

    VIII. **Exercises**   196

CHAPTER 10 – OTHER SUPPORTING INITIATIVES   199

    I.   **Rubric**   199

    II.   **Questions to Ponder**   199

    III.   **Why Maturity Models Are Important to the Project Manager**   199

    IV.   **TQM Project Manager Scenario**   200

    V.   **Capability Maturity Models**   201

    VI.   **Exercises**   228

APPENDIX 1 – CHANGE MANAGEMENT   231

    I.   **Change Management**   231

    II.   **Configuration Management**   231

APPENDIX 2 – TEMP EXAMPLE   **241**

    I.   **Overview**   **241**

    II.   **Integrated Test Program Summary**   **245**

    III.   **Developmental Test and Evaluation Outline**   **247**

    IV.   **Operational Test and Evaluation Outline**   **251**

    V.   **Test and Evaluation Resource Summary**   **253**

APPENDIX 3 – TIEMPO   **257**

APPENDIX 4 – PRODUCT VERIFICATION   **263**

    I.   **Product Verification**   **263**

INDEX   **267**

LIST OF FIGURES

Figure 1.1 The butterfly effect from chaos theory suggests small causes can have large effects.   2

Figure 1.2 Example of a well-defined organization hierarchy.   4

Figure 1.3 The Shewhart Plan-Do-Check-Act (PDCA) cycle.   6

Figure 1.4 PM balancing act of the stakeholder expectations and resources.   8

Figure 1.5 Program-project hierarchy.   9

Figure 1.6 No silver bullet for project management!   10

Figure 1.7 Process flow from supplier to customer, whether internal or external.   11

Figure 1.8 Organization chart outline showing bottom-up improvement and top-down improvement - one key to cultural change.   12

Figure 1.9 Relations of different engineering organizations in a typical enterprise.   13

Figure 2.1 A typical instrument cluster for truck.   18

Figure 2.2 Variety of product requirements and demands.   19

Figure 2.3 A typical test "buck," with all controllers centralized and powered.   21

Figure 2.4 The entire vehicle HIL rig, showing the electrical controller unit (ECU) cabinet.   22

Figure 2.5 Hardware in the loop rig with expanded graphical controls.   23

Figure 2.6 Pressure sensor calibration fixture.   24

Figure 2.7 Oscilloscopes perform key analyses for the design and testing teams.   25

Figure 2.8 Signal generator.   26

Figure 2.9 An improvement in tolerance philosophy results in increased margins. 27

Figure 2.10 Acceptable switch performance. Note the clean signal response.   29

Figure 2.11 Unacceptable switch performance.   30

Figure 2.12 Use the test tool to develop stimuli that replicate challenges generally found on the vehicle.   31

Figure 2.13 Radar diagram comparing project targets to actual.   32

Figure 2.14 Note how charts and graphs provide quick, intuitive indication of project status.   33

Figure 2.15 Examples of regulatory agencies in the automotive world.   34

Figure 2.16 Seen is a SAE transient fixture, which replicates EMC bulk current injection and SAE transient simulation/injection.   35

Figure 2.17 The effect of insufficient data; insufficient detail makes it difficult to draw conclusions.   37

Figure 2.18 Range of testing is defined by criticality of the function.   38

Figure 2.19 Simplistic icons on a dashboard mislead more than they inform.   38

Figure 2.20 Artifacts.   39

Figure 3.1 An example of a typical Pareto chart showing the order data. The line helps discern the 80% point.   43

Figure 3.2 This Pareto chart shows the issues with an instrument cluster on a motor vehicle.   44

Figure 3.3 Pareto of instrument cluster failures by cost indicates where we find the most monetary damage.   45

Figure 3.4 Scatter charts show the correlation (not causation) between two factors. 46

Figure 3.5 Scatter plot of vehicle preparation for systems integration test shows a
range of durations to make the vehicle a suitable test subject.   48

Figure 3.6 Problems found with vehicle test subject that must be addressed prior to
systems integration testing.   49

Figure 3.7 Old method of manually testing harness continuity checks.   50

Figure 3.8 Drawings and pinout descriptions at the ready for manual testing of wire
harness.   51

Figure 3.9 The NXPro graphic - the tool that does the point-to-point wire harness
checks comparing an input file.   51

Figure 3.10 Dynalab and cabinet test fixture for automated point-to-point testing. 52

Figure 3.11 An example of a multi-lead sensor calibration setup.   53

Figure 3.12 Example of a flow chart.   57

Figure 3.13 Ishikawa (cause-and-effect, fish bone) diagram helps catalog potential
failure modes.   58

Figure 3.14 A typical normal distribution from relatively random data.   59

Figure 3.15 Example of countdown to production checklist.   60

Figure 3.16 Simple Gantt chart of an arbitrary project.   60

Figure 4.1 If we have a set of separated tasks, we must link them based on dependencies.   66

Figure 4.2 Tasks begin to fall into place as we analyze them.   67

Figure 4.3 Example of a network diagram, providing more information than we get from a Gantt chart.   67

Figure 4.4 The beta distribution models the array of values we can use to predict our task completion.   68

Figure 4.5 PERT task variance in tabular format.   69

Figure 4.6 PERT probability for durations.   69

Figure 4.7 The impact of task variation on dependent tasks.   70

Figure 4.8 Bugs or failures reported by individual allows us to check for potential skills problems.   73

Figure 4.9 Performance over time with average lines showing trends.   74

Figure 4.10 We begin to connect our tasks in a network that reflects the dependencies, also known as a directed graph.   79

Figure 4.11 The closer we get to the target, the better our estimates.   81

Figure 4.12 One model for communications.   83

Figure 4.13 A good escalation process provides a rational approach to bringing attention to a situation.   85

Figure 4.14 A tabular view of a relatively "good" schedule performance index.   86

Figure 4.15 Organization A SPI for multiple projects.   87

Figure 4.16 EVM demonstrated with a two stage project.   88

Figure 4.17 Example of Schedule Performance Index from a company with a wider variation.   88

Figure 4.18 Organization A example of Schedule Performance Index from a company with smaller variation.   90

Figure 4.19 Organization B example of Schedule Performance Index from a company with a wider variation.   91

Figure 4.20 Cost performance index tracking including the running average.   92

Figure 4.21 Cost performance index weekly performance report.   93

Figure 4.22 Organization B CPI with variation.   93

Figure 4.23 Organization A with a less variation in CPI.   94

Figure 4.24 A high-quality digital multimeter is a required tool for initial troubleshooting.   95

Figure 4.25 Risk identification and course of action selected based upon those risks.   97

Figure 4.26 Example of a product under development.   99

Figure 4.27 Gate passing statistics of an organization.   100

Figure 4.28 Project gate failures can be broken down by the objective (cost, quality and function) to learn where to focus our attention.   101

Figure 4.29 Failure to pass gate audits by department.   102

Figure 4.30 Illustration of the failure rate when a particular organization skips some of its development phases.   103

Figure 4.31 Closing the project compares the expected outcomes to the actual outcome.   106

Figure 5.1 Typical sample test material for a subsystem on a commercial vehicle.112

Figure 5.2 For statistical testing, we need to have a meaningful sample size.   113

Figure 5.3 Connector pin out fixture provides identification of the wires populated within the connector for both the male and female connector.   114

Figure 5.4 Connector inspection fixture built as a cardboard piece to prove concept.   115

Figure 5.5 Closeup of connector pin out fixture for inserting and testing pins during point to point testing or to repin the connector.   115

Figure 5.6 Xbar-R plots with anomalies.   116

Figure 5.7 CuSum plot with anomalies.   118

Figure 5.8 Notice the decline in failure rate as the product "settles down."   119

Figure 6.1 An illustration of how the work packages or individual WBS elements are in the accumulation of the budget for the project.   127

Figure 6.2 A graphical representation of the layered AIAG model for product and process development.   131

Figure 6.3 Nearly all product development models use a phased approach with numerous gates.   132

Figure 6.4 The AIAG PPAP structure provides a method for ensuring requirements are met.   137

Figure 7.1 Schedule performance index with risk limits identified for severe action from the PM similar to a control diagram only not based upon control knowledge but acceptable risk levels or performance expectations.   150

Figure 7.2 Pareto of configuration issues found during verification and test.   154

Figure 7.3 NI chassis from which modern testing occurs. The testing can be automated. The tool allows improvement in the repeatability and is faster than by hand or manually.   155

Figure 7.4 Screen shot from the NI test chassis test report for a vehicle module. 156

Figure 7.5 Automatically generated test report from NI test fixture.   157

Figure 7.6 Hardware in the loop simulator interfaces with the various components of the system via conditioned input and output signals.   158

Figure 7.7 Hardware in the loop rigs are employed to simulate the system and the component interactions.   159

Figure 7.8 A simple change management process.   162

Figure 8.1 Decade box used for testing product response to variation on the resistive inputs of the product.   178

Figure 8.2 An example of a product that would need to be inspected.   180

Figure 8.3 Demonstration of window motor performance over a range of units. 181

Figure A1.1 The complete kit of electroluminescent decal for automotive windshield power supply, interface connector and harness.   232

Figure A1.2 Product night view in car.   233

Figure A1.3 Illuminated graphic in the car from a distance.   233

Figure A4.1 Partial testing fault distribution can be used to estimate what other faults may remain.   263

Figure A4.2 Rate of faults found in various releases of software.   264

I. Acknowledgments

We know a number of people who need acknowledgment here.

John Wyzalek, the acquisitions editor at CRC, has been a great help with development, encouragement, and promotion of all books we have written for them.

I (Jon) would like to thank those who have contributed to refining the content and the quality of this book: John Bate, Barry Smith, Luis Correra, and Bill Klodaski to name a few. I appreciate your help with the wire harness test fixture and wire testing tool discussions. I would also like to thank John Bate for assisting with the wire harness tool development, and writing that section. I would like to thank all of the 18940 group at Volvo Trucks.

I would also like to thank Mr. Kim Pries. I learn much from our collaborations and I am ever appreciative of the opportunity to work with you.

Last but not the least, I would like to thank my family: my wonderful wife Nancy, and my son, Jackson, the best boy a daddy can have.

I (Kim) would like to thank my wife, Janise Pries, for reviewing this work; regardless, all mistakes belong to Jon and me. She is the love of my life, the reason I work such long hours to make a change in the world.

II. About the Authors

Kim H. Pries has four college degrees: B.A. in History from the University of Texas at El Paso (UTEP), B.S. in Metallurgical Engineering from UTEP, M.S. in Metallurgical Engineering from UTEP, and M.S. in Metallurgical Engineering and Materials Science from Carnegie-Mellon University. In addition to the degrees, he has the following certifications:

- APICS
  - Certified Production and Inventory Manager (CPIM)
- American Society for Quality (ASQ)
  - Certified Reliability Engineer (CRE)
  - Certified Quality Engineer (CQE)
  - Certified Software Quality Engineer (CSQE)
  - Certified Six Sigma Black Belt (CSSBB)
  - Certified Manager of Quality/Operational Excellence (CMQ/OE)
  - Certified Quality Auditor (CQA)
- Texas State Board of Education
  - Professional teaching license
  - Certified in mathematics (8-12)
  - Certified in special education (EC-12)
  - Certified in technological education (6-12)
  - Certified in Technological Applications (EC-12)

Mr. Pries worked as a computer systems manager (IT), a software engineer for an electrical utility, a scientific programmer on defense contracts and for Stoneridge, Incorporated (SRI), he has worked as:

- Software manager
- Engineering services manager
- Reliability section manager
- Product integrity and reliability director

In addition to his other responsibilities, Mr. Pries has provided Six Sigma training for both UTEP and SRI, and cost reduction initiatives for SRI. Mr. Pries is also a founding faculty member of Practical Project Management. Additionally, in concert with Mr. Quigley, Mr. Pries is the cofounder and principal with Value Transformation, LLC, a training, testing, cost improvement, and product development consultancy. He is also a cofounder of Counselor Connection LLC, a consultancy providing training and educational services to the regional educational service centers of Texas. Email Mr. Pries at kim.pries@valuetransform.com. Mr. Pries's first book was *Six Sigma for the Next Millennium: A CSSBB Guidebook*, now in a second edition as *Six Sigma for the New Millennium: A CSSBB Guidebook, Second Edition*.

Jon M. Quigley has three college degrees: B.S. in Electronic Engineering Technology from the University of North Carolina at Charlotte, MBA in Marketing, and M.S. in Project Management from City University of Seattle. In addition to the degrees, he has the following certifications:

- Project Management Institute
  - Project Management Professional (PMP)
- International Software Testing Qualifications Board (ISTQB)
  - Certified Tester Foundation Level (CTFL)

In addition to the degrees and certifications, Mr. Quigley has a number of patents and awards:

- US Patent Award 6,253,131 Steering wheel electronic interface
- US Patent Award 6,130,487 Electronic interface and method for connecting the electrical systems of truck and trailer
- US Patent Award 6,828,924 Integrated vehicle communications display (also a European patent)
- US Patent Award 6,718,906 Dual scale vehicle gauge
- US Patent Award 7,512,477 Systems and methods for guiding operators to optimized engine operation
- US Patent Award 7,629,878 Measuring instrument having location controlled display
- US Published Patent Application 20090198402 Method and system for operator interface with a diesel particulate filter regeneration system

- Volvo-3P Technical Award for global IC05 instrument cluster project 2005

- Volvo Technology Award for global IC05 Instrument cluster project April 2006

Mr. Quigley has worked in a variety of capacities within the new product development organizations:

- Embedded product development engineer (hardware and software)

- Product engineer

- Test engineer

- Project manager

- Electrical and electronic systems manager

- Verification and test manager

Mr. Quigley teaches project management classes at Forsyth Technical Community College as well as being on their project management advisory board. He is also on Western Carolina University's Masters of Project Management advisory board.

Collectively, Mr. Pries and Mr. Quigley are the authors of the books *Project Management of Complex and Embedded Systems: Ensuring Product Integrity and Program Quality*, and *Testing of Complex and Embedded Systems*. Additionally, they have authored numerous magazine articles and presentations at product development conferences about various aspects of product development and project management.

- *Embedded System Design*

- *Product Design and Development*

- *Embedded Design News (EDN)*

- *Software Test and Performance (STP)*

- *Electronics Weekly* (online)

- *DSP Design Line* (online)

- *Design Reuse* (online)

- *All Business* (online)

- *Quality* magazine (online)

- *Automotive Design Line and Automotive Design Line Europe* (online)

- *Project Magazine* (online)

- *Tech Online India* (online)

- *Embedded Design India* (online)

Additional information about Mr. Pries, Mr. Quigley, and Value Transformation, LLC can be found at http://www.valuetransform.com. There are areas there to ask the authors questions and exchange ideas about product development.

III. Preface

Product development is becoming increasingly complex. Technology is advancing. Projects are often populated by a diversity of people in a plurality of locations.

Effectively managing these complex projects requires attention to details. When we understand the range of possibilities for our project's execution we minimize the risk associated with that project. We can make plans that meet our typical performance. Thus we minimize the schedule risks associated with a project that has dates based upon hope and want with little or no basis in reality. When we drive our people to a schedule that they are aware is a death march, we set them up for failure.

Consider the company management the coach of the team. Certainly like any coach, we will want to push our people to perform better every day. However, a coach does not push the team to boundaries that the coach knows are not possible. For example, you will not hear a football coach ask his wide receiver to fly in the air for 50 yards. That is not a possible task. He may, however, see how fast that athlete is, and believe he can get him to run a fifty-yard dash in fewer seconds. Imagine what we do to the employee morale when we ask them to do what they know is not possible. Additionally, like a coach, we cannot show our team where we can improve if we do not know how that team presently performs. Further, our game strategy hinges upon what we have for a team. Is our team fast? Is it slow and strong? We have to either plan our strategy for our organization's goals, or we have to adapt our present team and playbook to the team we need to achieve our goals. To do so, we must know what we have for a playbook and team. To know what we have for a playbook and team requires measurements and analysis.

This book is about applying those Total Quality Management tools to both the line functions in your project as well as the project management discipline. You must study your organization to know what *really* can be achieved. A fist pound on a conference table with an arbitrarily set date that has no basis in reality may not motivate many people. While the world is plenty uncertain, we can learn something from the activities our organization performs. We may find out many of the things we assumed valid are not really true. We may find areas of the organization where a little effort will produce great performance improvements. We will have to study these things to find that out and TQM tools are key instruments in achieving that understanding.

The genesis of this book is in part serendipity. We were setting up a class that merged the discipline of Total Quality Management with Project Management. We realized we have never seen a book that applies these tools beyond the manufacturing realm. The more we thought on this, the more we realized while projects are unique, in each organization there are similarities between projects that could help "read the runes" as it were, to improve project future success. In the text below, we discuss the organization as a project factory bringing the TQM tools into the project management and line management functions of an organization. We treat each area in the organization as if it were a station in our manufacturing facility. An organization's process can help move the project from "every time is like the first time" to something that is not entirely unique every time. For example, consider a test department in a company that designs systems composed of embedded (software and hardware) and electrical components. That department may employ similar tools and will have some set of processes to accomplish the test and verification tasks at hand. We can critique our past and present to improve the future execution of our projects. At a very bare minimum, we will at least see the range of possible outcomes for the tasks we are monitoring within our organization. We can use this information to help with the future estimating of projects tasks, while considering that variation that we have seen in those processes and tasks.

IV. The State of the Art?

Progress, far from consisting in change, depends on retentiveness. When change is absolute there remains no being to improve and no direction is set for possible improvement: and when experience is not retained, as among savages, infancy is perpetual. Those who cannot remember the past are condemned to repeat it. In the first stage of life the mind is frivolous and easily distracted, it misses progress by failing in consecutiveness and persistence. This is the condition of children and barbarians, in which instinct has learned nothing from experience.

The Life of Reason, Volume 1
George Santayana
1905

In the years we have been working we have seen ample examples of use of hope as a tool for product development and managing project's in general. We call it hope, because we make our decisions to produce a certain outcome though we may actually know little about what it may take to be successful. Even when we do "know" our organization may ignore what is being said to meet this objective. We are not talking about the occasional event where something falls between the cracks. We are talking about those times when the people around us have been taking measurements to understand the issues and possibilities of that organization. Instead of building upon this, we summarily dismiss this person that is proving us wrong with this information as not being a team player or just a naysayer with a negative attitude.

A manufacturing engineer will pay attention to the capabilities of his equipment. If, for example, the demanded or needed throughput of product through that piece of equipment is higher than the equipment is capable of producing, some other course of action will be required. It may be possible to adjust the machine – customizing the machine to improve performance. It may be deemed necessary to otherwise upgrade the equipment. Maybe purchase another piece of equipment that meets this new throughput demand. Maybe the solution is to purchase another piece of equipment and between these two pieces of equipment meet the throughput demands. The rational engineer will not likely try to force the demanded product through the equipment, if the equipment has a throughput limitation and expect all to be well.

Let us consider a product made of a particular type of plastic that has a specific melting point. It is not likely this product will maintain the features desired or meet the customer's demands above a certain level of heat stimulus. It would not seem likely that a sensible person would violate the physical properties of the material and complain about the predictable failure. The person designing the product would benefit greatly from knowing the attribute of the plastic prior to using the material in a design.

What do these things have in common? Well, this is exactly the sort of thing that goes on in organizations every day! This happens in product development and project management. Many believe that "the old college try" will save us. Those individuals who point to real data – to show the "reality" are derided as being naysayers; they are not team players. These people are overly negative. What does it say for those of the team that ignore the historical record? The time-honored saying attributed to George Santayana: "Those who cannot remember the past are condemned to repeat it."

CHAPTER 1 – INTRODUCTION

I. Rubric

	Novice	Sr. Novice	Journey-man	Sr. Jour-neyman	Master
Understand TQM	x	x	x	x	x
Understand need for TQM		x	x	x	x
PDCA loop			x	x	x
Project hier-archies				x	x
Scheduling				x	x
Budgeting				x	x
Meeting control				x	x
Quality					x
Reliability					x

II. Questions to Ponder

- Does TQM applied to project management (PM) provide any added value?
- Is TQM too abstract or is it really down-to-earth?
- Why is the standard flailing and floundering approach so seductive?
- Does the enterprise really need TQM in project management?
- If our organization transforms itself such that it achieves a higher level of performance, have we really accomplished anything?
- Does TQM/PM have any marketing value?
- Why are there so many quality tools and why are they little used by PMs?
- Why are the quality models different and yet the same (compare and contrast)?
- Isn't TQM just another way to make somebody some money?
- Is there an ISO version? Isn't ISO-9000 largely discredited?
- Why can't we just "roll our own" approach to process improvement?
- Are processes loose guidelines or should we use a disciplined approach?
- Does your organization systematically critique development and project processes to learn how those processes really work and to shorten and improve the processes and products?

III. Why TQM Is Important to the Project Manager

Total Quality Management (TQM) involves the application of quality techniques to all segments of the enterprise. We are recommending that TQM be applied to project management also.

Most of the project managers (PMs) we have known have focused first and foremost on the project schedule, next on the project budget, and lastly on the project quality issues. We suspect this approach may even be so topsy-turvy as to be backwards. At no point have we seen project managers applying any sensible quality techniques to their own process. Ultimately, each project we witnessed devolved into a weekly nagging meeting that lasted at least an hour as the PM desperately tried to assert some level of debatable control by doing a futile "time line review." We know that powerful methods exist to eliminate the flailing usually seen, particularly at the end of the project.

Figure 1.1 The butterfly effect from chaos theory suggests small causes can have large effects.

This project flailing my be visible at the end of the project; however, the reasons for the flailing are well before this point, usually in the planning phase (see Figure 1.1). The TQM tools demonstrated in the following chapters will show how planning that does not derive from past experience is really not planning at all, but going through the motions. TQM and developing a learning organization are tied together.

IV. TQM Project Manager Scenario

A. Situation

The project manager (PM) created a standard project schedule using Microsoft Project. This individual did not use the tool for budgeting and derived no project metrics (which are available readily in this tool). The PM did not understand resource allocation and the need to inspect the truth-value of statements from supporting departments. Product launch was soon to arrive and insufficient material was available to manufacture a sustainable stream of product. The purchasing activity was in the midst of switching over from MRO (maintenance, repair, and operations) buying where lot sizes are any size—to MRP (manufacturing resource planning) buying, where materials are purchased in bulk lots to ensure an economic order quantity. The enterprise was in danger of shutting down the customer.

B. Objective

Bring materials acquisition and release back to sanity.

C. Action

The initial action was to allow MRO buying as well as MRP purchasing. A company director indicated that "this is World War II and I want to see piles of the correct materials" as an alternative to misguided interference from a lean manufacturing initiative. This director also recommended that the materials handling people "kit" the material. "Kitting" occurs when the materials staff counts the required components for a build of X parts and puts everything in a kit. It is short of lean manufacturing, but it ensures the correct parts are available, although it does present the risk of shutting down the line if a part is missing (which would happen anyway).

D. Results

Production was brought back into a sane sequence. The PM was encouraged to inspect the stockroom to visually verify that the correct parts were available.

E. Aftermath

Sadly, this approach worked so well it was never used again. The enterprise continued to ignore the MRO/MRP discontinuity for all future projects. This painful lesson was not learned.

V. Total Quality Management Prerequisites

Before we can even begin to discuss total quality management for project managers the organization must fulfill some prerequisites. Some of these include the following:

- A reasonably well-established hierarchy (see Figure 1.2)
- A set of documented processes
- Individuals willing to champion the new initiative
- Management support for the new initiative
- An understanding of the benefits of total quality management
- A corporate culture that does not game the system

We're going to look at total quality management from two perspectives, that of total quality management on project management and that of project management on total quality management. Out of this dialectical relationship arises something better than either item by itself. It may seem a trifle odd, but most organizations do not apply their quality practices to the project management process. One would think that the launch of the new product for the creation of a new service would be sufficient to drive quality practices into project management. In our experience, this outcome is just simply not the case.

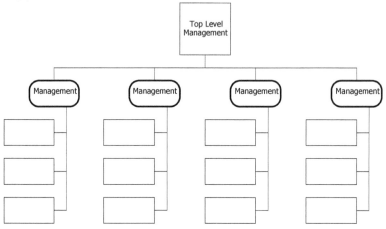

Figure 1.2 Example of a well-defined organization hierarchy.

Consider organizations that routinely develop a set of products or services. These companies have a set of processes and are structured in such a way to deliver these products to the consumer. We will call a hypothetical version of such a company a project factory for lack of a better name. Each stage or functional area (example systems engineering, embedded engineering, and verification) will have a set of activities that are performed using some set of defined processes. The same is true for the project management discipline. In the end, we want to show how these tools can be applied to these areas to continually understand how your organization works, and more importantly, how to continually improve that performance.

Some readers may feel that total quality management is passé in the age of Six Sigma quality and manufacturing Lean practices. Each approach has its place. Our take on the situation is as follows:

- Six Sigma is the obvious choice for cost reductions and other cost-cutting activities

- Lean is the primary tool used for waste reduction

- Lean Six Sigma is a conflation of the Six Sigma algorithm and hard-money approach with Lean objectives

- TQM is the approach of choice when an organization or a part of an organization desires to perform a total overhaul of the complete system

In most cases, Six Sigma is not applied to an organization as a systemic approach to effect organizational transformation, but rather, the approach is used to look for cost reduction opportunities that can improve the bottom line. When not afflicted with hucksterism, the Lean approach can be used to save more money, improve production flow, and improve the bottom line. The same applies to Lean Six Sigma. Unfortunately, the lack of a systemic approach doesn't always move these worthy methodologies in the direction of maximizing customer satisfaction. In short, we suggest that TQM is relevant when thoughtfully applied and we feel that the approach is particularly relevant when dealing with the frequent nightmare that pertains to project management, especially with regard to scheduling and budgeting—not to mention the quality of the product or service. In the end it is the project manager who must balance the competing demands from the project organization as well as other stakeholders in the project.

Project management activities produce metrics just as the line organization does. If an organization has aspirations of being a project factory, for example, these same tools would be required as they would in a manufacturing environment. Specifically the tools used in total quality management are applied to the manufacturing discipline. In our project factory world, the line organization would be the various stations in the production process.

While all projects by definition are unique, we can find considerable routine within that uniqueness. Consider, for example, an organization that produces embedded products for a vehicle. For any given organization or industry, there are certain steps often considered to be a prudent approach to the work. For our embedded automotive company we may always start with generating a set of concepts and then a critique of those concepts to improve the product before we start putting hardware together. In this way, the concept generation activity, for example, could be considered a step in the manufacturing process of the project. Taking the perspective that this is a manufacturing station, we can apply the TQM tools to understand the capability and variation in the production processes via the specific activity at that station. While this explicitly speaks to the line organization, it need not be limited to that. By extension, these tools can be applied to any of the developmental processes as well as the data that falls in the area of project management.

VI. Organizational Attributes

Any organization that chooses to pursue an application of total quality management to project management and, in some cases, program management must possess certain attributes. Some of these attributes are as follows:

- Training in total quality management (or Six Sigma)
- Enough structuring to support project management (in other words, we are not dealing with a fly-by-night entrepreneurial experimentation)
- Clearly defined roles
- Defining processes
- Willing to adhere to those processes

We have been surprised during our careers when we discover that some companies don't understand the flow of material, services, and information from suppliers into the enterprise process and out to their customers. These flows should be well-documented. If we are discussing an ISO 9001 company, then we know many of the processes will be documented because it is part of the requirements for ISO-9000 certification. With regard to the accounting and fiducial governance function in North America, the Sarbanes-Oxley regulatory requirements will drive a significant level of process documentation. Why are we focusing on process documentation? Documented processes make it easier to measure baseline activities to determine if our interventions have produced salutary results. Since our process description helps us to uncover the areas to improve, it becomes necessary to actually perform to that process definition. It is surprising how many companies seem to abandon any notion of process in the attempt to get a product out the door by an arbitrary date. The processes of corporate governance and fastidious product release can be thrown out the door in the face of a delivery date.

One of the most egregious areas of inadequacy in project management is an activity that lies at the very heart of what project managers do for a living. We are talking about scheduling. In our experience, product or service testing often occurs under pressure and at very short notice towards the end of the project—often with insufficient time to do a complete job! What we have seen too frequently is the release of a product or service before it should be released to any kind of customer. What often follows is a mix of customer dissatisfaction, product returns, and occasional recalls. Hence, one of our goals in this book is to highlight techniques and mindsets that will improve this situation and reduce post-product release heartburn. These launch miscues cost the organization dearly and often lead to fire fights of constantly fixing what was just delivered. There are not many organizations these days that have a surplus of available staff. Spending unplanned amounts of time fixing that which was just launched comes at the price of appropriate diligence for the next project or product in the list for the organization to complete. Thus we end up with the next product being launched with errors, taking away from the following product. The result is a seemingly never-ending forest fire that consumes resources and leaves the team perpetually behind schedule.

VII. PDCA—Shewhart Cycle

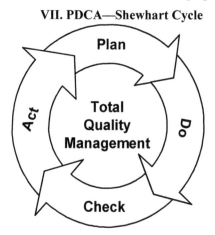

Note: The combination of Check and Act constitutes control

Figure 1.3 The Shewhart Plan-Do-Check-Act (PDCA) cycle.

We believe that the Shewhart cycle[1], while simplistic in appearance, is a potent weapon in the battle against incompetent project closure. The acronym PDCA refers to plan, do, check, and act. Before we start, we need to look at what the issues are and formulate a plan for action. Once we have a plan, we can begin to act, which is the "do" phase of the process. After we have executed the plan, we check on our results and compare them with our documented expectations. If results do not match expectations, then we act to correct our issues. We do not execute this loop one time: we continue to execute this loop in perpetuity; in effect, we have an infinite loop. This sequence has considerable common ground with the project management discipline. The project has a catalyst that starts the project activity, followed by planning, sampling, and controlling until the project closes.

The Shewhart cycle, then, lies at the heart of any good TQM initiative (see Figure 1.3). We must understand that the "infinite loop" idea is our future and always will be our future. We must continue cycling through the sequence because factors change and customer expectations shift and we certainly wish to remain competitive. Many project management people will no doubt recognize the PDCA as part of project management as well. This is yet another connecting point between these two areas.

VIII.   Project Management

Nearly all project management approaches bear a family resemblance. For each embodiment, we are balancing stakeholder demands and resources (see Figure 1.4). For example, here are the primary components as we see them:

- Customer's needs
- Functional analysis
- System synthesis
- Evaluation, options, and decisions
- Work breakdown structures
- Specification and/or requirements development
- Configuration management throughout
- Technical reviews, audits, reflective practice
- Test and evaluation
- Technical performance measurement
- Risk management
- Change management (usually tied to configuration management)
- Product life-cycle costing and management
- Manufacturing/producibility
- Product retirement and closure

The following table shows one set of activities in roughly the order in which they might occur in order to launch a product. Clearly, if we are launching a service, some of the items will be different or will disappear completely.

Activity	Responsible
System acquisition	Procurement / marketing / sales
Program initiation	Executive management
Concept exploration	Engineering / marketing
Concept selection	Engineering
Demonstration / validation	Engineering
Program kill or no-kill	Project management
Product development	Project management / engineering
Production / process specification	Manufacturing
Production	Manufacturing
Deployment	Manufacturing / logistics
Operation and support	Customer service
Disposal	Project management

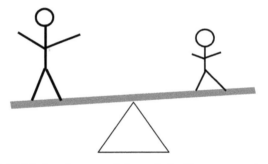

Figure 1.4 PM balancing act of the stakeholder expectations and resources.

Of course, not every project will follow exactly this sequence and, in some cases, we will want to break some of these pieces into smaller chunks for more detailed management.

IX. What Is Program Management?

Depending on how we define our terms, we usually understand a program to be composed of projects; hence, program management is a superset of project management. We provide an illustration in Figure 1.5. However, this definition is not always the case—one of us worked for a company that used the "program manager" title as an alternative to "project manager," probably because the customer referred to their new vehicle as the result of a "program."

One way to look at programs is to think about Department of Defense or NASA. An aircraft carrier is a program to be managed. Each major component of the program is also a project; for example, the steam catapult would easily be a sizeable project in its own right. Program management is management of project managers and requires a set

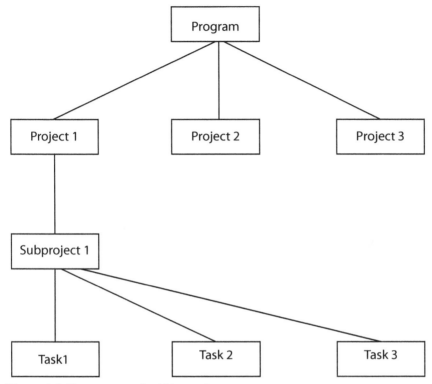

Figure 1.5 Program-project hierarchy.

of skills that include the ability to see the program as a whole as well as see the large configuration of the pieces. The program manager must consider relationships even more than does a project manager; except, in the case of a program, we may be dealing with entirely different suppliers and contractors during the course of the development.

If a program is composed of projects then of what is a project composed? We believe the term "subprojects" to be adequate, although it is easy to see how naming conventions could become inane if this idea is carried too far. Any project may break down into subprojects naturally; subproject are usually defined and documented during the creation of the work breakdown structure (WBS). Simple projects will often use the term "tasks."

This hierarchical breakdown is not directly a part of TQM, but the structure can make it easier to see how the pieces relate during a program or project and also allow us to determine the impact on the total program of a modification to a subproject or task. The study of parts and wholes is called "mereology." We will not spend much time on this philosophical topic; however, we think it important that the program or project manager maintain a level of "systems thinking." A systemic approach is one of the few ways to reduce the unintended consequences of a course of action, since we are balancing the details against the totality.

Figure 1.5 shows a representation of one approach to the program-project hierarchy.

Note that we are saying "one" approach, since other aspects could easily be defined for a particular enterprise. The names do not matter so much as the concept of the hierarchy, which resembles a taxonomy.

X.   Why TQM Is Not Another Management Fix

People who remain current with the popular business literature have seen many flavors of the week cross their desks; for example:

- Re-engineering
- Six Sigma
- Lean
- Lean Six Sigma
- Total Quality Management
- Business Process Management
- The Management Matrix
- Management by Objective

Sometimes we have been victims of the search for a silver bullet (see Figure 1.6) that will suddenly convert a mediocre company into a great one. Is TQM any different? That depends on how we internalize our view of this methodology. If we view it as

Figure 1.6 No silver bullet for project management!

another management trick to get workers to push harder to gain some hypothetical reward, then we will have a self-fulfilling prophecy. However, if we sincerely use this collection of techniques from our own point of view rather than that of upper management, we can make our workplace a better place to be.

Ultimately, as with Six Sigma or any of the other methodologies, we will basically get out of it what we put into it. A cliché, yes, but a meaningful one in this case. The rest of this book shows how we can use TQM to improve our project and program management activities. Keep in mind that we wish to implement TQM using sound project management practices, much in the same way that Six Sigma projects are managed.

XI. How to Change the Culture

We have often heard upper-level managers orate about "transformation" in the enterprise in hyperbolic terms, as if one could establish a magic program and in a matter of months, change the enterprise. We suspect upheavals of this nature are more counter-productive than productive.

In our experience, a cultural change will either occur naturally or as the product of thousands of small changes focused on a goal or set of goals. The small changes work if we have high-frequency feedback so that we can make course corrections and adjust either our goals or the thousands of small changes. One of the TQM approaches is called "Kaizen," which dovetails well with the thousands of small tactics approaches. We have never seen a successful cultural change without one of these two events occurring: evolution or planned adaptation.

One of the difficulties in the "myriad" approach is the method for managing this substantial amount of activity and staying on track. One tool that can help is the Hoshin Kanri management method, which is effectively a top-down and bottom-up method that aligns all parts of the organization when executed well.

Why do we have to use the tactics of a thousand changes? We have seen employees balk at massive, "transformational" changes because they are afraid of what may come and prefer the familiar to the unknown. By using this "myriad" method, we are able to slowly manifest change without the churning and fear present during large changeovers. Likewise, we have seen a bottom-up approach used at one company where all of the groups within a department designed how the individual groups would work. Each group clarified its responsibility and identified what it needed to successfully deliver (see Figure 1.7).

- Supplier
- Input
- Process
- Output
- Customer

The output to each downstream customer was considered as well as what constituted a successful delivery well-provided with reviews at the handoff points. In

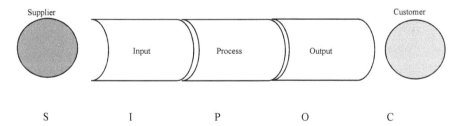

Figure 1.7 Process flow from supplier to customer, whether internal or external.

the end, it was a clearly defined, rational approach that never arrived at completion, at least in part due to lack of upper management endorsement. The results on those developing the processes could easily be witnessed and were quite negative. Exclusive top-down or bottom-up approaches seldom work (see Figure 1.8) thanks to the lack of coordination and buy-in. From a personal perspective, not only does bottom-up not

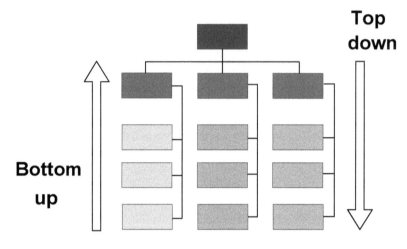

Figure 1.8 Organization chart outline showing bottom-up improvement and top-down improvement - one key to cultural change.

work, the failure comes at a price to the morale of the people that were looking for the change to an improved state, those performing the work.

XII. Eliminating Junk Activities

We address non-essential activities here because this task is not often considered during TQM activities. What is a junk activity? We might suggest several non-competing criteria, any one of which might be sufficient:

- It doesn't improve profitability
- It is in a procedure but seems to have no purpose
- "We always did it this way"
- "The customer wants it this way" when we are really speaking about a customer representative who may or may not have that authority
- The standards book appears to recommend an activity that makes no sense (an example of this occurs when we retest features we have already tested because we are now doing "validation" instead of "verification." A test that tells us nothing new is a worthless test!)
- Our activities are performed mechanically according to somebody's scheme of how project management "should" be done (could be a national "standards" organization)

- Team meetings last over fifteen minutes or half an hour
- Full time line reviews occur in the name of "making sure everybody knows," which is sort of like casting sand on the wind and hoping the result will be the Taj Mahal

Figure 1.9 is a crude illustration of the areas for developing an embedded product that is part of an entire system. Each of these areas can be considered a station within the production process. It does not matter if the production process is a design. Tools such as value mapping make it possible to understand how the pieces fit together and allow for determination of the critical parts used to deliver the desired quality in time. In matrix organizations, we have the project manager and the line manager working together and sharing the responsibility for project delivery The line manager is the person responsible for the performance within a specific cell or area. The project manager would work with the verification group manager and some portion of the verification line team to identify the scope of the work for testing and verifying the project's product. In this case, the line manager or members of the verification line organization will provide the project manager with the processes for performing their part of the project work.

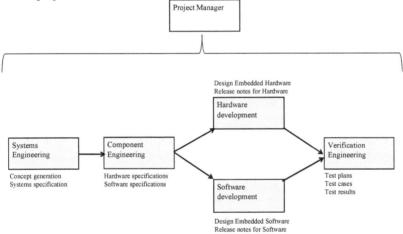

Figure 1.9 Relations of different engineering organizations in a typical enterprise.

Each line manager must work with the other line functions to understand how upstream parts of the organization contribute to the downstream portions of the organization. Ultimately, each link in the chain knows what it gets from the preceding link, and what it will deliver to the subsequent part of this metaphorical manufacturing line.

We don't think it is necessary for the project manager to identify these interfaces for every project, however, the project manager must make sure the contributions of each team and the requirements of the dependent groups are met. If the project manager is fortunate, he or she brings a variety of personal experiences from various line organizations and understands the rationale for each part of the organization.

XIII.   Exercises

- Explain why total quality management (TQM) is an important concept to the project manager (PM).

- Create 5-10 variations of the Shewhart PDCA loop (one example is Six Sigma with the define-measure-analyze-improve-control sequence).

- Create a protocol for project sustenance; in short, explain the role of the PM subsequent to product launch.

- Explain the role of the PM during project maturity/decline and project closure/ termination.

- Explain whether or not you believe Hoshin Kanri brings anything new to the strategy and tactics table—make sure you understand the approach used in Hoshin before you begin.

- Decide whether TQM was, in fact, superseded by Six Sigma and defend your point of view with well-reasoned arguments.

- Explain why quality practices have not been applied to the project management process—was this an oversight or deliberate?

- Suggest some reasons for the lack of formal contingency planning among project managers.

- Define the role of the project manager in the enterprise and how he or she fits into the prevailing hierarchies, particularly if you have a personal example.

- Write an essay that defends a management approach: project-based, matrix, weak matrix, and pyramid.

- Create a protocol for capturing "lessons learned."

- Why are lessons learned so easy to speak about and so difficult to do? Come up with an explanation for this anomaly.

- Difficult: brainstorm 100 ways to capture lessons learned and choose 20 of these for future assessment.

Endnotes

1. Deming, W. Edwards. *Out of the Crisis*. Cambridge, MA: MIT Press, 1982.

CHAPTER 2 – METRICS AND REQUIREMENTS

I.   Rubric

	Novice	Sr. Novice	Journey-man	Sr. Jour-neyman	Master
KPIs	x	x	x	x	x
Pareto chart		x	x	x	x
Priority set-ting			x	x	x
Require-ments tear-down				x	x
Attribute re-quirements				x	x
Variables require-ments				x	x
Software re-quirements				x	x
Require-ments templating					x
Super-re-quirements					x
Testing re-quirements					x
Testing breakpoints					x
Test results acceptability					x

It is not enough to know the requirements, although that is a leap forward. We also need to know how to prove that requirements have been satisfied. Even more troubling is the responsibility to elucidate requirements that the customer has not specified and for which we may have no standard.

II.   Questions to Ponder

• Do requirements metrics provide any added value?

• Are requirements metrics too abstract or are they really practical?

• Why is the "winging it" approach so seductive?

- Does the enterprise really need requirements metrics?
- Does our ability with requirements metrics have any marketing value?
- Why do we have so many metrics?
- Why are requirements metrics different and yet the same (compare and contrast)?
- Are requirements metrics just another way to make somebody some profit?
- Is there an ISO version and is it better than the other models?
- Why can't we just "roll our own"?
- How does your organization decide what areas to measure and what metrics to follow?
- Should project management office help identify those measurements or is it strictly line management? Or both for matrix organizations?
- List activities a project manager can use to elicit customer requirements.
- How are customer needs translated into product requirements?
- How are the requirements validated?
- How does variation impact the project manager's job?
- What is the role of the project manager regarding competing demands and goals?
- What project and product risks are associated with the use of standards?
- What does our project management organization do to continuously improve?
- How does the variation in the product and project cost impact the bottom line of the organization?
- What is the difference among tampering, natural optimism, or self-preservation?
- Is your organization data and information driven – or is it "the old college try"?

III. Why Metrics and Requirements Are Important to the Project Manager

If we do not measure, we have no idea where we are in the continuum of enterprise accomplishment. Likewise, if we are conducting a project, then, without metrics, we neither know where we are or what it takes to get to where we desire. One starting point for metrics is during the conceptual specification and requirements phase.

The project manager should enforce metrics acquisition from the onset of the project and never let up. The only time metrics capture should stop is for a specific metric and only if that metric has been clearly shown to be meaningless. If we start off well, then we increase the chances we will finish well!

IV. TQM Project Manager Scenario

A. Situation

The customer supplied a written specification with requirements for a specific communications protocol, previously unimplemented by the supplier. The supplier "analyzed" the specification, but did not do a specification tear-down as a means to elicit all the requirements.

Unfortunately, the requirements analysis was so inept, nearly half the desired implementation did not occur, causing the customer substantial anguish, real and imagined.

B. Objective

The goal was to meet all customer requirements, or failing that, to have the customer modify the requirements to something that was achievable.

C. Action

The full protocol was later implemented by the supplier; in fact, years later. The supplier claimed a communications error on the part of the participants was the root cause for the issue. The relationship with the customer was damaged by this interchange.

D. Results

An engineering executive subsequently implemented a technique for using the table function in a word processor as a tool for a specification tear-down. After this change, no requirements were lost so long as this individual was in charge of the engineering function. Heroic leadership is not the same thing as systemic improvement.

E. Aftermath

This enterprise quit using this approach and fell back into the same pattern of self-indulgent assumptions seen previously.

V.   Product Requirements

Product requirements come from a variety of places. The sources of our requirements can be legal or specific to industry origin. The customers can be internal and external to the company. For example, the manufacturing portion of our company may have specific requirements for how the product is to be put together. We may have requirements based on the capability of our pick and place machines (for reflow soldering and surface mount electronics). These requirements are in addition to the requirements from the end customer. Some requirements point to other requirements; for example, the life expected from a battery-operated unit and the weight of that unit. These two requirements may point to a certain battery technology for power density and size.

Capturing requirements is not a simple matter either (an example of a product is illustrated in Figure 2.1). Requirements elicitation requires attention to prioritizing and balancing of many demands from both internal and external customers. We have to know what is really meant when we ask questions of our customers. This requires interviews and clarifying follow up questions until we achieve mutual understanding. If we do not already know the sorts of stimuli to which the product will be subjected we may have to learn this information through field studies. We can have competing requirements such as the cost of the product and the number of features or the weight and the battery power required.

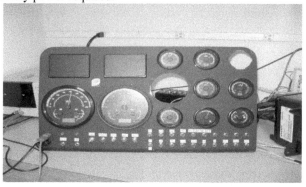

Figure 2.1 A typical instrument cluster for truck.

Product requirements set the stage for any project (see Figure 2.2). The approach of our project to meeting the customer's need will depend on these requirements. Our project approach in turn establishes some of the risks to which a project will suffer. For example, if we have a microcontroller-based product, we know we are going to be exposed to software risks. If we select a microcontroller that is still under development, then we expose our project to the possibility the microcontroller will not make it to production and this will affect our product delivery schedule.

A. Specifications and Requirements

Designing and building a new product is not really possible if the requirements for that product are unknown. If we don't know the target, we will be lucky if we hit any meaningful target—including the business applications of the product. A dialogue between the engineering or technical community and the customer is necessary to clarify the goals of the product. Ultimately, this activity will put details into the product scope and will identify the success criteria for the project as well as the product (see Figure 2.2).

According to the Department of Defense *Systems Engineering Fundamentals*, the characteristics of a good requirement are:

- Achievable or obtainable
- Verifiable (objectively and quantitatively)
- All information to understand customer's needs (complete)
- Expressed in terms of need, not solution
- All requirements are consistent – no conflicts among the requirements
- Appropriate level of detail for the hierarchy under definition (systems definition does not contain component detail requirements)

Figure 2.2 Variety of product requirements and demands.

According to IEEE Standard 830-1998: *Recommended Practice for Software Requirements Specifications*, the characteristics of good SRS requirements are:

- Correct
- Unambiguous
- Complete
- Consistent
- Ranked for importance
- Verifiable
- Modifiable
- Traceable

According to the Department of Defense *Systems Engineering Fundamentals*, there are six types of requirements:

- Customer requirements
- Function requirements

- Performance requirements
- Design requirements
- Derived requirements
- Allocated requirements

We list a number of ways of culling the product requirements.

- Customer interviews
- End user interviews
- Walk (talk) through
- Requirements decision tools
    - Requirements and constraints matrix (juxtapose the product requirements to design constraints)
    - Pugh matrix (prioritize product needs and evaluate design meeting those needs)
- Design documentation reviews
- Simulation or visualization

Understanding the demands and key metrics for the product with the customer goes a long way to confirming that we met targets. It is possible to meet the letter of the requirements and still have a product that does not meet customer expectations. While this may provide an "out" for the supplying organization ("we built what you asked for!"), it will not help the relationship with the customer.

We have seen specifications written using one of two major viewpoints:

- The customer puts together a specification based on market research and understanding of end user needs
- The customer contracts the supplier to put together the specification, since the supplier is presumed to possess significantly more expertise for the specific product than does the customer

A product or service specification is a description of the desired product. If we are fortunate, this document will contain enough requirements for us to begin a requirements analysis. Of course, if we write the specification ourselves, we have little excuse for leaving out requirements.

In our experience, most specifications are written by engineers and use large amounts of narrative text in addition to drawings, tables, graphs, and other information. The difficulty with narrative text is that it can quickly and easily become ambiguous. Ambiguous specifications lead to mistaken requirements, particularly if the customer/client review system is not functioning correctly or we have inadequate communications.

In the early 2000s, we did some experiments with tagged text in XML to see if we could rationalize the production of requirements. We chose a small set of meaningful tags and expressed the specification in this format—it was not great literature. Subsequently, we used an XSL script to transform the XML source into an HTML

Figure 2.3 A typical test "buck," with all controllers centralized and powered.

requirements document and we ran another XSL script to generate information for later importation into a spreadsheet to use in testing. Both of the derived documents were usable and demonstrated the feasibility of using this approach. Unfortunately, this initiative received little or no management support and faded away quickly.

In some advanced organizations, we will use simulation and modeling to develop the requirements (see Figure 2.3). Using the right equipment—a systems simulator that would use a combination of hardware and software such as hardware in the loop simulator (see Figure 2.4 and Figure 2.5)—we can investigate the way we can meet the requirements in advance of making the product. Using such a device, it is possible to model the performance of a set of components, allowing exploration as part of the requirements elicitation. This helps guide our work in developing the specifications and minimizes some of the risk associated with capturing requirements. With these tools, it is possible to show the customer and other stakeholders how a proposed system could work, even to the point of understanding performance demands. However, this work is only as valuable if the models in the simulation are accurate and how well they account for system variations.

Figure 2.4 The entire vehicle HIL rig, showing the electrical controller unit (ECU) cabinet.

We believe the introduction of a new product or service is really a proposal to solve a problem. Like any other problem-solving technique, we need to define the problem precisely and accurately insofar as we are able (it is not always possible to make a problem concrete!) and then proceed through the problem-solving steps. We suspect a more concise format for specifications would lead to fewer requirements analysis errors although we have no statistical data in this regard (...remember, the initiative died on the vine!).

B. Quality

Quality requirements, insofar as they are known, should be defined as early as possible in the project. Early definition of quality requirements allows the development team to adjust their design to meet customer quality expectations.

Sometimes exploration is needed to understand the requirements. Figure 2.6 is a piece of test equipment that is used to calibrate flow rate sensors. A known quantity of defined fluid is pushed through the hoses. The calibrated sensors are then used to measure the flow rate of various fluids (radiator fluid being one) of a vehicle when used in the dynamometer (a dynamometer is a device that simulates road loading on the wheels and tires of a vehicle).

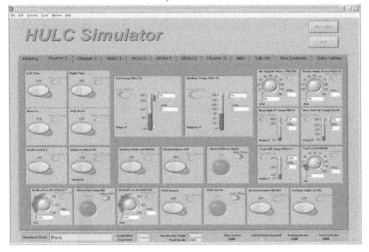

Figure 2.5 Hardware in the loop rig with expanded graphical controls.

The development team will also have to consider relevant standards and regulatory requirements; for example, for the automotive industry:

- Society of Automotive Engineers (SAE) standards

- Automotive Industry Action Group (AIAG) requirements

- United States Department of Transportation (USDOT) regulations, including the Federal Motor Vehicle Safety Standards (FMVSS)

- U.S. Code regulations

- Potential insurance requirements

- State requirements

- Other national requirements if the product will be sold in other venues; for example, Canada or Mexico

- Internal quality requirements

The last item my raise some eyebrows! Can we not redefine our internal requirements? The answer to this question is a qualified "yes." We can change our internal quality requirements when we can *prove* we have a new requirement that produces better results. Keep in mind that our internal quality requirements have often evolved from a sequence of "lessons learned" in the most difficult way.

If our internal quality requirements exceed those of the customer, we do not see a good reason for diluting those requirements. We must also show caution in the other direction—higher internal requirements—since we may end up driving up the cost of the product while not appreciably improving the real quality. Driving up the cost of the product erodes the profits the enterprise expects to earn on the product. If the improvement in quality improves the range of sales or reduces the warranty, margin per se may not improve, but we will be reducing "anti-margin." However when the cost increases and no additional markets are open, with no new opportunities to sell and increase volume, then the cost is just a penalty on the company and the product.

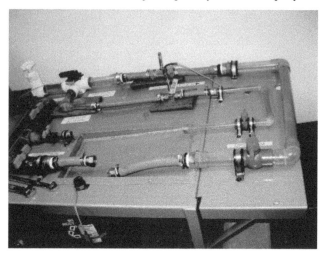

Figure 2.6 Pressure sensor calibration fixture.

There are a number of quality techniques and systems that aid in meeting the quality targets for the product. Our experience suggests that frequent reviews add value to the process. Reviews are especially productive at transition points in the organization; for example, when the specifications have been written and the developers are to begin their work. The frequency should be no less than a month and high-speed, focused reviews can occur weekly (daily, if we use scrum). Basically, the reviews provide the feedback portion of a closed-loop control system (the audit function), allowing the various development and production teams to perform "in-flight" corrections in order to control project variances. Adequate time to analyze the material under review is itself a project requirement. Often, specifications are passed out carelessly and the next day the team is expected to show up for reviews. There must be sufficient time to read and prepare critical questions before the review. We have witnessed field failures where the symptom of the failure is reported to the supplier and the supplier found the probable source of the failure by reviewing the software. We wonder, had the review happened as part of the product development work, would the problem have made it through manufacturing and to the customer?

Any product, be it software or hardware, should be assessed for manufacturability. In general, the approach involves special reviews called design for manufacturability (DFM) reviews that assess the product from both the hardware and software points of view. A good DFM review will look at mechanical assembly, electronic issues, and potential software-related issues.

Finally, the product requirements should receive aggressive and critical reviews

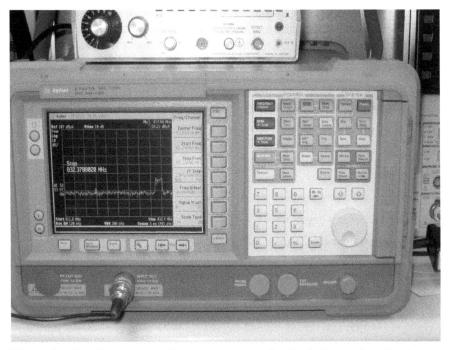

Figure 2.7 Oscilloscopes perform key analyses for the design and testing teams.

by key development staff as well as by the customer to make sure that a common understanding of the goals and attributes of the product are known. Our experience suggests that formal sign-offs are appropriate at this point and indicate reasonable levels of acceptance by both sides of the development process. We will use tools such as those in Figure 2.7 and Figure 2.8 to measure and evaluate the product.

A typical automotive example might look like the following: the development group is using a flashable microcontroller ("flash" is a form of nonvolatile electronic memory)—the software is developed and a dedicated programmer used to program the flash, after which the production team discovers a flaw in the software; that is, where is the connector and boot loader that allows them the ability to reflash the part? In other words, a manufacturable part should have the designed-in capability for reflashing if that is a goal (otherwise, why go to the expense of re-writable memory?).

Revision control

Revision control is a necessary tool for hardware, software, and firmware development. It allows the development team to retain the development history of the product while always providing the most recent files by default. In the best of all worlds, the revision control system will have off-site backup that helps to protect the intellectual investment of the enterprise.

Sophisticated revision control systems also allow for branching, merging, and backtracking of project software. In every case, the developer should always be able to revert to any previous version of software that he or she checked into the revision control system. They also handle feature revision levels not just the software revision level, meaning, within a software package 1.2, there is a define collection of capabilities. Feature "A" at revision 0.4 and feature "B" at revision 0.6.

Revision control is not limited to the software and hardware of the product under development. In fact, everything from the product to the development processes should be under revision control; for example:

- Product software

- Product hardware

- Test cases

- Software for test equipment

- Hardware for test equipment

- Development process (work) instructions

- Manufacturing process (work) instructions

Change management

What are not errors in software and hardware (non-conformance to specifications) are changes—which may be developed internally or be an output of the customer. Both require tracking; however, scope changes are of interest since these are often

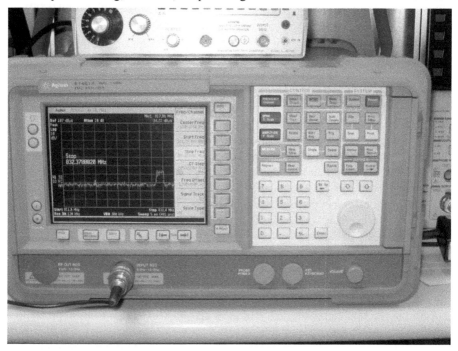

Figure 2.8 Signal generator.

new features or attributes to specified features that were unplanned; that is, the time, resources, and costs for the changes were not included in the project plan. The inclusion of these new features or attributes requires determination of the existing software, hardware, and project status and a differential assessment of effects of the changes.

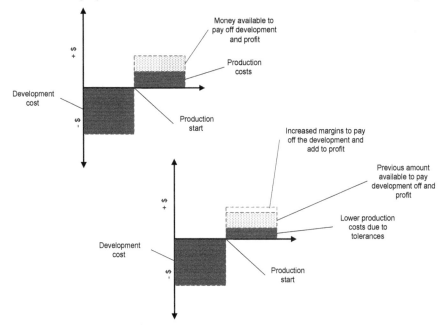

Figure 2.9 An improvement in tolerance philosophy results in increased margins.

A good change management system must:

1. Be able to track each individual change proposed and status through the change management system

2. Present the details of the change (requirements)

3. Allow for proposed integration of the cost and schedule of the change

4. Define a reviewing body to determine if and how

5. Update requirements and plans for the new integration

6. Be understood, used, and followed

The reality is we often see occasions when the specification is interpreted in one way by the developer and the product is actually required to perform differently. This then becomes a source of contention as to whether the feature meets the intent or is a change request. The end result is an alteration of the specification or an update to the product. We suspect that adequate reviews between customer and developing organization of specifications would go far in reducing the probability of occurrence.

C. Product Cost

The project team on the supplier side will probably have already provided some kind of cost estimate before the project truly commences. Often, the initial quote is called a "spin" quote, based on historical data and a hastily constructed bill of materials (or bill of services). The TQM-driven project manager needs to stand firm on the real cost once we have an assessment based on a more meaningful design solution (see Figure 2.9).

The spin quote should be called exactly that and the potential for cost increases made clear to the customer. If we have a healthy relationship with our customer, open booking the quote should not be a major issue. If we are dealing with a new customer, quote changes will have to be negotiated.

Note that we have use the word "quote." A quote will be the estimated cost times a multiplier that provides for some previously established margin. One way to establish these values occurs when the enterprise sets "hurdle" values using discounted payback, internal rate of return, and net present value metrics. We can use the solver function in a spreadsheet to provide us with the desired information if we have a reasonable cost model.

D. Performance Requirements

Performance requirements are objective requirements based on the actions to be performed by the product or service.

Performance requirements can cover a variety of areas. Often these requirements are associated with behavior rates of specific aspects of the product. In the automotive world, these are often referred to as key product characteristics (KPC)—what makes the product deliver the results the customer demands of the product. Looking only at the KPCs of a product is not the best way to deliver a successful product. Variation exists throughout systems and understanding these variations and the contribution of each to the total product really constitute the performance requirements. Additionally there can be more than one key product characteristic for a product. For example, consider a tire pressure monitoring system. The transmitter is mounted in the tire via the valve stem. A key product characteristic would be the frequency of broadcast—specifically the carrier frequency. The receiver must pick up this signal and decode to determine the pressure within the tire. Another would be the way the product mounts into the tire, and if this is poorly designed or does not meet the needs of the rim, the rim and tire combination may not retain air. Hence, we have dual KPCs.

We can use sophisticated tools such as signal generators to model signals and the respective interpretation by an electronic control unit. We can use this signal generator (see Figure 2.8) over the range of possible signals to help establish performance requirements of the product. With this tool, we can vary the frequency of the signal as well as the shape of the signal to understand the performance has an impact based upon this variation.

Consider also the individual components of the product—not just the product as a system. The performance of the system will be based upon the performance of those parts composing the system and any emergent properties. For the response of a system to meet the performance objectives, we must have the correct individual parts to meet those needs. Figure 2.10 and Figure 2.11 show the performance of two switches. Both switches are from the same manufacturer; both switches are the same model from that manufacturer. One of the switches has the desired response (see Figure 2.10). The other switch performance not only does not meet the desired response of the system, but it also causes problems within the system.

Both switches are able to do the same function. However, the performance of the switch in Figure 2.10 is the performance required for the component interpreting the signal to respond appropriately, thus making the system function properly. The variation in components must be considered through the entire product development cycle.

Performance requirements do not end at the component level. To know the component part needs, we should have a good idea of the performance needs of the entire system. We can use simulators to help establish these performance needs. These

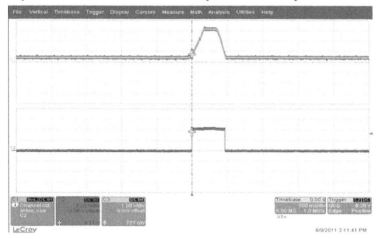

Figure 2.10 Acceptable switch performance. Note the clean signal response.

simulations can be solely software models or some combination of software and hardware such as hardware in the loop simulation.

E. Functional Requirements

Functional requirements may be the most common form of requirement seen by most engineers. A functional requirements document will detail the following items:

- Input, output, and processes tied to those inputs and outputs

- Any known workflows

- Any known scripts

- Necessary reports such as those for change management, databases, and test reports

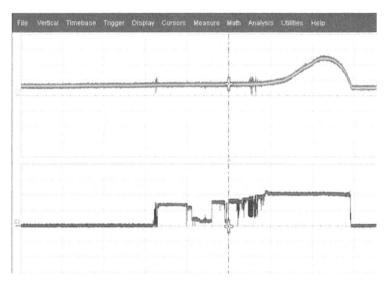

Figure 2.11 Unacceptable switch performance.

- Any and all known standards
- Enough information to apply interface control
- Input, process, and output or concepts used in the well-known input, process, output (IPO) format developed by IBM decades ago

Existing workflows need to be documented so that both customer and supplier understand how the process is to proceed.

The functional requirements will often provide fodder for the TQM project manager to consider improvements to the product. The reason for this is that the functional requirements document is usually the primary source for product information. While the functional requirements document may be the primary source of information, it is not the only source of information; for example, the performance specification is extremely important in setting both product parameters and test parameters. Both documents should provide enough information such that a good test team can verify that the product does indeed meet requirements, internal, external, regulatory, and standards-based.

We can use tools such as simulators to help generate the functional requirements. Using these tools we can uncover interactions needed to meet the functional requirements. Simulations of the system help us to derive functional requirements by a virtual replica of the system (see   Figure 2.12). Our test engineers will use hardware products from suppliers such as National Instruments, including software such as LabView (also from National Instruments). We can then explore many ways to achieve the functional content of the product without going through the entire development process—including the generation of prototype parts. We do, however, need to ensure our simulation reflects the real world possibilities. In the case of integrating a new component or product feature into an existing system, we must have realistic modeling of the system in its present embodiment. From there we can configure a number of approaches that we expect would meet the new functional requirements. We can run each of these simulations, exploring how the variations in the system affect the new functional performance. We can then select the appropriate concept as the design possibility that will meet the performance needs when placed within the larger system context.

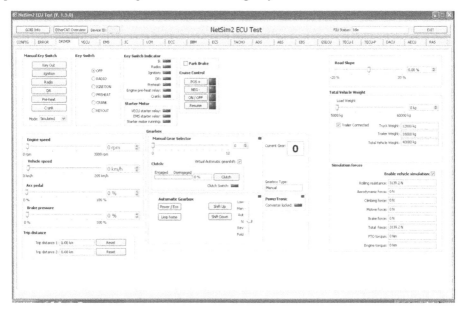

Figure 2.12   Use the test tool to develop stimuli that replicate challenges generally found on the vehicle.

One of the important uses to the project manager of this functional requirements document includes the concept of scope management. Scope creep is a phenomenon that occurs as the customer or the supplier starts having additional ideas for improving the product beyond the original definition. In some cases, these improvements are hardly real improvements; in other cases, we may be looking at real improvements. In either case, the well-informed project manager will have to recalibrate the schedule and the budget for the project. If the project manager does not take care of these two items, then it is highly probable that product quality will suffer.

VI.   Project Requirements

We generally measure projects typically using several attributes. Though these attributes can have the goal of meeting "the customer's needs," the successful attributes can also be stated as "must be able to profit from the result of the product". At times, these things can be seemingly at odds with each other (see Figure 2.13); the goal is to balance all of these attributes to produce the best solution.

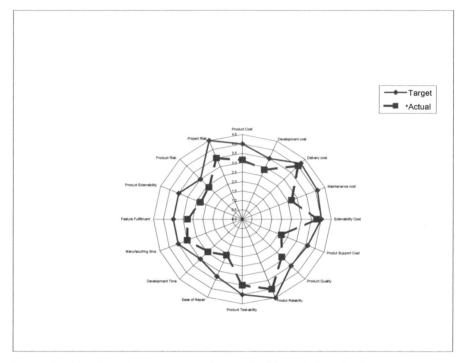

Figure 2.13 Radar diagram comparing project targets to actual.

A. Project Cost

Project cost will include all costs associated with the project and provide yet another reason for developing a complete work breakdown structure. It should be clear, then, that we will be considering human resources costs, setup cost, development cost, testing cost, manufacturing cost, and a host of other related costs. Even simple project costing is a difficult exercise.

Any costing done by the project manager will need review by the accounting department. This method allows us to have a check against error by the project manager. If costing and quoting is a particularly laborious activity due to substantial customer customization of what would otherwise be standard products, then we have a candidate for either a Six Sigma project or some total quality management activities. In some cases, we might use the Kaizen approach of progressive refinement. This true kaizen approach is not a Six Sigma project–it lacks the specificity and the time boxing normally seen with Six Sigma projects. However, progressive refinement allows us to start relatively quickly and then cycle through our quality adjustments as long as it makes sense.

Project costing is an area ripe for application of TQM tools. The track record of the company's project costs and product costs provides an historical basis for decision making. Consider the company that supplies embedded products to the automotive industry. This company could even specialize in certain components such as engines, brakes, or instrument clusters. The product the company delivers has historical continuity; that is, we find abundant similarities in the product from generation to generation. The technical details and level of sophistication may increase; however, as an aggregate, the products are similar. The result of the delivered products—the accuracy of estimates—is the variation of the result to those original estimates, which allows us to improve subsequent projects.

B. Schedule

Scheduling can go through the same kind of progressive refinement as does project cost. Obviously, we want to maintain open and clear lines of communication with our customer during this process. In fact, we will let them know what our process is from the very start of the project; that way, we will have no surprises, producing customer consternation, later in the project.

Scheduling may seem to be a type of black art. If we have historical data we may be

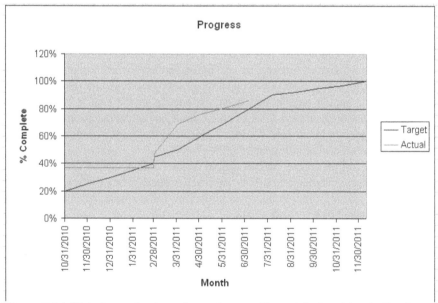

Figure 2.14 Note how charts and graphs provide quick, intuitive indication of project status.

able to analyze that data using a variety of quality tools, such as distribution analysis, and be able to build a simulation tool for ourselves that will give us some kind of mean and variance to our estimates. We are not saying that the mathematics will simplify scheduling to the point where we can pinpoint the milestones to within a day, but rather, we are trying to provide a statistical basis for our schedule estimates.

Tracking the progress (see Figure 2.14) in such a manner that we communicate the state of the project in a meaningful way is essential to project management yet often seems missing. Progress need not be via one of the ubiquitous project management software tools, but could be as simple as tracking the actions and deliverables according to some expected delivery date. This provides some feedback on how the project is progressing.

Every time we hold a review or if we discern an anomaly and schedule, we must inform the customer. Any delay in passing on scheduling or costing information to a customer will result in much greater exasperation as we proceed through the project. We have never favored hiding bad news from the customer or from our own upper management.

VII. Derived Requirements

As the name suggests, "derived requirements" are generally those requirements that we discern in the customer specification or from other sources (e.g., regulatory requirements).

VIII.   Internal Requirements

Why worry about internal requirements? Didn't we set these ourselves? Yes, if we did. As we have already indicated, we created those internal requirements for a reason. One of the most common reasons for creating an internal requirement occurs when we have what we call a quality spill. Let's take a brief look at the automotive industry: we will generally have a set of rules for the use of temperatures when doing reflow solder on printed circuit boards. These rules constitute a set of internal requirements that are either based on supplier recommendations, experience, or the results from designed experiments. Obviously, it pays to check these limits on regular occasions or when we observe a degradation in our solder joints. Regardless, these internal requirements are still a part of the overall requirements for the project.

We recommend that these internal requirements be documented and included as part of the project documentation. We may reach a point during the life cycle of the product where that information becomes important; for example, when we are faced with either a lawsuit or a product recall.

IX. Regulatory Requirements

Regulatory requirements are generally industry-specific. For example, in the automotive industry we have United States Department of Transportation and its federal motor vehicle safety standards (FMVSS), the Society of Automotive Engineers and its SAE standards, the legal requirement of the United States code, state requirements,

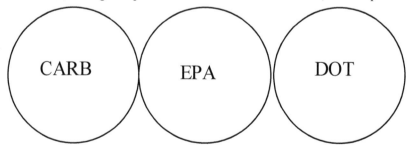

Figure 2.15 Examples of regulatory agencies in the automotive world.

international requirements, and expectations from other professional engineering organizations. Regulatory agencies also include the Environmental Protection Agency (EPA) as well as the California Air Resource Board (CARB) (see Figure 2.15).

Because regulatory requirements are nearly always part of the law, we have no choice as to whether we implement them or not. It is important that we document these standards as applicable and that we indicate in our documentation how we have implemented these regulatory requirements. We do this for at least two reasons: so that we can assure ourselves that we have done the job correctly, and in the case where we are under a lawsuit or recall.

X. Standards

In any industry, a variety of standards can be applicable. In the automotive industry, for example, we have SAE standards (see Figure 2.16), ISO standards, software development standards such as CMM, ANSI standards, and even military standards. The medical industry will have some of the same standards as well as many others; for example, those of the Food and Drug Administration.

In some cases, the standards are not product standards, but rather, they are process standards; in short, they tell us how to proceed rather than telling us what the product must comply with. As part of the total quality initiative, the project manager will look for ways to make more systematic use of all applicable standards as well as, perhaps,

Figure 2.16 Seen is a SAE transient fixture, which replicates EMC bulk current injection and SAE transient simulation/injection.

creating a few of his or her own.

Another possibility occurs when we take a collection of appropriate standards and use these to create our own set of super standards. If the super standards do not lead to significant increases in product development cost, we can use them to drive quality in both the product and the process (and, of course, services when that is our product). The benefit of taking this approach to standards is that we can create a consistent set of practices for all customers; thereby providing a stable platform of behaviors for our own employees. If our employees are not chasing moving targets, we enhance the probability of superior compliance to the super standards. Furthermore, we can use the concept of the super standards for marketing purposes—pointing out that we meet or exceed any standard the customer can provide.

Make no mistake—the idea of the super standards, in our experience, usually meets with resistance. The primary reason for this seems to be that neither management nor employees can see the long-term benefit in using this approach. We strongly recommend that a TQM project manager consider such an initiative as part of the overall TQM activity. We can use the idea of bootstrapping enterprise quality to drive a super standards project. As with all projects, we will still have to do the inaugural work to provide meaningful financial benefit for this laborious initiative.

All that being said, the reality is that standards can either help or hinder. We have also seen instances where the product met performance standards and promptly failed in the field. Standards allow the project to reduce the research work regarding the product use; however, standards also may not account for the exact population of customers and usage that the product will experience in reality. For example, a product may be required by the customer to adhere to the electrical and electronic transients in the SAE J1455 standard. However these signals may not reflect the typical electrical transients from which the product suffers. With technology quickly changing, we may even be using an obsolete standard! We suspect that it is no doubt true that during the development of the standard all possible combinations of vehicle use and field exposure were not considered.

A. Limitations of Metrics

Information on the exposure of the product to assorted stimuli should not be estimated without data. In some cases standards are used when an objective body has performed some sort of quantitative analysis on the field stimuli to which a component is exposed. The expediency of these standards can sometimes cost in the future of the product. Unless these standards are derived from measured data from products in the field, there is risk that the definition is arbitrary.

To find the real answer, it is often necessary to set up instruments in the environment that the component must survive and gather real data (see Figure 2.17). One solution is to pick a situation that represents the worst case scenario. This information, gathered over a relatively short time, is used to estimate the exposure of the component to the variable over the life of the component using known formulae (e.g., the Arrhenius equation). For example, in an instrumented vehicle that drives 1,000 miles, exposure to temperatures above 80° Celsius happens after 10 miles. Then, in 100,000 miles the projected exposure would be 1,000 miles as well as the related time duration. This would be the same scenario that would be conducted on a number of vehicles that represent the typical or maximum exposures to the stimulus. All of this information is then analyzed to produce a description of what happens in the field.

Regardless of the development methodology used, it is important to understand and track the requirements. We do this by ensuring specifications are traceable and the

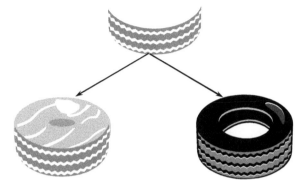

Which one of these is the top graphic from?

Figure 2.17 The effect of insufficient data; insufficient detail makes it difficult to draw conclusions.

requirements within them are traceable. Unique identifiers for the requirements and a method for tracking the changes to those particular requirements (revision tracking of the individual requirements as well as overall specification document) are all part of requirement management (or change management). It is not necessary to have a special software package to track the requirements. Tracking can be done with any one of the ubiquitous spreadsheet or document programs. A clever way to do this tracking using Microsoft Word involves the markup function, which will show the changes in the form of colored bubbles on the page. It is important to note that changes in requirements drive changes in the verification activities. For each requirement, there must be related verification. Therefore, change management must consider the ripple effect further into the project and the effect these changes will have on project schedules and budgets.

The testing exposure time or severity is generally dependent upon the role of the function or component. A radio, a convenience feature, is not valued at the same level as an antilocking brake system (see Figure 2.18). The ABS system will be required to perform over a wider range of possibilities and correct itself when things go wrong. All of this must be known at the time of specification. This often includes specifying the failure response, forcing it to a particular reaction.

Many times the customer organization has identified categories of performance or deviation from the expected performance based upon the type or criticality of the system. For example, a safety system would have to be quite immune and perform as expected under a wide range of stimuli (i.e., it must be robust). On the other hand, a convenience feature may be allowed to have anomalous performance but revert back to the expected performance without intervention from the operator.

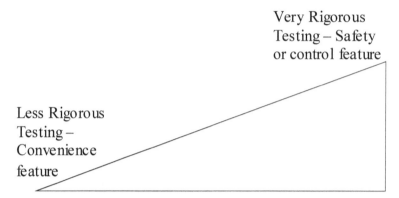

Figure 2.18 Range of testing is defined by criticality of the function.

B. Distortion of Understanding

One of the little known problems with the use of metrics lies in the interpretation of exactly what the metrics mean. Our first consideration should be whether or not we are measuring a factor that has a meaningful causal relationship with the effect we wish to understand. Next, we need to ensure that we are measuring enough different factors to yield a complete description of what is occurring. To top all this off, even if we are using the correct factors as part of our metrics, we will still only see what those specific metrics represent. Herein lies the difficulty with tools such as the balanced scorecard.

Balanced scorecards are not deadly to the enterprise but they can be deceptive. We understand the rationale behind the original fourfold system, which was designed to eliminate many of the distortions present in a one-dimensional measurement system. However, we would still recommend that those using the balanced scorecard go out on the shop floor, deal with real customers, and speak with client employees. The Japanese call this "going to the *gemba*," the place where the action is occurring.

In an effort to streamline the process and understanding, we see degradation of the balanced scorecard approach at it moves to smiley faces and green, yellow, or red circles to convey the state of the process or project. The need to reduce the complexity

Figure 2.19 Simplistic icons on a dashboard mislead more than they inform.

can be understandable, with quick comprehension of the status of either process or project being desirable in the face of "more with less." The truth is, metrics can only be made so simple. Understanding can't be achieved by looking at smiley faces as illustrated in Figure 2.19.

We can anticipate some level of reality distortion regardless of the measurement system we choose. We think it important to remember that metrics can produce a picture that is a distortion of reality.

C. Artifacts

In most cases, artifacts (see Figure 2.20) for our projects consist of what ISO would call "records." Not only do records help prove our cases, they also provide a source for "lessons learned," allowing our organization to move in the direction of becoming a self-optimizing enterprise. Experience suggests this area is often overlooked. Keeping good notes and records do not appear to produce the results we need now. Taking time to identify the data needed helps when we make decisions based upon some level of fact. The TQM project manager will understand the limits of the organization and what is possible without a great deal of "give it the good old try."

Figure 2.20 Artifacts.

XI. Exercises

- What is the objective of product testing?
- Create a map of a hardware test bench.
- Create a map of a software test bench.
- Create a map of a hardware-in-the-loop (real subsystems) software test bench.
- Define how much subsystem simulation you consider to be appropriate.
- List the types of simulation available (for example, discrete-event) and define for each one the most applicable scenario.
- As a PM, when would you start testing? What tools allow you to do this? List your assumptions and probable tool use. How would you know when you are finished with testing?
- Summarize the main goals of testing.
- Explain how you would test a process.
- Pick a process for simulation and summarize how this approach could help with process analysis and improvement.
- Explain how you would determine which metrics are significant.
- Make a case for a specific number (count) of metrics.
    - How many are too few?
    - How many are too many?
    - What is the goal?
    - How do you consolidate metrics for presentation to management?
- Write a protocol that defines how the various developmental, product integrity, and order fulfillment teams will report to you.
    - Which metrics do you need?
    - How do you avoid becoming overwhelmed?

CHAPTER 3 – TQM TOOLS

I.   Rubric

	Novice	Sr. Novice	Journey-man	Sr. Jour-neyman	Master
X-bar R	x	x	x	x	x
X-bar S		x	x	x	x
Median			x	x	x
np				x	x
p				x	x
u				x	x
c				x	x
EWMA					x
CuSum					x

II.   Questions to Ponder

- Do TQM tools provide any added value?
- Are TQM tools too abstract for real use or are they really down-to-earth?
- Why are tools so seductive?
- Does the enterprise really need another toolbox?
- Does the use of the toolset have any marketing value?
- Why do we have so many tools?
- Why are the toolsets different and yet the same (compare and contrast)?
- Is toolset just another way to keep the quality people employed?
- Is the ISO version better than the other models?
- Why can't we just "roll our own?"
- How does dispersion affect a project manager's schedule?
- What variation in your organization's process gives you the most heartburn?
- How well-planned are your organization's processes?
- How much does the project manager rely upon the line manager for understanding variation?
- How can a Pareto plot help with project scheduling?
- Who decides what data / information should be used to build the schedule?
- What happens when the historical record is ignored?
- What does the project manager do when the expected delivery date dictates

neglecting the process? How does this impact the subsequent measurements?

- How do you know the capability of a process that you frequently abandon?
- Who manages the transition points from one group to another?

III. Why TQM Tools Are Important to the Project Manager

TQM tools add to the armamentarium of the project manager. At a minimum, the TQM project manager should understand what he or she is seeing when presented with results in one of these formats.

IV. TQM Project Manager Scenario

A. Situation

We were asked to deliver a project on a very specific date. Investigation revealed that the delivery date was not based upon the work required, with key areas of project execution unlikely to happen.

B. Objective

Our goal was to deliver the best possible project with the time available. We wanted to ensure that stakeholders were aware of the state of the project at all points. We wanted to document missing activities or describe where significant business processes were cut short, so we would have a sense of the risks, particularly once the product was delivered to the customer.

C. Action

We identified the most important set of requirements to be met by the product. We prioritized the delivery of that portion of the project. We identified the testing needed to confirm those sets of requirements, including exploratory testing, to find breaking points not identified by the product requirements. We made sure the levels of project management as well as line managers and the executives, knew the probability of success—as defined by our company's typical expectations from projects—was not practical or even possible. We procured additional contingency funding. We scheduled numerous quick releases of the system components, used automated bench testing as much as possible on the requirements, and promptly reported faults into the tracking system. We used quick iterations and testing of those as much as was feasible.

D. Results

The product was still delivered more than ninety days later than demanded by management due to problems found during testing and the time required for corrective action releases and subsequent retesting. The problems found would have been catastrophic to the customer had the product not had been tested so intensively!

E. Aftermath

Quick software builds and testing went a long way in mitigating the risks. We learned that those who made the arbitrary decision to launch based on subjective impressions don't know the damage it did to the employees, especially when management made requests for heroic effort and overtime. Even so, the extra effort did not produce the desired—wishful—time objective. We learn that while the product delivery date can be demanded at a particular time, that does not necessarily trump the laws of physics and the demand for attention.

V.   Benefits to the TQM Project Manager

This section may seem targeted to the quality manager for the enterprise, but we think it is critical that the project manager understand the use of the these tools. For example, one of the most useful tools is the Pareto chart. A project manager could use this plot to analyze which customer complaints are most frequent during a project (by category) or, perhaps, look at complaints from the point of view of cost in currency or in time.

While the tools are traditionally or typically applied to manufacturing endeavors, these same analysis tools can be applied to both line management as well as project management activities. To be able to do either, you have to understand the strengths and weaknesses of the tools. Then learn how to apply them to better understand your organization and solve the complex problems.

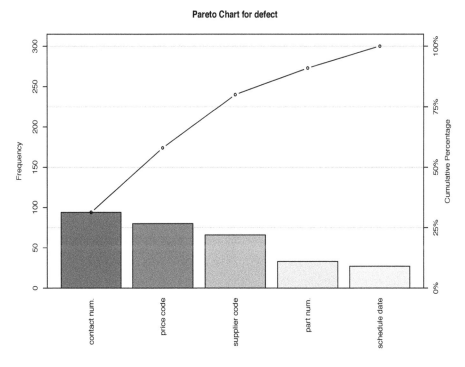

Figure 3.1 An example of a typical Pareto chart showing the order data. The line helps discern the 80% point.

VI. Pareto Chart

A Pareto chart[1] is effectively a sorted bar chart or shorted histogram (see Figure 3.1). The great frequency will be on the left and the least frequency on the right-hand side of the chart. The purpose of the Pareto chart is to quickly identify those items that are significant, and in so doing, simultaneously identify those items that are not currently significant. The so-called "80-20" rule comes from this plot; for example, we often observe that 20% of our customers provide 80% of our revenue. The Pareto chart and the 80-20 rule are simplifications of Zipf's Law—the power law observed in many natural phenomena.

A. Potential Distortions

The Pareto chart can introduce distortions in our understanding when we chart information that is not truly relevant. For example, suppose we simply chart frequencies of issues with regard to returned warranty products; frequency may not be nearly as revealing as making a Pareto chart of the **cost** of each issue. The frequency chart may

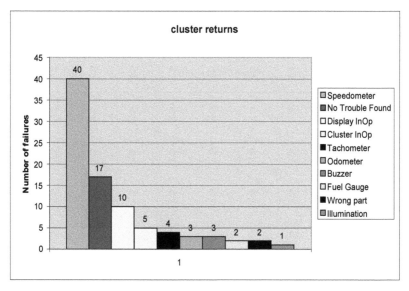

Figure 3.2 This Pareto chart shows the issues with an instrument cluster on a motor vehicle.

give us a clue to the most important niggling problem but it will not enlighten us as to the product giving the most financial pain to the customer.

Consider the Pareto chart of failures (see Figure 3.2) witnessed with an instrument cluster for a particular vehicle. We see the best place to start to investigate and fix, in terms of number of failures, is with the speedometer. We would then set up some exploratory testing to understand why this is so. However, just because the problem or failure is more prevalent than others, may not mean that the money at stake or customer impact is the largest. When we know what the returns cost, including our handling of them, we can rework the Pareto chart to illustrate the dollars (Figure 3.3)

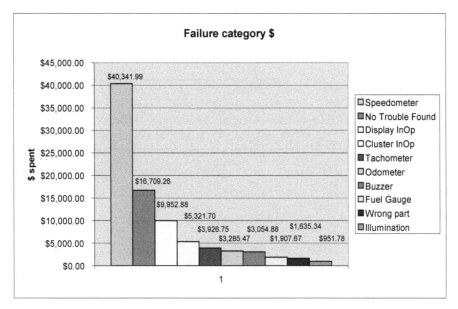

Figure 3.3 Pareto of instrument cluster failures by cost indicates where we find the most monetary damage.

at stake and not just the number of units. In this case, we see that the dollar amount associated with the failures follows the number of failures closely. We can then use this information to determine our plan of attack to improve the situation.

B. Limitations

The Pareto chart really only uses count data, which means we are looking at integral frequencies (categorical data) and not variables data. In other words, we do not have as much information as we get from variables data. We have never found this to be an issue in practice, but we also remain cognizant of the kind of data we are actually plotting.

C. Power of the Pareto Chart

Even with recognized distortions and limitations to our Pareto charts, they form one of the most significant decision support tools we have. In general, the 80-20 concept is easy to explain to upper management and provides a good support for our decisions.

D. Pareto Charts and Project Management

If our project management office retains historical data of the issue discovered during the course of numerous projects–and they should–we can plot the frequencies of issues we have seen and generate a Pareto chart of undesirable behaviors. Once we know who the "heavy-hitters" are, we can begin to train out or introduce corrective actions that eliminate or reduce the most common issues. We suspect putting a dollar value on project management issues may not be worth the effort and, hence, we are willing to accept some potential distortion in our understanding.

VII. Scatter Plots

A. Correlation

Scatter plots are used to look for potential correlation. Correlation is exactly what the name suggests—we relate one variable with at least one other variable (see Figure

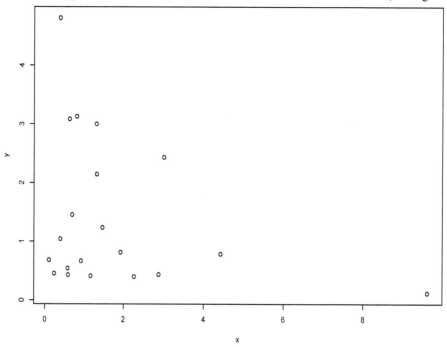

Figure 3.4 Scatter charts show the correlation (not causation) between two factors.

3.4). Note, however, that we relate but we do not prove causation. True causation is difficult to prove. John Stuart Mill ruminated on this topic in his *System of Logic* (1843):

- "If two or more instances of the phenomenon under investigation have only one circumstance in common, the circumstance in which alone all the instances agree, is the cause (or effect) of the given phenomenon."

- "If an instance in which the phenomenon under investigation occurs, and an instance in which it does not occur, have every circumstance in common save one, that one occurring only in the former; the circumstance in which alone the two instances differ, is the effect, or the cause, or an indispensable part of the cause, of the phenomenon."

- "If two or more instances in which the phenomenon occurs have only one circumstance in common, while two or more instances in which it does not occur have nothing in common save the absence of that circumstance: the circumstance in which alone the two sets of instances differ, is the effect, or cause, or a necessary part of the cause, of the phenomenon."

- "Deduct from any phenomenon such part as is known by previous inductions to be the effect of certain antecedents, and the residue of the phenomenon is the effect of the remaining antecedents."

- "Whatever phenomenon varies in any manner whenever another phenomenon varies in some particular manner, is either a cause or an effect of that phenomenon, or is connected with it through some fact of causation."

As we can see, causation is a non-trivial concept, although to see some organization's approach to root cause analysis, we might interpret this otherwise. Mere correlation is insufficient to be conclusive since it is primarily suggestive. Insufficient understanding of all of the relevant parameters and variations will result in less than the entire root cause of the problem.

The Pearson correlation coefficient is a parametric measure of the correlation between two or more variables. Correlation, as the name implies, is the relation between or among variables. In short, we attempt to determine how variable y (presumed dependent) varies with changes in variable x (possibly independent). In multivariate regression, the idea of variable independence may have little meaning although, just as with analysis of variance, it is possible that a given factor may have little influence and, hence, be effectively independent. However, this kind of independence is not what we are looking for in correlation analyses.

What are we seeking in the bivariate linear correlation coefficient? Notice in the. As for this resultant value, the rules are as follows:

- The correlation is 1 in the case of an increasing linear relationship (positive correlation)

- The correlation is −1 in the case of a decreasing linear relationship (negative correlation)

- For all other cases a value between −1 and +1, denoting the degree of linear dependence between the variables

- Understand that the closer the coefficient is to either −1 or 1, the stronger the correlation

- In the case of values near zero, the correlation is weak or nonexistent

If too few paired values are used, say four or fewer, the distribution of the correlation coefficient widens sufficiently that the value of the correlation is suspect.

Because the Pearson correlation coefficient is parametric, we know the underlying distribution is significant. Alternative non-parametric correlations exist, to whit:

- Spearman's ρ

- Kendall's τ

As is typical with non-parametric tests, the power of the correlation coefficient is less than that of Pearson's; on the other hand, it is almost miraculous in some cases that we can say anything about correlation, particularly with messy data.

One other topic of concern is the relation of correlation to causality—there is none directly. Correlation may imply causation, but it cannot prove causation. Ever since the meditations of David Hume in the *Treatise on Human Nature*, the concept of causation has been fraught with difficulties. Always proceed with caution when claiming a correlation represents causation. The safest path is to avoid claims of causation altogether.

Consider for example, a certain vehicle manufacturer who builds prototype vehicles in a special area at their manufacturing facility. The prototype vehicle built at this off-site location is shipped to the design and test facility. From the time the vehicle arrives, there is preparation work to ready it for testing. The vehicle does not arrive on the first day and testing starts that day or even the next day (see Figure 3.5). The graphic shows the historical range of days that it takes to prepare the vehicle for testing—to make the vehicle a suitable test sample. This vehicle preparation work must happen before any planned tests can occur. We can see there are few times a vehicle is ready in fewer

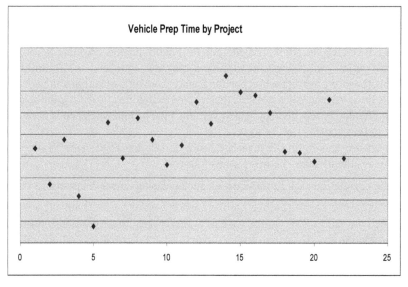

Figure 3.5 Scatter plot of vehicle preparation for systems integration test shows a range of durations to make the vehicle a suitable test subject.

than five days. In fact, for four times, the event happens in fewer than five days out of twenty-two times. This is not portending success in the schedule that assumes testing will start that first day or week the vehicle arrives.

If a project manager does nothing else differently, simply placing the testing task to start as soon as the vehicle arrives on his or her project plan will almost certainly fail. This result is especially true if this testing is on the project critical path. The end date *will* change. The historical record indicates that this attempt to start testing on the

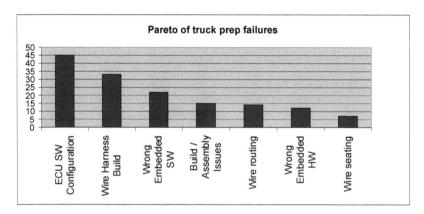

Figure 3.6 Problems found with vehicle test subject that must be addressed prior to systems integration testing.

first day has little or no probability of success based on past performance. A look at the Pareto chart of the faults found on the vehicles before testing will provide the project manager with some ability to shorten the time between vehicle arrival and the start of test by addressing the causes.

We see in the Pareto chart (Figure 3.6) of the vehicle failures, that prototype configuration is a significant contributor to the time to prepare the vehicle. In this particular organization some of the electronic control units (ECU) contain hundreds of parameters and each ECU's configuration depends on the feature set of the vehicle and other ECU configurations (e.g., those for the anti-locking brake system, the transmission, the instrumentation, and any other ECUs that are hooked to the data bus). At prototype level, the configuration of the vehicle is often performed manually. Additionally, the wire harness is another significant contributor to the vehicle preparation time. The prototype harnesses are built in ways that are under far less control than the production parts. Addressing these known failure points within the project could shorten the time between vehicle arrival and the start of testing. Actions taken to improve these problem areas could improve the start of testing. The project manager that would have his testing start immediately upon vehicle arrival will have to do something about the variation in time it takes to make a prototype vehicle a suitable vehicle for testing. In essence, the wise project manager will include some padding in the schedule to account for the expected variation around the start time for testing the vehicle.

Let us consider the wire harness portion of the Pareto chart. The incoming prototype material is used to build the early prototype vehicle (see Figure 3.7 and Figure 3.8). At this point, the organization performs manual checking of this material. This manual checking consists of:

• A dimension check of the harness and all legs of the harness

- The use of a voltmeter and one to two people performing a continuity check against the paper design document (sometimes continuity is the only real check for a wire harness)

This checking consumes numerous hours just to test one part, and we always have multiple wire harnesses on each vehicle—a few of these harnesses have a large number of wires contained, often in excess of 100 leads and sometimes to the level of hundreds of leads. Unlike most automotive applications, heavy, commercial vehicles are built

Figure 3.7 Old method of manually testing harness continuity checks.

with a large variation of electrical/electronic configurations and content. For example, we can find options where only the passenger door has a power window. This means there is ample diversity of harnesses for the total vehicle offering.

Manually checking amounts to a spot check, since the manual check is time intensive and there are so many different parts and variations on the vehicle. Further complicating the ability to test these prototype parts is that the material can be a long lead time item. In situations where the prototype material arrives late, the material can go directly to the prototype vehicle build. The prototype vehicle builds are scheduled well in advance of the test date. The test team generally expresses great reluctance to reschedule these builds. Eventually these vehicles are used for various testing activities. When this unqualified material is placed on the vehicle, we find problems when we go to work with the vehicle. The results of which can be seen in the Pareto chart from Figure 3.6 elements 2, 5, and 7. In this situation, our project consumes many man hours to tear down the vehicle to fix the prototype material problem.

So now we have a range of dates to prepare a vehicle for test, and a list of typical issues associated with that duration that impacts our ability to start the vehicle testing on day one. We know our present process and tools don't meet the brief time schedule demanded by the project time line. So, how do you reduce the faults found in the

Figure 3.8 Drawings and pinout descriptions at the ready for manual testing of wire harness.

vehicle builds due to the harness errors? One possibility is to automate the testing of the wire harness. Automation of this testing is a good candidate since the work consumes human effort and is not a creative activity.

The NX Pro+ fixture from Dynalab Test Systems (see Figure 3.9) is set up to import

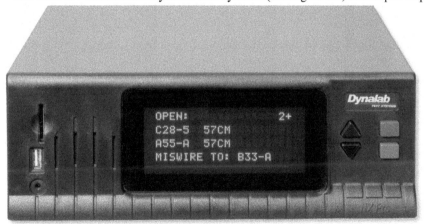

Figure 3.9 The NXPro graphic - the tool that does the point-to-point wire harness checks comparing an input file - DSI from the harness design folks to the received product from the supplier, especially useful on the early prototype parts when deviations may abound with uncertainty of what content is in what harness part number due to the deviations.

the design documentation directly from the designer's computer into the test fixture, minimizing documentation handling errors. The fixture has 32,768 test points! An adapter harness is made to connect this fixture (see Figure 3.10) to the wire harness device under test. A configuration file is loaded into the harness tester. This file contains a list of all harness test pins and the corresponding DUT (device under test) harness. This fixture then compares the harness to the design documentation in seconds. The tool performs continuity checks, discontinuity checks, cross-continuity checks, and

Figure 3.10 Dynalab and cabinet test fixture for automated point-to-point testing.

intermittent connection feedback in a fraction of the time and more accurately than the manual method. The scope of coverage is much more than what is possible through manual means and takes a fraction of the time.

Assuming that the harness has four hundred connection points, a manual test might take (assume an expedient tester who averages 10 seconds per check) 400! * 10 = 4000 seconds (or 66 hours)—a *very* long time (and don't forget that it might take more than one person to test the harness). The harness tester is able to test one hundred wires in one second so (400! * 0.01) equals a much smaller time. A manual test might be 95% accurate. The harness tester would run the test with a 99.999999% accuracy rate; the failures depend on the probably of a failure in the harness tester or in the harness test adapter cable.

Other problems are possible—the configuration file feeding the harness tester needs to be correct. Examining the process to create the configuration file can lead to additional time savings. Creating this file by hand is not always conducive to an efficient use of engineering time. In one case it was measured to take at least five hours to create one configuration file. We developed a simple program and we managed to reduce the execution time to about five seconds, a cost savings of at least five hours. It took two days to create the program, for a payback after about four harnesses.

Additional features for a harness tester might be a time domain reflectometer. This feature can measure the length of a wire by pulsing one end and measuring how long it takes the signal to travel the length and back. However, our present Pareto chart does not seem to indicate there are problems in this area.

We may choose to vary the loads that can be put on the wire harness ends to make sure the mathematical calculations or simulations of the wire performance over the range of current draw is acceptable and the product meets these demands. We can use a load tester like the one in Figure 3.11, where we can increment or decrement the resistive load to decrease or increase the current through the harness. This will provide us with some information on harness performance over the range of expected amperage seen on a vehicle, including catastrophic short circuits and non-performing open circuits. We would then know the limits of the product, and more importantly, how the product would fail in under these circumstances.

This example clearly illustrates the use of the tools of TQM and how they can be employed to enhance project delivery through improvement of the line function. Automated inspection reduces the burden upon the inspectors to have a critical eye on every aspect of the prototype material. Some parts of the inspection could not be automated—for example, the dimension checks and mechanical angles of the wire harness as it routes through the vehicle (angles can lead to inductive alteration of impedance), the size of the wires in the harness, and the connector pin sizes. We can do spot checks on these aspects. However, from our Pareto list, we see little if any evidence that harness lengths and angles have caused any logistical problems with performing the subsequent testing, although we have some anecdotal evidence that

Figure 3.11 An example of a multi-lead sensor calibration setup.

inductive impedance can cause a vehicle fire under very special conditions. The automation of the length does not appear to be of much value to the organization. It is probable that the mechanical aspects are addressed in simulations or models of the parts before the parts are built, making this area of less concern.

B. Difference between a Line Graph and a Scatter Plot

Line graphs provide a way to map independent and dependent variables, each of which can be known. We all recall linear equations, where we calculate the slope and y-intercept and how we made determination of the other points on the line based upon the slope and where the line fits on the Cartesian plane. This mathematical formula defines all of the points associated with that *line* for any given variable. Scatter plots are similar in that we are still mapping quantitative data. Instead of the unique single points along the way, we are viewing a range of possible points that ultimately express a trend and range of possibilities. There is no line connecting the individual points— and if there were, it would not tell the same story. The closer the points, usually the easier it is to assess and arrive at some conclusions.

Because the data points represent real data collected in a laboratory setting rather than theoretically calculated values, they will represent all of the error intrinsic to such a collection process. A regression line can be used to statistically describe the trend of the points in the scatter plot to help tie the data back to a presumed ideal function, although we must be careful with higher order polynomial fits. This regression line expresses a mathematical relationship between the independent and dependent variable, but not necessarily a causative relation.

VIII.   Control Charts

A. Controlling Process Performance

A look at our terminology leads to the following recognition about control charts[1]:

- Statistical = sampling.
- Process = coordinated activity.
- Control = modification of behavior by comparing desired response with actual output.

The ultimate goal is reduction of variation. Simply gathering data and putting it on a chart is clearly insufficient.

These tools have been used most typically in production processes. However, that need not be the case. The concepts apply directly to the line functions of a product development organization. Variation exists in this area of work as well. In later chapters, we will demonstrate the concept of control chart as applied directly to line management as well as the project management discipline.

B. Special versus Common Causes

A special cause is an assignable cause. We use a special tool called a control chart in order to separate the assignable causes from those expected from normal random variation. In fact, common causes lie behind the random variation.

Of the two causes, the special cause is "easier" to handle because we can assign a reason for it. To reduce the effect of a common cause, on the other hand, frequently requires a profound knowledge of the process being measured and a subsequent process change to improve the situation.

Type I SPC errors occur when we treat a behavior as a special cause when no change has occurred in the process. This item is sometimes called *overcontrol*.

Type II SPC errors occur when we DON'T treat a behavior as a special cause when, in fact, it is a special cause. This situation is sometimes called *undercontrol*.

C. Tampering

Tampering occurs when operators or technicians "nudge" a device or process in a direction that they believe will reduce the variation. Because these individuals do not make their changes using a predetermined "gain," they will often make the situation worse rather than better.

Tools exist that permit changes to common causes. Two related examples come out of the work of Box and Jenkins and Box and Luceño. These studies were initially used as forecasting tools, predictive indicators of observed patterns. However, engineers realized early on that the tools could also be used in a control scenario and they have since been applied to dynamic control with control charts.

Tampering does not just apply to the physical aspects of "nudging" as demonstrated above. It can be difficult to get objective perspective on the status of a particular activity or project. Tampering in these cases consist of overestimation or approximations and down playing the risks. While less physical, you can witness the impacts of tampering when you see project passing gates with the rest of the team scratching their head in amazement. The impact of tampering becomes more prominent when the project activity duration or the detailed description of the desired end state is not so clearly articulated. If you can't describe the output in a tangible way, measurement becomes difficult.

D. Box-Luceño

A powerful alternative to the woes of tampering lies in the technique advocated by Box and Luceño[2] in their book on control of processes. First, they look at detecting small shifts in process performance and they recommend either the exponential weighted moving average (EWMA) control chart or the accumulated sum (CuSum) control chart since both of these are more sensitive than Shewhart control charts. Then, they propose a control system where the deviation of the process from the desired value is adjusted using a gain (a percentage of the total deviation opposite in value to the deviation itself). Then, they present data to support the benefits of using this technique.

IX. Selection of Variable

Variables selected for variable control charts should be critical to quality. How do we know what is critical to quality (CTQ)? Because it is:

- Important to customer perception
- It can be counted or measured
- We can tell whether we are achieving it

If we have performed a quality function deployment (QFD), we will have an idea of the items that are of concern to the customer (the voice of the customer). Alternatively, we can construct a hierarchical CTQ tree to try and clarify the items that are critical to quality.

If we are in a true process control situation, we can also measure the control variables. That is, which variables contribute to the ability of the process to remain on target?

A. Other Considerations

A process that is completely out of control is not a good candidate for control charts. An out of control process will have little else but special causes. Hence, in order to use the control charts, we would want to bring the process under some kind of reasonable control. In the beginning, it may make more sense to track the data of interest with a simple run chart, which will show the variation without having to concern us with control limits. Remember, however, that a control chart can be calculated even in a situation with substantial amounts of random data (noise); what is questionable is the business advantage achieved from those measurements.

Once we have chosen the variable of interest, what will be our sampling plan? Keep in mind that although variable control charts are incredibly efficient with regard to information, they really don't tell us a whole lot about reject rates. An attribute chart is more appropriate when the topic of concern is the level of product rejection. Additionally, attribute-based sampling schemes have a substantial literature: ANSI Z1.4, MIL-STD-1235C (continuous sampling), Dodge-Romig, and various other sampling schemes.

X.   Flow Charts

Flow charts[1] are exactly what they sound like: graphical representations of flow. Generally, the flow of which we speak or write is that of a process. The process flow can be that of software, a manufacturing sequence, a set of instructions, or a recipe. In some cases, flow chart usage will tend to reduce extraneous terminology, particularly with instructions. When we use instructions, we are always in the imperative mood (verb followed by nouns and qualifiers) except when making a decision, in which case, we use something more like a material conditional (if this, then do ....; if that, then do ...; and so on).

An organization may have its processes illustrated via flow charts (see figure 12). Since projects are by definition unique, the project manager may find it necessary to tailor fit processes for the specific project. It is possible that the organization may not have a defined process for a particular set of circumstances. In that event it would be better for the project manager to produce flow charts for the missing or unique processes for the team. If the project manager is missing the requisite understanding of the needed process, the line manager can aid or be the source for developing the flow chart. In short, we use whatever resources we have to enhance our comprehension of our own processes.

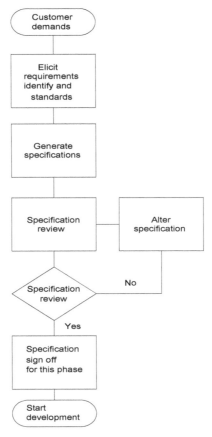

Figure 3.12 Example of a flow chart.

A. ANSI standard

Flow chart symbols were definitively defined by ANSI in standard X3.5 in 1970 (see Figure 3.12). Since that time, a few additions/extensions have been made unofficially, but the standard is generally well-understood by people who have never even heard of X3.5

B. UML

The Unified Modeling Language (UML) is an object-oriented alternative to the ANSI X3.5 standard. While some of the symbols remain the same (e.g., the diamond for selection), UML provides a much richer set of constructs. UML is also able to provide symbols for data modeling, which were not part of X3.5, but belonged to other standards such as the military "iDef" standards.

XI. Ishikawa Diagram (Fish Bone Diagram, Cause and Effect Diagram)

The Ishikawa diagram is named in honor of the Japanese quality expert and scientist, Kaoru Ishikawa, who promoted the use of the tool. The concept is simple, which explains the widespread use of the tool.

In essence, we define a problem and place it into a box (see Figure 3.13). From that box we draw a spine; from the spine we draw some "bones." For each "bone," we might have topics such as: man, machine, methods, measurements, materials, environment, and so on. We choose topics that make sense for our particular issue, although alliterative choices are not uncommon (e.g., people, policies, purchases, programs, etc.).

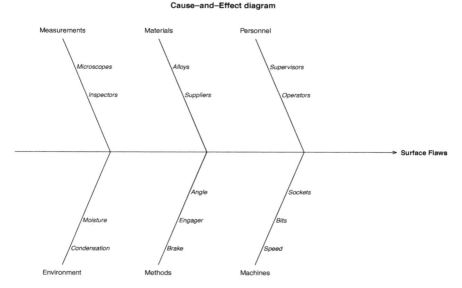

Figure 3.13 Ishikawa (cause-and-effect, fishbone) diagram helps catalog potential failure modes.

Ishikawa diagrams provide a structure to imagining the possible causes for the particular effect under consideration. With this tool, the project manager can trace the effect through a number of "why does this happen" questions to the possible roots of the item under consideration. There can be interactions among the various proposed causes that produce the end effect and the same cause may end up in a variety of places in the structure of the fish bone.

XII. Histogram/Bar Graphs

The histogram[1] is similar to the Pareto chart in that it produces a graphical representation of data frequency. However, the histogram has no requirement that the data on the abscissa be sorted from most frequent to least frequent. The histogram has been around for more than a century and was created by Karl Pearson.

The histogram will sometimes present data in a specific order on the abscissa (x-axis); for example, intelligence quotient (IQ) test results are normally presented from lowest to highest and most frequently replicate a facsimile of the normal distribution, which may be an artifact of the measurement system itself. The data on the abscissa is usually collected into intervals called "bins" and the ordinal (y-axis) represents the frequency (see Figure 3.14); hence, multiplying the number of bins times the frequency for each bin and adding them up will give us the totality of the counted data.

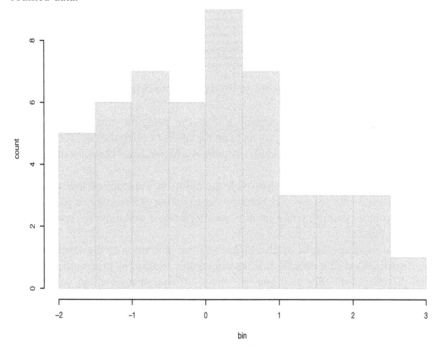

Figure 3.14 A typical normal distribution from relatively random data.

If the histogram has no order on the abscissa whatsoever, we might call this a bar chart. This situation occurs when the data is purely categorical and applying an order would be utterly arbitrary; for example, we are counting the number of blind individuals by species and representing the results visually.

How is this kind of chart helpful to the project manager? A project manager might want to track the number of discovered and later-discovered software errors over time, which would be a time series version of a bar chart, since the data is clearly count data.

XIII.   Checklists/Check Sheets

A checklist is an ordered table of activities or items that need to be completed or acted upon (see Figure 3.15) In the most primitive case, we can create handwritten checklists and literally check off each item. One of the great features of a checklist

Project Checklist

Project	Project Title	w -18	w -16	w -14	w -12	w -10	w -8	w -6	w -4	w -2	SoP
###	Name	complete	complete								

(Column group headers across the top, repeating for each time period: Production releases done, Design Change release, Test chassis build, Integration test complete, Set production introduction date, Spare Parts released, Pre-builds complete, PPAPs planned 100%)

Figure 3.15 Example of countdown to production checklist.

from the program management aspect is that the program manager can nearly completely control the actions of project team members through the use of exhaustive checklists. In fact, the work breakdown structure is a hierarchical checklist of the tasks and deliverables for the project.

We have seen checklists used to provide the objective evidence on the state of the project for staged-gate reviews. If parts of the checklist are missing, a judgment is made as to whether that infraction inhibits passing the gate and moving on to the next stage of the project.

Of course there are limits to checklists, and one limitation is the level of detail of that item itself on that checklist. What constitutes success or achievement of that item on the checklist? For example, we check off design review, but we had few people participate with insufficient time with the documentation prior to the review. It

Name of project
project number
check list

Project	Date	w1126	w1127	w1128	w1129	w1130	w1131	w1132	w1133	w1134	w1135	w1136	w1137	w1138	w1139	w1140	w1
Kickoff meeting																	
Customer clarification																	
Concept generation and selection																	
Release schedule and content defined																	
Prototype builds																	
Tooling needs identified																	
Concept/requirements freeze																	
Systems specification review																	
Systems specification release																	
Schematic reviews																	
Schematic freeze																	
Detailed specifications																	
Packaging design																	
Packaging design review																	
Packaging released																	
Prototype parts released																	
Detailed specifications																	
Review of detailed specifications																	
Tooling frozen																	
FEMA Analysis																	
Design review																	
Test scope																	
Test case generation																	
Test case review																	
P parts released target																	
Receive parts for the field testing trucks																	
Install parts on test vehicles																	
Testing system integration																	
Test and fault reports issued																	

Figure 3.16 Simple Gantt chart of an arbitrary project.

is difficult to glean all of that information from a checklist item labeled design review. Would that constitute closure of this item on the checklist?

From the negative point of view, we see some people balk at being provided with checklists, even though the use of checklists virtually assures success when followed completely and correctly. These people may think the process of the checklist unfairly restricts their ability to produce the deliverable item (see Figure 3.16). The same could be true for the project management activities. We often get the feeling that these people hide under the word "pragmatic" when it comes to product development. They wish to not be encumbered by a process—which generally produces ad hoc results.

A check sheet is a different kind of document than a checklist. With a check sheet, we record the frequency of items on the sheet often with handwritten hash marks. If we only have one order column of titles for the data and we record the data frequency as horizontal hash marks going to the right, we will end up with a rough estimate of the discrete distribution for this data. We must take care with bin sizes and also verify that the data is appropriate to a statistical distribution.

XIV. Exercises

- Explain in a well-reasoned essay which tools seem to be the most useful for the TQM project manager.

- Explain the relationship between the project manager and the line manager in a matrix organization.

- Describe how TQM tools allow the project manager to understand and mitigate risks to the project.

- When would you use a Pareto diagram?

- Create an Ishikawa diagram for an effect you wish to understand the cause.

- Create a checklist for the quality activities for a product with which you are familiar.

- Explain the difference between checklists, and check sheets.

- Draw flow chart for a project change management process.

- What is a control chart?

- Provide two examples of tampering. Show how tampering is not always a physical event.

Endnotes

1. Brassard, Michael, Lynda Finn, Dana Ginn, and Diane Ritter. The Six Sigma Memory Jogger II. Salem, NH: GOAL/QPC, 2002.

2. Box, George E. P., and Alberto Luceno. Statistical Control by Monitoring and Adjustment. New York, NY: John Wiley and Sons, 1997.

CHAPTER 4 – PROJECT MANAGEMENT TOOLS

I. Rubric

	Novice	Sr. Novice	Journey-man	Sr. Jour-neyman	Master
WBS	x	x	x	x	x
Dependen-cies		x	x	x	x
Project Gates			x	x	x
Brain-strorming techniques				x	x
Risk man-agement				x	x
Estimating techniques				x	x
EVM				x	x
White book					x
Project clos-ing					x

II. Questions to Ponder

- Do maturity models provide any added value?
- Are maturity models too abstract or are they really down-to-earth?
- How does scope change impact the WBS? Does your organization have a controlled way of updating the WBS with this content?
- How can the project manager understand the organization's ability to respond to changes?
- Can you really count on a normal distribution for the estimates?
- Does your organization recognize the input from the experts? What happens when the "truth" is told about risk to the project?
- How can the project manager account for task variation on the critical path items on the time line?
- Why is the maturity model approach so seductive?
- Does the enterprise really need a formal audit?
- If our organization transforms itself such that it achieves one of the "higher" levels, have we really accomplished anything?

- Does the maturity model designation have any marketing value?
- Why do we have so many maturity models?
- Why are the maturity models different and yet the same (compare and contrast)?
- Does the stage gate model of project management work?
- Is a maturity model audit just another way to make somebody some money?
- Is the ISO version better than the other models?
- Why can't we just "roll our own?"

III. Why Project Management Tools Are Important to the Project Manager

Our toolbox provides us with a standard means for achieving project and program objectives. The tools provide a kind of working language common to most project managers and well-known industry-wide.

IV. TQM Project Manager Scenario

A. Situation

We were worked on an automotive project that was initiated to develop a new subsystem for the vehicle. This meant a few new parts and a number of new functions for existing parts. Repeated requests for detailed functional content of each software delivery produced nothing but heartburn for the test and verification group— seemingly disregarded. The challenge was to understand all of the functions and when these would be delivered, so the testing of the components and the system could be optimized. In other words, only test the features that are to be delivered—when they are delivered. The problem is, nobody could or would provide the individual software and hardware content information in detail.

B. Objective

For this project we did not have adequate configuration management or functional synchronization among the myriad changing controllers on the vehicle. The objective was to comprehend the content of each software package from each component (and ultimately, the system). In that way, the testing focuses on the parts that are delivered and does not waste time testing what does not exist. In the end, the scope of the testing was to cover all of the changes as well as regression testing for the previous and unaltered functions.

C. Action

In the early releases we tested only those parts that were explicitly defined— this being many fewer than the quantity contained in the entire scope of the project. However, it was a place from which to start. When the subsequent releases of the software were delivered by the various subsystem and component owners, we still did not have this detailed list of software delivery, functions, and dates. So we started testing all of the expected functions that would end up in the final software package.

The test group tested top down from a prioritized list of specifications. This meant that at times the verification people would find problems within a software package—because that function was not yet delivered by the development group. The development staff would say after the fact "oh that function has not been built." The test group would still produce a fault report for the missing feature. At the end of this round of testing the project had a list of fault reports that were associated with requirements. Thus the fault list became also the list of feature content as well as the list of missing feature content.

D. Results

The suppliers typically identified fault reports clearly so that the new software could close out in their software release notes. Thus, for each subsequent package the suppliers provided a list of fault reports using the test report identifiers (Example: FR1209) found in the fault tracking system. From then on, the requirements met in each software package were much more identifiable, and hence, the testing was much more focused upon what was delivered and not the functions and features that did not exist.

E. Aftermath

We used the tools that were in place to achieve the objective. When it was not possible to get the specific contents of the software for each component in the system, we used the system that was available to log the failures and track the failures that are really the definition of the system. We found out what these organizations measure and used those mechanisms to get what was needed to meet the objective. This method produced many reported faults that were not, in fact, faults; however, fault reports were monitored. The suppliers provided detailed information to close a fault report—actually reporting the fault report number in the software release notes. One person remarked that maybe we need this "tough love" to keep the organization in progress while highlighting the absent functionality.

V.   Scope

A. Work Breakdown Structures

We address the WBS elsewhere. One of the primary purposes for the WBS is to allow the project manager to manage scope. The unplanned trip to a more complicated product is called scope creep, leading to unbilled work and schedule disruption. The WBS is a tool we can share with our customers because they should observe the effect they have on the general prosecution of the program or project. This is also where we lay the groundwork for applying the TQM tools. Sufficiently decomposing the tasks required to deliver identifies the key areas of the project and the product to which we can compare future measurement. This identification of the key areas will be exactly where we want to ply our TQM tools. It does not matter if those measures be product area, functional area of the organization, or the project management area of the organization. In this section we will see how the TQM tools can be applied to the project management discipline and those metrics.

VI. Project Estimating Techniques

Aside from scope, the next most important thing is identifying what it takes to achieve the objective or scope. During the scope elicitation we have gathered the tasks and dependencies that are needed to meet the project demands as dictated by the scope. Once we identify the tasks we have to find a way to quantify those tasks. How long does it take to complete each of those tasks? How do we arrive at those estimates? We have seen project schedules put together that show the delivery of tasks that are point source durations. For example, that task will take exactly 32 hours as if there was one possibility. There are few times when you can say with some certainty how long a task will take to complete. Even when the task is something that we have performed a number of times, there are still issues or problems that can be encountered that we have not seen in the past. There are ways to reduce some of the risk to the estimating process such as:

- Program evaluation review technique (PERT)
- Expert knowledge
- Historical record

A. PERT

PERT planning involves the following steps:

- Define specific tasks and milestones
- Determine the sequence of the tasks
- Build a network diagram
- Estimate the duration for each task
- Determine critical path (if one exists)
- Update the PERT chart throughout project

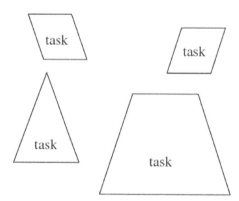

Figure 4.1 If we have a set of separated tasks, we must link them based on dependencies.

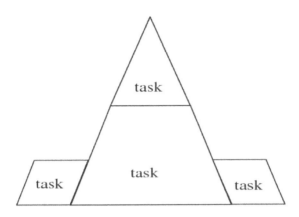

Figure 4.2 Tasks begin to fall into place as we analyze them.

1. Define tasks and milestones

The tasks are the things required to complete the project. The milestones are the events marking the beginning and end of one or more tasks. It is helpful to list the tasks in a table that in later(see Figure 4.1) steps can be expanded to include information on sequence and duration.

2. Determine task sequence

This step may be combined with the task identification step, since the task sequence is evident for some tasks (see Figure 4.2). Other tasks may require more analysis to determine the exact order in which they must be performed. The manner in which we assemble the tasks of our project defines what tasks will end up on the critical path. .Thus we should give attention to these dependencies we create and not violate those dependencies that are required, such as software availability, before testing starts. Neither should we create artificial dependencies.

3. Construct the network diagram

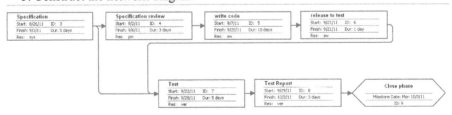

Figure 4.3 Example of a network diagram, providing more information than we get from a Gantt chart.

Using the task sequence information, we can draw a network diagram showing the sequence of the serial and parallel tasks (see Figure 4.3). For the original task-on-arc model, the tasks are depicted by arrowed lines and milestones are depicted by circles or "bubbles."

If done manually, several drafts may be required to correctly portray the relationships among tasks. Software packages simplify this step by automatically converting tabular task information into a network diagram.

4. Estimate task times

Weeks are a commonly used unit of time for task completion and we find the use of weeks is often more realistic than using days or hours. For each task, we define three duration estimates:

- Optimistic time—the shortest time in which the task can be completed. We usually define our optimistic time as three standard deviations from the mean; hence, there is roughly a one percent chance that the task will complete within the optimistic time

- Most likely time—the completion time having the *highest probability*. Not the same as expected duration

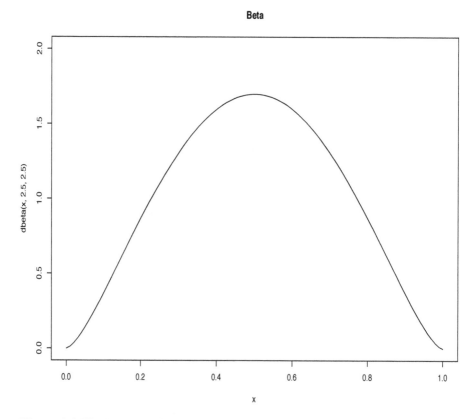

Figure 4.4 The beta distribution models the array of values we can use to predict our task completion.

- Pessimistic time—the longest time that a task might require. We again use three standard deviations from the mean

PERT assumes a beta probability distribution for the time estimates (see Figure 4.4). For a beta distribution, the expected time for each task can be approximated using the following weighted average:

Expected time = (Optimistic + 4 x Most likely + Pessimistic) / 6

To calculate the variance for each task completion, we select three standard deviation durations (see Figure 4.5) for the optimistic and pessimistic times, giving us six standard deviations between them (*if* we *assume* a beta distribution); hence, the variance is given by:

[(Pessimistic — Optimistic) / 6]^2

Task variance can be important because it provides clues to the level of risk

WBS designation	WBS description	Estimate responsible	Optimistic estimate (hours)	most likely estimate (hours)	pessimist estimate (hours)	task variance	68.26%		
1.1.2.	review hw content	JMQ	3	5	5.31	0.385	4.3	4.7	5.1
1.2.2.	review sw content	KHP	1	2	3	0.333	1.7	2.0	4.4
			2	5	10	1.333	4.0	5.3	13.1
			2	10	20	3.000	7.3	10.3	25.8

Figure 4.5 PERT task variance in tabular format.

associated with the estimates. An estimate with a large variance in the task estimate implies that we have some discomfort in the estimate or a lack of certainty. Tasks that have a lower variance suggest some level of comfort with the estimation by the person performing them. This comfort may not be for any real reason—it could be the person has none of the prerequisite knowledge to perform the estimates. Maybe we have an overly optimistic person performing the estimates. Follow up with questions when reviewing the variation may provide some additional clues as to the reason for the estimates as they are. If the variation is large, we should approach that task with some caution (see Figure 4.6). How does this uncertainty work in the project schedule?

task variance	68.26%			99.46%		99.73%		99.99%	
0.385	4.3	4.7	5.1	3.9	5.5	3.6	5.9	2.4	7.0
0.333	1.7	2.0	4.4	1.3	2.7	1.0	3.0	0.0	4.0
1.333	4.0	5.3	13.1	2.7	8.0	1.3	9.3	-2.7	13.3
3.000	7.3	10.3	25.8	4.3	16.3	1.3	19.3	-7.7	28.3

Figure 4.6 PERT probability for durations.

5. Determine the critical path

The critical path is determined by adding the times for the tasks in each sequence and calculating the longest, contiguous, slackless path in the project. The critical path determines the total elapsed time required for the project; that is to say, the longest path will give us the shortest time estimate! If non-critical path tasks accelerate or decelerate down, project duration remains unchanged. This statement will hold true until non-critical path tasks consume their slack time.

If the critical path cannot be readily calculated, we can look at the following four estimates for each task:

- ES—Earliest Start time
- EF—Earliest Finish time
- LS—Latest Start time
- LF—Latest Finish time

These times are calculated using the estimated time for all the selected tasks. We determine the earliest start and finish times of each task by scheduling *forward* through our network and establishing the earliest time at which a task can start and finish, all the while considering its dependent tasks. The latest start and finish times are the latest times that a task can start and finish without delaying the project. LS and LF are found by working *backward* through the network. The difference in the latest and earliest finish of each task is that task's slack. The critical path then is the path through the network in which none of the tasks *in that path* has any slack.

The variance in the project completion time can be calculated by summing the variances in the completion times of the tasks in the critical path (see Figure 4.7).

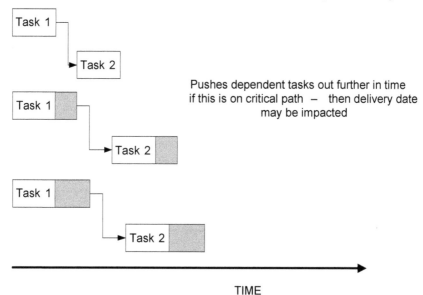

Figure 4.7 The impact of task variation on dependent tasks.

Given this variance, we calculate the probability that the project will be completed by a certain date, assuming a normal distribution for the critical path (we need historical data in order to make this assumption—otherwise we are assuming the risk of a specious statistical model). The normal distribution assumption will hold if the number of tasks in the path is sufficiently large to apply the central limit theorem (meaning, we have the means of the items we measured).

Because the critical path determines the completion date of the project, we might be able to accelerate the project by adding the resources required to reduce the duration of the tasks in the critical path. When we apply this method for schedule diminution, we call it "project crashing."

6. Update as Project Progresses

We must adjust the PERT chart through the duration of the project. We replace estimated times with actual times. When we have the inevitable slowdowns, we may request additional resources to remain on schedule and we must modify the PERT chart to communicate our new information.

Benefits of PERT

PERT can be useful to the project manager because it provides the following information:

* Estimated project completion date

* Probability of completion before, on, or after a specified date

* The critical path tasks that have an impact on the completion time

* The tasks with slack time—they can lend resources to critical path tasks

* Task start and end dates

Limitations

The following are some of PERT's weaknesses:

* The task time estimates are usually subjective and depend on opinion

* Even when task durations are well-estimated, PERT assumes a beta distribution for these time estimates, but the real distribution can be significantly different

* Even if we buy the beta distribution, PERT assumes that the probability distribution of the project completion time is the same as that of the critical path. Because other paths can become the critical path if their component tasks are inhibited, PERT will consistently underestimate the estimated project completion time.

The underestimation of the project completion time due to alternate paths becoming critical is generally the most serious of these issues. To overcome this limitation, we can employ Monte Carlo simulations on the network to eliminate optimistic bias in the estimated project completion date; however, good Monte Carlo simulation will require historical bases for assuming probability distributions.

B. Experience / Experts

Like an experienced carpenter who can look at a project and estimate the amount of material required, technical experts can provide some insight into the steps and the amount of time to achieve the specific deliverables. The expertise can be especially worthwhile if the expert has the knowledge of the specific organization as well as the domain knowledge. Specific experiences within the organization impact the estimation process. For example, an expert in testing may know the typical order of activities, but may not know the amount of time required to perform the specific activities. The expert could estimate based upon past experience; however, if that experience is outside the present organization much may be different. Domain experience (process understanding) as well as organization experience can go a long way to improving WBS content and subsequent schedule estimation.

It is beyond the scope of this book to identify all of the methods for extracting expert perspectives, though a brief list is provided below. In the absence of explicit historical data that is known to be accurate, expert perspective is an alternative for gathering this information. The scope sets the stage for uncovering this perspective, industry and organization processes and practices. Specific domain experience as well as organizations experience can help fill the void of lack of data. By way of example, the Delphi Technique elicits expert perspectives from answers via questionnaires.

With the Delphi Technique, a panel of experts is asked questions. The answers to these questions are compiled by the person performing the activity, into a set of answers and rationale for those answers as reported by the experts. This compiled work is then passed back to the experts, so they can see the perspectives (anonymously) of the other experts participating. The result is a collaborative effort without the risk of groupthink or other contamination of the individual perspectives. It is also possible to perform statistical analysis of the results, for example the mean, median, or mode on specific answers.

Another example of the use of experts is "consensual estimating" found in *Project Planning Scheduling & Control* by James P. Lewis. This methodology counsels gathering individual estimates for the WBS areas and then reviewing the results collectively (in a meeting) to clarify the various perspectives. The subsequent meetings are a forum to define the reasons for differences in the estimating process. Lewis continues counsel regarding the benefits of such an approach:

- No one person "on the hook" if there are repercussions
- Team learning
- Gathering all factors that could impact the estimates more likely with divergent or differing perspectives
- Commitment to the estimates and making things happen

C. Historical Data

Historical data in project parlance can also be referred to as analogous data. This works when the project is similar to a previous project—for example instrument clusters for an automobile. If we have been performing a multitude of these sorts of projects, we can estimate what it takes to produce this product based upon our past experience. We may know, for example, the dollar amount to produce the product based upon a certain level of technology. All things remaining equal, this can be an adequate starting place for developing specifics (cost, time, quality) regarding the product. A single point source (a sample of one) may be of some help in estimating, but does not consider any possible variation in the project outcome.

We show examples of how historical data is used throughout the book. For historical data to be useful you must have confidence in that data. For example, Figure

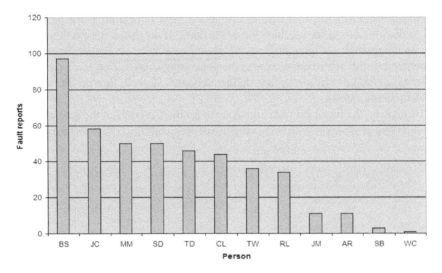

Figure 4.8 Bugs or failures reported by individual allows us to check for potential skills problems.

4.8 shows the fault reports for a particular test group over a period of time. We can use these faults reported and see we have a distribution of faults reported. There could be a number of reasons for the Pareto chart to have this appearance, including the suspicion that some of the staff are more capable than are others. If that would be the case, we would find ways to bring the rest of the staff up to similar performance. There really is insufficient information in the graphic to tell!

You must not suspect or believe there is manipulation or gaming of the system to produce the "acceptable" values on which to build. After all, we are building a new project and product based upon a course of actions and estimates from this historical record. Invalid data may put the project onto the same failure path as the previous project if the data is invalid.

This may mean you have to cheat the system to make the results work out favorably. Like all data, it is only as valuable as the validity. This accuracy of data frequently affects the project management discipline when considering the question from the employees "against what WBS should I put my time."

Additionally, changes in the organization's processes may have an impact on the validity of that historical data in future context. That is what process improvement is all about. Presumably the changes in the organization's processes were precipitated by a need to improve performance, reduce cost, or otherwise reduce the risk. It should be expected to see some change in the outcome of that particular process. To develop a correlation between any process changes and the recorded historical data requires tracking of the process changes. As an example, consider a company that has previously employed the waterfall method of development and is migrating to scrum or some hybrid approach, or If the project is more distributed than those contained within the historical record. In those cases, the deviation from the past methods must be considered. Does this new data belong in the same collection as the other? What can be discerned from the combination of the data? If the data is messy, then not much can be interpreted; for example, are we seeing new data, an outlier, or the start of some trend. If this is a trend, what was the generating cause? That is why we need to understand changes that were made deliberately and, as such, is a portion of the data collection requirements.

Ultimately, the historical data allows us to produce models of the area of concern, which in turn provides us with some measure of predictability. The better the model, the

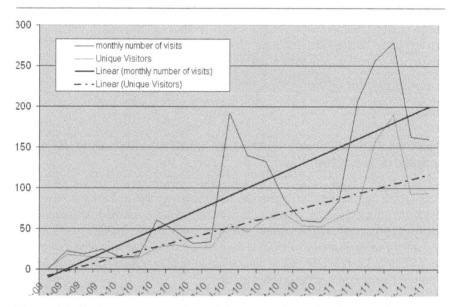

Figure 4.9 Performance over time with average lines showing trends.

better the prediction, or as in the case of project management, the better possibility the planning and controlling actions will meet the requirements of the project. In fact, when we have enough historical data to allow us to model the situations encountered, we are in a position to effect early project control—anticipating the areas that generate over-runs, poor quality, and late delivery. Historical data allows us to see what variation we really have in the performance of an organization—and this variation supplies inputs for business management philosophies such as total quality management (see Figure 4.9). Analysis of historical data by using TQM tools turns this data into actionable information. It allows the project to organize and plan to meet the actual possibilities. These possibilities range from our example of the vehicle availability to test to the distribution of the possible durations for specific tasks, to the calculation of potential project termination dates.

VII. Project Budgeting

Project budgeting is not relegated solely to the monetary portions of a project—being the most obvious area. However, the fact is that this is only part of the story. Budgets are also part of outsourced work and material purchases and acquisitions. Project budgeting, to maximize efficacy, requires budgets associated with the work breakdown structure as well as with different organizational functions as well as different organizations. These budgets are driven by the scope of the work as defined in the work breakdown structure as well as the attributes of that work—such as level of quality or refinement of the output of that part of the organization. The previously discussed historical data helps fill in the gaps. All of this goes into the cost estimating for the project and the allocation of the resources as defined by the needs or argument. Due to the transient nature of projects and the fact that projects are not operations and take on different scope, we can still find unaccounted-for variation. This will be discussed further in the risk section.

If we are an organization that has mature processes or performs a similar set of projects; for example, software development for automotive applications, we can develop checklists to make sure we include the appropriate activities to achieve the goals of the project. Even if the processes are not mature, we can rely upon the experts to put these activities together to assist the project manager in determining the set of tasks required for that portion of the project, and eventually, the durations and associated budgets.

A. Time Phasing

In planning our project, we will have a list of activities that are recorded in our work breakdown structure. This list encapsulates the project objectives in an easy-to-decipher format. We identified the attributes for success of each of these elements in the breakdown structure. How will we know that we have met each specific deliverable? This information is contained in the work breakdown structure dictionary. From this list of qualified activities, durations and a schedule are developed. This schedule shows the use of project human resources. In turn, this provides the baseline of the project—a road map if you would—of the use of time and money (instantiated as schedule and budget) for the project. This time phasing will be compared against the actual time taken during the execution portion of the project. Comparing the expected hours consumed (the road map) to the actual values provides an objective indication of the state of the use of resources by the project.

In addition to the human resources, project-incurred expenses such as tools or fixtures should also have a place in time phasing. This provides the organization with the same road map for the tools and other project-related expenses. Again, comparison of the actual values with those on the expected road map provides clues to the state of the project. Depending upon the variation of the actual values, the project manager can take necessary counteractions to manage the risk of the project exceeding the budget. We will discuss this in further detail in the metrics and control section where earned value management is explored. Once we have established our schedules, dependencies, and complete list of deliverable items, we move to the next step.

VIII.   Cost Estimating

Cost estimating can be derived much as we did with the estimations of duration. Historical data can be used for projects that have similar themes. Consider, for example, an automotive company that routinely develops an instrument cluster for cars (colloquially referred to as a "dash," although this name really refers to the entire assembly in the vehicle cabin). Given a consistent supplier base and good records, it should be possible to provide a range of possibilities for the cost of such a project. This is especially valid if the technology employed has not changed appreciably between releases of the product. The use of the historical information can help reduce the risk associated with variation in validity of the estimates. In fact, the more data that exists for these similar projects, the better. In that case, a distribution of the possible project costs provides insight into the range of possibilities for the effort. Of course, the historical record will only take us so far. Basing the future cost estimates upon faulty historical records is unlikely to provide us with data integrity we desire.

Let's consider material acquisition for a project. For specific commodities—an example would be copper for wire harnesses—we can monitor the cost of the raw material and use this to predict the future cost and account for this in our material acquisition. We can use the TQM tools such as histograms and time series analyses to predict, or at least, be aware of the cost volatility of the material for the project. If the business case for the project is based upon an end cost for the product—and most business cases are—to maintain the margins in the face of increasing material costs will require increasing sales costs, or we will see erosion of the profit margin contribution by the product to the company. The result would be a product that does not produce the desired revenue generating impact expected by the enterprise and becomes a loss until the material cost returns to the point assumed in the financial calculation. Maybe this material cost never goes back to that of the original estimate. In that case, the company has lost the development money as well as the opportunity cost for pursuing other projects that may be more profitable. We also have the option to salvage the product; we can pour many resources into removing content and numerous design changes to bring the product back to profitability.

Estimating can be further complicated when the project covers a significant time—say many months to a few years. In these cases, organizational, procedural, and technological changes can affect the validity of estimates at the start of the project. It may not be easily foreseen that availability of a particular skill set may diminish over time. The more scarce the resource, the more probable it is that we will see a risk of higher cost for that particular talent or resource over time. This may not be known at the start of a project unless there is considerable expenditure of effort in forecasting and even then we must bear in mind the perils of extrapolation.

If the estimations are a response to a request for proposal, we have yet another complication. We still have the business case issues where overestimating may remove our organization as a candidate for the project. If we underestimate the project, we either have to renegotiate or suffer the loss—depending upon the contract type this could be unpleasant. Cancelling the project may not be as simple as cancelling an internally-developed project when we learn more about the costs associated such a cancellation. For external customer work, we must be cognizant of the contract and cost implications at a higher level due to legal conditions imposed by the contract.

So we can see that cost estimating is not a single event that happens at the start of the project, though cost estimating at the start of a project is important as well. As we work into the project, we learn more about the details, requirements, and impediments that allow us to make better predictions of the cost for the product and the cost of the development effort. In our staged-gate project management model, discussed later in this chapter, we progressively improve the estimates. As we move through the project some of the possible early risks to the project do not consummate. This situation means any costs associated with these risks were avoided. Essentially, as we work through the project, the risks become fewer (fewer items remain that could go wrong), but the consequences of the remaining risks can be quite severe—termination of the project. The termination of the project would mean all (or a significant amount) of the money put into the project to that date is likely lost—as well as any opportunity costs associated with our decisions.

As stated earlier, the validity of historical data depends upon the scope of the work included. Making radical departures from the past technical solutions may affect the reliability of the historical data (the probability that events will occur in a similar way). Additionally, major changes in the process may affect the validity of that historical data in a future context. Consider a company that has previously employed the waterfall approach to development and moves toward model-based development. In this case the previous material cost historical data may not directly apply. Instead of developing individual parts, the models fulfill the role of the actual material and this will probably affect the material costs. Once again, the expert perspective can help to reduce these risks. We can use domain experience, such as:

- Project budgets
- Prototype material construct
- Material handling
- Manufacturing
- Product development
- Engineering
- Purchasing

Ultimately, knowledge of the costing is similar to schedule estimating. As we progress through the project, just like our GPS system, we learn more about the probable distribution of the cost.

A. Project Budgets

Budgets are assigned to the work areas responsible for the deliveries. In our WBS we have identified the work to be done. We have estimated what it takes to successfully deliver the respective pieces of the project (success as defined in the WBS dictionary). Typically those that perform the work own the budget for their part of the work. Control accounts plans (CAPs), also referred to as cost account plans, are the beginning of prerequisites for the earned value management activities discussed later. This plan juxtaposes the work to be performed—the WBS element and the responsible entity—with the money to achieve the work package objectives. All of which is done under the guidance of the project manager—after all, the project manager is responsible for the entire budget. The result is a WBS that links the performing entity (the line function responsible for the particular delivery) to a definition of success, and the budget for achieving the objective. The line function could be systems engineering, for example, delivering the concept to be detailed to meet the customer and organizations needs. All of these budgets roll up to produce the entirety of the project budget.

Budget control becomes more complicated depending on the organizational structure. To fully take advantage of the benefits requires taking the time to deconstruct the project to the "atomic" level and to have the dollars and hours linked to each "atomic" element. Another area of concern is how we measure the state of the particular task. If sufficiently deconstructed, it boils down to a binary discussion. The task/deliverable is either complete, or it is not. When the task requires multiple weeks, assessment of the state of progress becomes difficult to determine, or allows loop holes for manipulating the system. If we can't definitively and objectively associate the level of completeness, we will see problems using the earned value management techniques discussed later. Finally, as is sometimes seen, the duration must apply in the service of that specific activity. For example, it is inappropriate to place time on office moves onto a project activity that has nothing to do with that office move. Neither should non-billable hours be substituted for this project work. At the time of evaluation, the hours to accomplish the WBS as defined in the CAP must be for performing the work in that WBS.

B. Cost Containment

We know the baseline of the project costs with our time phased budget. The time phased budget we produced, now is used as the measuring stick to compare the future project expenditures. The tighter the review (weekly or monthly) the finer or coarser the granularity of cost sampling, the quicker or slower the response time. The longer time between reviews of the actual budget compared to the baseline, the more latency or slower response time possible by the project manager and team to attend to the correction, ultimately containing the potential cost overrun. This focus upon the project execution and comparison of the performance to the planned activities is one of the benefits of the agile project management methods. The sooner we find a misstep, the sooner we can offer up a corrective action or otherwise make adjustments. Experience suggests that this review of the baseline to the actual events happens all too infrequently if it happens at all. When we take this approach we agree to relinquish some level of control response to cost for the fewer resources required to do the work. In this way we can have one project manager attempting to manage a multiplicity of projects and budgets and not performing particularly well.

C. Competitive Bidding

When we know the sources of our cost and control our costs, we are in a position to provide a competitive bid for the work. Knowing the capabilities of the organization in mathematical terms establishes the envelope of possibilities for our project delivery. In knowing this information, we then are able to account for this variation in our response to the request for quote (RFQ) in a way that addresses our customer's desire to maximize the value and our own organization profit motive.

IX. Project Scheduling Fundamentals

We have already covered the prerequisites of scope, work breakdown structure, budgets, and dependencies. It should come as no surprise that resource availability has an effect upon schedule development. Yet, experience suggests, that behind incomplete or unknown scope, resource availability and use are the next trouble areas for project managers. There is a difference between hours to complete a specific task, and the number of days it would take to complete these, neither of these factors necessarily being equal. This situation depends upon utilization of the resources; for example, what are the typical non-billable hours (hours consumed that are not associated with project work) per week. How many other projects require these same resources at the same time? How many of these resources are committed to these projects as well? These are the sorts of things that impact the available hours for doing the work. This same constraint applies when the resource carries portions of multiple projects—for example verification activities for a number of different projects that run concurrently. We suggest that common sense makes it folly to assume 100% utilization of resources.

The responsibility for the schedule depends upon the organization structure (functional, project, or the various levels of matrix organizations). For functional

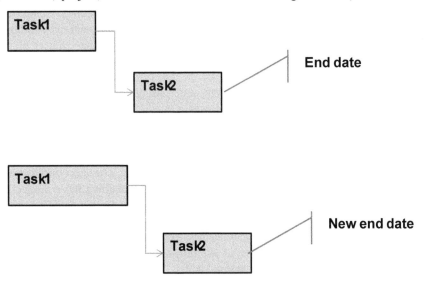

Figure 4.10 We begin to connect our tasks in a network that reflects the dependencies, also known as a directed graph.

organizations we can expect the schedule to be in the responsibility of the various line functions. The more complicated would be the matrix organization in which the schedule is put together through a collaboration of the line functions and the project manager. Or lastly, and seemingly all to frequent in occurrence—an upper level manager who sets an arbitrary date that has no basis in the actual work required—we have no task list, no work breakdown structure, and no knowledge of what it takes to deliver. This is really where the definition of the dependencies to each task really becomes obvious. We discussed dependencies earlier in the text. If we get these building blocks in the incorrect order, or we do not know what constitutes successful delivery of a particular block, we will have problems when it comes to producing the schedule and more importantly executing from the schedule. For example (see Figure 4.10), a delivery is made from one group to the downstream customer. Let us say it is a specification from which the test and verification group will be required to test. When the specification is delivered, there are missing pieces of information—and only now we start to make the necessary corrections to make testing of the product to the specification.

The more the project manager knows of the processes required to produce the product, the better he can contribute to the project schedule and will understand the various line functions and risk associated. For example, if a project manager does not understand the role of verification and test within the organization and a project, he is not likely to be able to make informed decisions. In fact experience suggests the interface between the project management and the verification and test activities are areas of contention, particularly because product validation tasks normally occur towards the end of the project after all the slack time has been consumed. As we have heard project managers say, "If we did our job correctly, we would not need testing." Additionally, this lack of knowledge makes it difficult to consider counsel by the experts and this is the only recourse left if the project manager does not have some level of skill in the processes.

Nothing can solve the seemingly arbitrary date setting enacted by the uninitiated and uninformed people in management. However, resource management is an often overlooked area regarding schedule development and control. Companies increasingly look to accomplish more with fewer resources. The focus upon the activities required to produce the desired results has consequences for resource utilization. This could be one of the reasons for scrum project management success. The short duration and daily focus ensure the resources that are identified are in fact doing those things that were committed. Barring this sort of intense focus, diffusing the available resources among a litany of projects is not a recipe for success. The "good, old school try" will not obtain the repeatable results that business demands. The approach of coercing employees to work significant amounts of overtime to make up for the fact that project schedules are unrealistic is at best a temporary fix. This approach is a great way for an organization to drive down the morale of the staff. Additionally, we suggest that overtime only nets a positive result for the company for a week or two. After that, you are making more mistakes and the focus on the details diminishes.

The job is not complete just because you have a completed schedule. Tracking the actual delivery dates to the scheduled delivery dates is an important part of controlling of a project. This includes defining how the progress of the activities in the time plan will be assessed. Examples include:

- Milestones
- Calculations
- Percent complete
- Audits or inspections
- Distribution over time

The goal is objective evidence on the state of the project's execution. To do that at the time the project is executing requires that the work be well defined and planned in time.

A. Project Accuracy Funnel

No matter the tool used, project estimating has a cone of uncertainty much like the way your GPS works. As you move through the project and tasks are completed, the risk associated with the delivery of those tasks either finish or don't. This provides real information for the project manager to base a recalculation of the project deliverable in terms of probable date of delivery and cost for the project and the result of the project. Much of this work is done by most project management software. A Gantt chart shown earlier can show the consequences of a task over-run in the time to deliver. If the

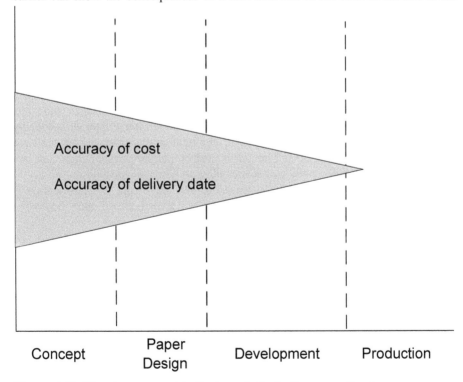

Figure 4.11 The closer we get to the target, the better our estimates.

dependencies are set up correctly and the project is correctly baselined, it is possible to see the new probable date of product release and compare it to the previous possibility The consequences of a task duration over-run are especially sensitive for the critical path. By definition an extension of this path through the project will inevitably lead to an effect on the probable delivery date. Figure 4.11 illustrates how the accuracy of the predicted date of conclusion improves over the time execution of the project.

B. Time Quanta (Weeks versus Days, versus Hours)

There is a relatively new project management methodology known as the agile approach. With agile project management, we find an emphasis on communications and constant monitoring of the project status with the team members. This constant monitoring and review of obstacles, ways to overcome hurdles, and altering of the plan based upon what is known, makes this a formidable project management approach. We cover these techniques in detail in our book *Scrum Project Management*. We make the analogy of a project as a control system, where we sample the output to provide feedback on current system performance, which we then compare to the desired performance and then make the necessary adjustments to bring the system back to the desired value or course[2]. This constant monitoring and adjusting by the project means we are never too far off from our base course when we know we have a problem, and therefore we are in a good position to expediently correct. The sooner the correction to the project direction, the less time and effort spent in this errant direction—essentially less time off course This is true whether we are considering schedule or cost performances of the project. The more lag in the response time, the longer the error or direction goes unchecked.

Some organizations employ the staged-gate model for their project management; in fact, we suggest that all project management models use some form of staged-gate even when this is not explicitly stated in the model. The project manager who waits until days before the gate review to understand the state of his project will probably have trouble surviving the gate untarnished. The total quality management tools are beneficial when deploying either method of project management. In each case, we can use tools like Pareto charts and scatter plots to better understand our ability to execute our projects. We monitor key variables and make sure this information is communicated to the team, allowing them to make decisions based upon the known state of the project and the project objectives.

X.   Communications Basics

A good project manager establishes communication with all stakeholders and provides an update mechanism to keep them involved and aware of project progress— enhancing meaningful communication improves organization and integration of development.

It can be argued that communication ability within a project is a success factor. In fact, in a paper by the Gartner Group titled "Project Management Skills: Avoiding Management by Crisis" in January 1996 identified "insufficient involvement of stakeholders and infrequent communication with sponsors as leading causes of project failure."[3]

Communication is one of the forces that can pull people together or tear a team apart. With effective communication, we do not have to arrive at the same conclusion or same direction only by luck. We use communication to:

- Understand the project sponsor's objective

- Make sure the team understands the project objective

- Uncover possible project risks and risk responses

- Initiate risk responses

- Communicate the state of our project to the project sponsors and team members

The total quality management tools can facilitate communication of the project objectives and status.

We should take active steps in creating a common understanding and conclusion. One way to make that happen is if we are communicating within the team and with the stakeholders. Communications challenges can abound. Many of us may recall the game we played as kids where a secret was whispered into the ear of one person and that secret was serially relayed to the rest of the group. Very seldom did the output

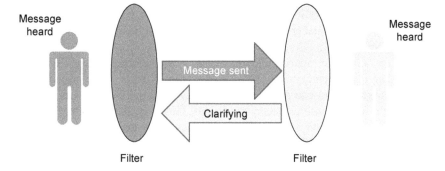

Figure 4.12 One model for communications.

secret match the original input secret (see Figure 4.12). Often this game was played with people who have the same native language. One could imagine how diverse the result is if we convey the secret among a variety of languages.

Communication is so important to project success that there are communications planning documents to facilitate and control this aspect of a project. The communications plan articulates the communications needs for the project to meet the stakeholder and team member needs. For small projects, a communications plan may not be necessary. The larger or more distributed the project, the more need for a formalized communications plan. Part of the communications plan includes progress reporting frequency and hierarchy for escalation situations as well as defining responsibilities and authorities. Who should be consulted and for what?

A communications plan facilitates communications among the required stakeholders, particularly when there are competing perspectives and demands upon a project. Within the communications plan resides the escalation to a higher level of management. The communications plan forces the project team to consider how information distributes among participants. The typical communications plan contains:

- Information distribution
- Information description
- Information schedule
- Progress reporting
- Communications plan revision
- Administrative closure

A. Stakeholders

The definition of stakeholder at project stakeholder management is "any person or organization that is actively involved in a project, or whose interests may be positively or negatively affected by execution or completion of the project." Using this definition, it is easy to see the stakeholders for the project are not just those who are providing the funding, though those people are also important members. The project participants are also part of this group. Conflicting perspectives, for example, performance and product cost, may have differing stakeholders. These conflicts must be resolved and quickly to keep the project on track.

A resource allocation matrix helps to clarify how the stakeholders fit. Without such a tool, all team members may believe they own all parts of the project and, at a minimum, they will not coordinate well. Like any good or effective team, there are times when these relationships become nebulous. However, the day a team member playing offensive guard on a football team decides to go out for a pass instead of block—that is a day that will cause a problem for the team in the loss of a quarterback. This matrix goes far to help understand the entirety of the stakeholders, and the areas in which they should respectively contribute. This resource allocation matrix describes what people are responsible for and attempts to depict the interaction of the team of stakeholders. Ultimately you want to:

- Identify who is responsible for what
- Understand their priorities
- Uncover and understand competing priorities (balancing)
- Know how and when and to whom to escalate
- Capitalize upon opportunities
- Minimize and deal with threats
- Know how to treat non-stakeholders behaving like stakeholders

B. Communications Channels

When we speak of communications channels, we are talking about the myriad possibilities for communication within the project: e-mail, voice mail, phone, face-to-face, virtually face-to-face, signage, documents, and tables. The more people, the more communications complexity that exists. Communications complexity does not consider the complexity of the communications, but solely the number of points of exchanges. If we add the number of channels to the intra- and inter-personal complexity of communications, we can readily understand why miscues, errors of understanding, and misdirections occur.

C. Escalation

There must be some way of resolving conflicts that can't be resolved by the project

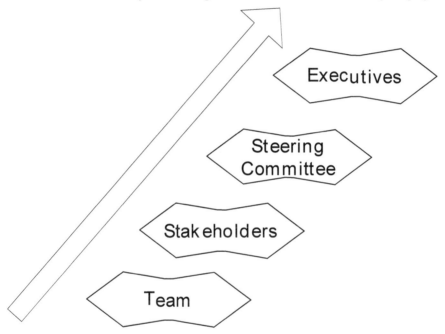

Figure 4.13 A good escalation process provides a rational approach to bringing attention to a situation.

manager within the project team (see Figure 4.13). This is the escalation plan, often included in the communications planning document. For large projects with many stakeholders, escalation may be what saves a project from being in a state of limbo while a decision on direction is *not* being made. Many organizations develop steering committees for large projects. This is one way of escalating any conflict that can't be managed within the project team and stakeholders. However, this is not the only way, and sometimes these committees meet at very specific times that may leave a project in a position where a decision needs to be made immediately but we have to wait for the steering committee to meet.

XI. Project Metrics and Control

We have previously been discussing the setup of the project and specific characteristics such as schedule and budget. These form the baseline from which we will compare our gathered information or metrics during the execution of the project. We have picked things in the project that we believe are key success factors. Since a project is measured at least in part upon its ability to deliver:

Organization B
Schedule Performance Index
Project Level A

	wk30	wk31	wk32	wk33	wk34	wk35	wk36	wk37	wk38	wk39	wk40	wk41	wk42
Project 1	1.00	0.98	0.97	0.95	0.89	0.88	0.88	0.85	0.83	0.82	0.82	0.79	0.77
Project 2		1.00	0.95	0.90	0.89	0.89	0.86	0.85	0.80	0.79	0.77	0.78	0.75
Project 3		1.00	0.99	0.98	0.96	0.97	0.98	0.97	0.96	0.99	0.96	0.95	0.94
Project 4		1.00	0.98	0.95	0.92	0.89	0.90	0.89	0.85	0.82	0.79	0.77	0.72
Project 5			1.00	0.92	0.89	0.87	0.82	0.80	0.81	0.79	0.77	0.73	0.70
Project 6			1.00	0.90	0.86	0.84	0.84	0.81	0.74	0.70	0.68	0.69	0.65
Project 7			1.00	0.93	0.90	0.88	0.85	0.80	0.79	0.72	0.69	0.64	0.62
Project 8			1.00	0.94	0.90	0.85	0.83	0.86	0.81	0.78	0.78	0.72	0.73
Project 9			1.00	0.95	0.96	0.93	0.92	0.90	0.94	0.88	0.89	0.87	0.89

Figure 4.14 A tabular view of a relatively "good" schedule performance index.

- Quality
- Cost
- Timeliness (Delivery)
- Customer's need

The specific metrics compare the state of the project to the expected outcome and will be associated with these areas. If, for example, the project were not to care about the development or the product cost, we would not bother with monitoring these areas.

A. Scheduling

For scheduling, we have a number of ways to compare where the project expects to be with where it actually is. The easiest, though least sophisticated, is the comparison of the original (baseline) time plan to the course of execution of the project. To do this requires constantly updating the project time plan that has all dependencies accounted for compared with the actual execution performance. There is no substitute for this attention to the details and the project support software can often identify a major shift in an important metric such as the critical path. The problem is usually in the construction of the plan to include all dependencies and to maintain the actual execution and compare it to the original project baseline. Additional difficulty arises in the determination of the state of completion of the task. If we built our WBS to the smallest level of detail the answer become either:

- Yes, the task is finished
- No, the task is not finished

If the WBS is other than this level of detail, gaming of the system or too optimistic a perspective can provide a false sense of the state of the project. Few project managers have not experienced the task that is well under way. At every point the progress is where the task should be. Then the end of the task draws near, and it turns out that we are only half complete, or the task otherwise ends up days or weeks late.

Another way to manage the schedule is to focus on the critical path of the project. A study of the critical path provides one possibility of the completion date for a project. This is true, because the critical path definition is "the longest sequential path of essential activities to meet the project objective." Prediction of the end date possibility can be done by reviewing the present state of the execution on this path in the project. Delivery of a late piece of work on this path will have an effect on the subsequent dates by pushing out the expected completion date of the sum of these tasks. Any one of the project management schedule tools will calculate the new conclusion dates of the project based on the assessed completion date of the previous tasks and the critical path dependencies. The Gantt view and, to a lesser extent, the network diagram will show the impact of late deliveries upon dependencies.

Another more complicated method provides a much clearer picture, a subset of the earned value management or EVM techniques. The reality is you still must have the project baseline information and even more. However, these tools provide a much more objective and clear perspective on the state of the project.

The basis for this work will be our time phased budget and our schedule complete

Organization A
Schedule Performance Index
Project Level A

	wk30	wk31	wk32	wk33	wk34	wk35	wk36	wk37	wk38	wk39	wk40	wk41	wk42
Project 1	1.00	1.05	1.10	1.03	1.05	1.02	0.99	1.00	0.98	0.97	0.99	0.95	0.92
Project 2		1.00	0.98	0.97	0.97	0.99	0.98	0.94	0.95	0.97	0.99	0.99	0.98
Project 3		1.00	0.99	0.98	0.96	0.97	0.98	0.97	0.96	0.99	0.96	0.95	0.94
Project 4		1.00	0.98	0.95	0.92	0.91	0.90	0.89	0.88	0.85	0.86	0.88	0.89
Project 5			1.00	0.95	0.94	0.94	0.92	0.93	0.90	0.94	0.96	0.96	0.97
Project 6			1.00	0.96	0.95	0.95	0.95	0.95	0.96	0.95	0.96	0.96	0.95
Project 7			1.00	0.97	0.95	0.94	0.93	0.94	0.92	0.90	0.88	0.87	0.85
Project 8			1.00	0.94	0.93	0.92	0.90	0.88	0.87	0.89	0.86	0.88	0.88
Project 9			1.00	0.98	0.99	0.97	0.95	0.95	0.95	0.94	0.92	0.9	0.89
Project 10				1.00	1.00	0.99	0.96	0.97	0.95	0.94	0.95	0.94	0.91

Figure 4.15 Organization A SPI for multiple projects.

with the hours to accomplish the tasks and deliverables within the project. This forms the basis of our planned value since this is how we plan on executing the project at any given point in the project. This is also referred to in other documents as the Budgeted Cost of Work Scheduled or BCWS. We can compare our road map to the Actual Cost of Work Performed or ACWP.

The specific earned value techniques that apply to schedule are:

Schedule performance index, or SPI, is the ratio of the work performed to the value of the work planned. An SPI of 1, means the project executes exactly as planned.

Let us consider two organizations and their portfolio of projects. We are tracking

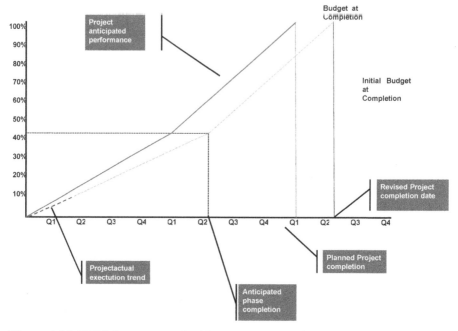

Figure 4.16 EVM demonstrated with a two stage project.

the schedule performance index for all of their respective projects to generate Figure

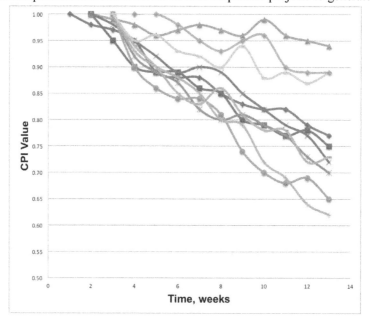

Figure 4.17 Example of Schedule Performance Index from a company with a wider variation.

$$EV = \sum_{t=0}^{t=now} PV_{workpackage\_completed}$$

$$Cost\,Variance = BCWP - ACWP$$

$$CPI = \frac{BCWP}{ACWP}$$

$$Schedule\,Variance = BCWP - BCWS = EV - PV$$

$$SPI = \frac{BCWP}{BCWS} = \frac{EV}{PV}$$

$$EAC = AC + \frac{(BAC - EV)}{CPI} = \frac{BAC}{CPI}$$

$$EAC = \frac{BAC - EV}{CPI_{cumulative} \times SPI_{cumulative}}$$

$$ETC = EAC - AC$$

$$TCPI = \frac{BAC - EV}{BAC - AC} = \frac{BAC - EV}{EAC - AC}$$

4.14 and Figure 4.15.

We can see that not all projects are executed precisely. We would expect our organization to show a variety of execution capabilities. From this view, we can't really make any statements or comments on the organization. We know that we would have some performance variation. There are a multitude of risks that may or may not consummate on any one project. One project cheats the risk—takes the chance and does not encounter a specific risk. Other projects may adjust for the risk and the management actions do not work, thereby causing suffering from all the implications of the risk. All that being said, we can still learn something about the organization's ability.

Consider organization A and the distribution of the SPI (see Figure 4.15) for their tracked project portfolio (see Figure 4.18 and Figure 4.19). We see that the range for this measure is quite broad. There are a number of obstacles for this organization in achieving the schedule performance they planned. This graphic does not show those impediments. In general we can expect our future projects to be delivered within this range of possibilities.

Schedule variance (SV) is the dollar amount difference between actual spending and planned spending at specific points in the project. The calculation provides quick feedback on whether the project spending occurs according to plan.

Of course, since this metric is developed based on estimates, we have some risk that the estimates themselves are suspect.

To make EVM work (see Figure 4.16), the organization must have tight links to the WBS elements. Each person working upon the project has to bill hours to that specific WBS element (budgeted hours and costs). Faulty time reporting amounts to a "garbage in garbage out" situation. Without these constraints, EVM is useless.

For scheduling, the project manager uses the technique to assess the current

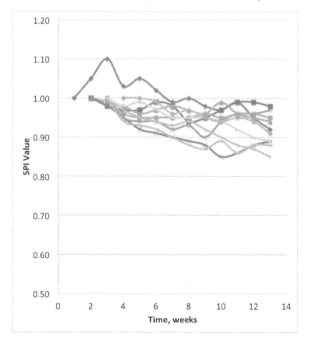

Figure 4.18 Organization A example of Schedule Performance Index from a company with smaller variation.

schedule status of the project measured in terms of cost. The methodology evaluates the project schedule against the planned time to determine the status of the project. As stated earlier, a critical dependency is part of the initial work, including the detailed WBS and associated budgets, all of which must be linked to the people executing the project, logging hours accurately against the WBS element for which the work applies. Here is a list of significant EVM values:

1. Schedule performance index by project
2. Schedule performance index by class of projects in portfolio (for example we may have are project classes defined by the dollar amount)
3. Cost performance index by project
4. Cost performance index by class of projects in portfolio
5. Schedule variance by project
6. Schedule variance by class of projects in portfolio (for example we may have project classes defined by dollar amount)
7. Cost variance by project

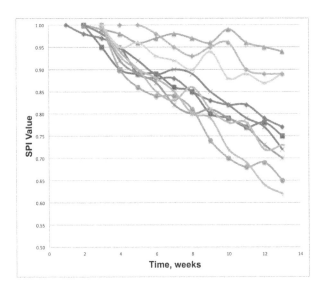

Figure 4.19 Organization B example of Schedule Performance Index from a company with a wider variation.

8. Cost variance by class of projects in portfolio (for example we may have project classes defined by dollar amount)

9. Estimate at completion

10. Estimate to complete

11. To complete performance index ((BAC-EV)/(EAC-AC)) or ((BAC-EV)/ (BAC-AC))

12. Actual task variation—may be covered in the truck preparation for testing area

So how does EVM apply to total quality management? The same tools that are applied to manufacturing and other process disciplines, apply to project management. The information collected in EVM can be accumulated and used to understand the capabilities of our organization; for example, scatter plots of the organizational SPI or CPI information for their respective projects. If this information is known, a view of this data from the TQM PM may tell the organization how well they are performing.

Budgeted cost work scheduled (BCWS)—the approved budget identified for an amount of work for a defined amount of time.

Budgeted cost work performed (BCWP)—also known as Earned Value, this is the budgeted cost of the work that was scheduled and delivered during a defined amount of time.

Actual cost work performed (ACWP)—the actual amount spent for a unit time of all expenditures—labor, overhead and material

Cost variance—the difference between the actual cost and the estimated or budgeted cost

Cost performance index—the measure of efficiency of the cost controlling activities of the project. A CPI greater than 1 means execution is better than planned and less than 1 means the execution is worse than planned (for either event the estimates could be suspect).

Schedule performance index—the measure of progress made in the project to the progress planned at a point in time. A SPI greater than 1 means the project is making more progress than planned and less than 1 means the project is progressing slower than planned.

Estimate at completion—estimation of the cost to deliver the project to completion

Estimate to Complete—estimation of the total costs to deliver the project results from a point during the execution of the project

To complete performance index—helps define the performance required for the project to attain the desired goals.

B. Budget (Cost)

Just as there are earned value management techniques for the project schedule,

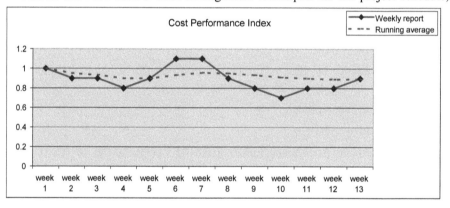

Figure 4.20 Cost performance index tracking including the running average.

there are EVM techniques for the budget or costs of the project.

Cost performance index, or CPI, is an important metric for any project manager. This measurement tells the project manager how well he is controlling his budget as compared to his plan to control the budget. Of course CPI will not work well if the estimates are incorrect.

At a minimum, a project manager must keep track of the project CPI over the weeks (see Figure 4.21) the project is executed. We suggest a quick evaluation point such as a week, as monthly or longer duration means the response to any unplanned or uncontrolled event will be slower. This situation is analogous to the response rate of a control system. We can only react or make adjustments to the plan if we understand that we are not performing to that plan.

Another possibility is to keep a running average of the performance (see Figure 4.20). Evaluation in this way, allows the project manager to see how the team is

performing in a less dynamic but meaningful way, We can see if we are improving
in our execution or not, as a trend instead of a discrete numeric value due to the week

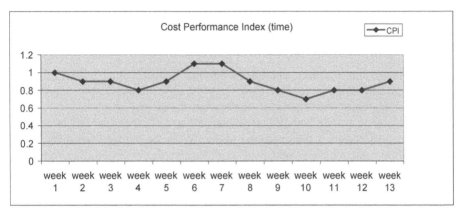

Figure 4.21 Cost performance index weekly performance report.

evaluation.

The cost performance index for an organization's portfolio of projects could be
used to understand the capabilities on a macro level of that company. Projects are
populated by human beings and there can be considerable differences between teams
in terms of output. However, it is also true if the organization has a defined set of

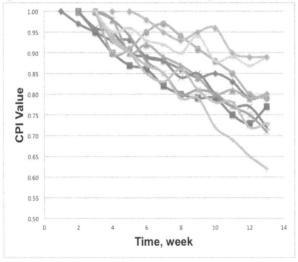

Figure 4.22 Organization B CPI with variation.

processes that are followed, it would learn how well it can perform. We can then
start to make some assessments of capabilities and therefore areas for improvement.
Knowing the envelope of an organization's performance allows us to better anticipate
the future needs of other projects. We can, for example, secure additional contingency

money if we know our organization habitually has a CPI performance of less than 1.0. Let us see how we can do that.

Let us review the product portfolio of two companies (see Figure 4.23 and Figure 4.22). We can look at the cost performance index information collected on the active projects under way. We will call these organizations A and B. The projects for these two organizations are of the same level of expenditure and comparable in complexity. Each row represents a project, and the columns are the weekly gathered CPI for each of those projects. We can see that each week the CPI changes as the project team moves through the activities and costs to complete the project.

With this view, we see both of these organizations have the capability to meet the cost of the project during the execution phase. While the numbers are there, it is a bit difficult to make a blanket statement on either organization's ability to deliver the project to the agreed-on cost targets. We can see that neither organization maintains a 1.0 CPI (the elusive perfect value for CPI). However, we can't easily describe either organizational capability as a whole.

We can, however, have a clearer understanding of each organization's capability

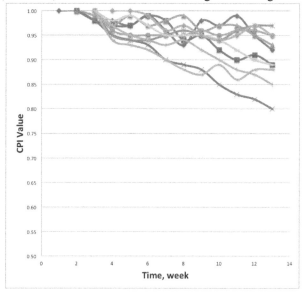

Figure 4.23 Organization A with a less variation in CPI.

by viewing the distribution of CPI through out the portfolio. We can see from this view that one organization has a tighter distribution than the other. The dispersion for organization A is much more broad than that of organization B. We do not know why, but if we do not like either distribution, if we would like greater control over the span of possibilities, we would then determine how to find the causes of the distribution and make adjustments to those processes or training of personnel to narrow the dispersion. We can acquire new employees with the missing skills or find a person in our present team that we can train to fill the need. There may be parts of our process that limit

Figure 4.24 A high-quality digital multimeter is a required tool for initial troubleshooting.

our success in achieving our cost objectives. Additionally, it could be the estimates on which our plan was built, and our organization has no room for improvement other than the estimates.

With our CPI known, we know it is possible to calculate the cost variance—or CV. This is the dollar amount difference between that which the project has actually spent and that which was planned to be spent at that point in time. This calculation provides a quick overview of the spending of the project. Knowing this budgetary value makes it possible for the project manager to estimate the cost of the project to complete.

C. Quality

The project manager is responsible for the overall quality of the project. The project manager along with the line organization determines the best way to achieve the quality targets for the customer and the developing organization. This is part of a balancing act for the team, quality cost and delivery schedule, or time. This is where TQM really has an impact upon a project and its outcomes. Deciding on the right variables or attributes to pay attention, we can put a high level of focus to draw our project and its collective subtasks to successful conclusion.

Figure 4.25 provides a list of possible solutions for access to a vehicle for systems integration testing. The matrix evaluates the possible courses of action a project manager can take to secure this key portion of the project. Derived from expert perspectives, we see under consideration five possible solutions (the first column). The scale was arbitrary at one hundred points maximum for each of the areas of critique (dependencies, quality of test, etc.). Each of these areas was deemed a critical success factor. The evaluation pointed to the best solution based upon these criteria. The process need not be unnecessarily complicated.

XII. Risk Management Fundamentals

A. Qualitative Risk

Like everything else, the scope for the project sets the risks that are possible; if we have no software development, then late software delivery is possible. The scope of the project and the course of actions proposed to take to achieve the project objectives create an environment teeming with risks. The team works through these risks as the strategies and tactics for achieving the project objectives become known. We will generate a list of risks that our team believes it is possible that this project will encounter.

Brainstorming the risks possible as seen from the stakeholders gets the team and stakeholders involved as a group, and it provides much needed boundary spanning or reconnaissance for the project. Qualitative risk analysis is performed to make the various stakeholders—including upper level management—knowledgeable of the risks that could have an impact on them. To acquire the complete picture of the risks associated with the project requires a variety of perspectives and a critique of the methods of achieving the project's objectives. One of the worst things a project manager can do is to ignore a risk a team member brings to his or her attention. It is exactly this individual experience and expertise that will uncover the risks of the project. Unless you want to hear "I told you that would happen," it is good to attend to this admonition.

We now have a list of most probable risks associated with the project. On identification of the risk exposure, we investigate the symptoms of that risk; or even better, we examine the precursor to the symptom of that risk consummating. We do this so we are able to recognize the risk event is no longer just a possibility, but a reality. We document the symptom we would expect to see, and find a person that would be in a position to detect that the risk event has happened to verify our intuition.

We have brainstormed the things that can possibly go wrong. We have identified the symptoms that we expect to see when things in fact are going wrong. We need to think of ways to mitigate the risk. Risk mitigation happens using any or a combination of the following behaviors:

- Transferred the risk (outsource)
- Absorbed or accepted no mitigation – ignoring the risk
- Eliminated the possibility of the risk (change the strategy or scope)
- Shared the risk through partnering
- Absorbed the risk by taking actions to reduce the effect

So what does quantitative risk have to do with total quality management? Learning from these events—that is what TQM has to do with risk management. The risks themselves are items that can be tracked. This is especially true for the risks that have a regular recurrence in an organization's projects. For example, a Pareto chart analysis of the most common and severe risks could lead to a deeper understanding about the organization's risk exposure resulting in process improvement. Putting together a collection of these risks and using TQM tools on them will make the organization aware of those things that are indeed risks compared to those things that are more of a certainty. For example, consider our earlier truck availability example demonstrates that knowledge of the distribution of the days before a vehicle is suitable for testing allows you to realistically assess the risk.

	Dependencies	Vehicle to Test	Quality of test	Use of time	Vehicle use later	Total
New EE trucks	100	100	100	100	100	500
Old EE Trucks	100	100	66	66	X	333
Old any truck updated	100	66	66	66	X	300
New Shared	X	X	X	33	66	100
Old Shared	X	X	X	33	X	33

Figure 4.25 Risk identification and course of action selected based upon those risks.

B. Quantitative Risk

According to a paper from the SANS Institute (an organization that specializes in internet security training), the benefits of qualitative risk analysis are:

- More objectivity in its assessment

- More powerful selling tool to management

- Offers direct projection of cost/benefit of proposal

- Can be fine-tuned to meet the needs of specific situations

- Can also be modified to fit the needs of specific industries

- Much less prone to arouse disagreements during management review

- Analysis is often derived from some irrefutable facts4

Quantitative risk analysis requires an understanding of what (usually how much) is at risk. This is the first step in the prioritization process by quantifying what is at stake should a specific risk come to fruition.

Once we know the amount we can lose, we must determine or otherwise assess the probability of the actual risk happening. Is this a probable or improbable risk? Where on this continuum from not possible to certain does this particular risk reside?

Once we have this information we multiply the two together. This number is the dollar representation of the risk to the project. If we are a smart project manager, we will use this information in the following ways.

First, we will prioritize our risk mitigation activities around this dollar amount risk associated with the project. After all, if project management is the discipline of minimizing risk and maximizing efficiency, we should address the highest monetary risk to the company first. We will then develop actions to reduce either the severity of the impact of the risk or the probability of the risk coming to bear upon the project.

We will also use this information to determine our contingency budget. We will add the highest risks; that is, what dollar amounts and probabilities we can address and manage.

C. Representing Risk

There are many ways to represent risk. The project manager may be wrestling with whether to reserve specific vehicles for the electrical and electronics testing of a major project. The project has a number of embedded software changes included in the schedule and the test group would need vehicles for part of the integration testing of the various iterations of software for a number of components in the system. The project manager consults with the manager of the testing and verification group. The ideas for meeting the demand are:

- Retrofit old vehicles (already in possession)
- Secure new vehicles
- Share new vehicles
- Share old vehicles (already in possession)
- Acquire yet another unknown vehicle

We find that software delivery dates, especially for one of the key suppliers, moves routinely. The scheduling of fixed time for testing on the vehicle with the other groups that would need the vehicle would have to be flexible enough to alter to the actual delivery dates for the software.

	Ahead of due date	On due date	1 week late	2 weeks late	3 weeks late	> 4 weeks late
Supplier A	0	6	1	1	0	0
Supplier B	2	6	0	3	2	0
Supplier C	0	3	4	7	2	3

This amounts to two schedules varying as the demands for vehicles also move and as other divisions of the company procure vehicles for the schedule changes they are encountering. The project manager and the higher-level manager create a list of the possible solutions and then assign points to the solutions based upon the assessment of the risk associated with that course of action. We are drawing upon expert judgment as well as analogous projects (historical projects of a similar sort encountered by the line manager). The prioritized areas for the critique or assessment are:

- Dependencies—varying software schedule and vehicle schedule

- Quality of the test articles (truck)

- Use of the available time for testing

- Use of vehicle after the testing for the maintenance phase of the product

We see in this evaluation that the best solution would be acquiring vehicles for the specific testing. In this case, the vehicle availability is not subject to intervention from the other parts of the company. The delay in software availability would not have an impact on the date of vehicle availability. The quality of the test specimen is deemed better as the vehicle would not be a rebuild or be a vehicle where it would be difficult to determine the quality of the constituent systems as well as configuration management issues and time to tear it down and make it suitable for testing. In the end,

Figure 4.26 Example of a product under development.

two solutions are workable with one being deemed the best least risky solution.

D. How Helpful Is This Task?

Of course, it is not possible to predict every event that can go wrong and impede the performance of a project or the ability to meet the defined objectives. In those cases, the ability to adapt to the demand is necessary. However, trying to find solutions to problems in the face of ever dwindling slack time or diminishing resources is not efficient. Planning is really the best alternative, even if some of the risks do not occur, because, if done correctly, we will know immediately when the risk has been encountered and what the consequences will be for our project. Preemptive activities for items that we know can go astray is generally more effective than letting the events occur and only then applying corrective actions.

XIII.   Project Termination Techniques

Projects are closed by a number of mechanisms. Successful project completion requires termination techniques, as does a premature termination of a project for any of a number of reasons:

- Successful delivery of the desired scope
- Need for project no longer valid
- Profitability expected from the project no longer possible

The closeout of the project as well as the gate reviews for the project, afford an opportunity to learn about how your project organization works. To understand this better, let us review project gates and the goals.

A. Project Gates

Gates are also known as project kill points. An organization that employs the staged-gate method of project management has regular reviews of the project at certain points throughout the process. The list below provides examples of the various phases for a project.

- Voice of the customer
- Concept
- Product design (see Figure 4.26)
- Process design
- Manufacturing
- Launch
- Post launch support

Each proceeding phase provides input to the subsequent phase. At the end of each phase, we conduct a review to see if the deliverables that will be used for the next phase are complete. We use check sheets to assess the project's specific deliveries for that phase against what was expected or needed from that phase. Questions are asked such as whether the organization will make a profit from the results of the project? Here is another area TQM tools assist the project manager and ultimately the project

Organization
Gates Cleared
Project Level A

	Jan-11	Feb-11	Mar-11	Apr-11	May-11	Jun-11	Jul-11	Aug-11	Sep-11	Oct-11	Nov-11	Dec-11
Total gate reviews	4	13	4	10	6	12	2	6	4	11	7	11
Gates cleared	4	6	3	8	4	6	1	6	3	10	7	6
Gates missed	0	7	1	2	2	6	1	0	1	1	0	5
Percent gates passed (month)	100%	46%	75%	80%	67%	50%	50%	100%	75%	91%	100%	55%
Running percentage	100%	59%	62%	68%	68%	63%	63%	67%	67%	71%	73%	71%

Figure 4.27 Gate passing statistics of an organization.

management office and the company.

This continuous critique of the goals of the project requires data that has been converted to information to make a rational and objective assessment of the project state. Some of this assessment would be the same if the project were to be allowed to continue to completion and will be part of the closing activities of the project. Essentially, closing the project—whether because the objective has been met, or because of early termination—requires the same attention to detail and provides a learning opportunity for the enterprise. These "lessons learned" should be used to

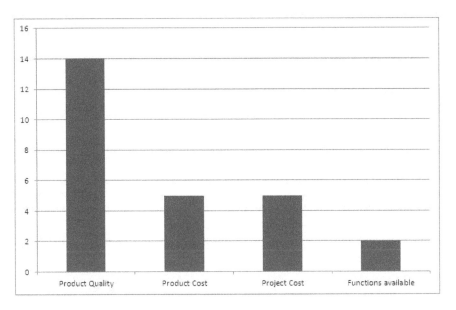

Figure 4.28 Project gate failures can be broken down by the objective (cost, quality and function) to learn where to focus our attention.

help future projects. It is possible to learn enough from the failures such that the organization will be able to spot a losing project earlier, saving the company both money and opportunity costs.

For example, we should be tracking whether we pass through the gates on time. If we know we have trouble meeting our gate targets, we can then investigate further to understand why we miss these targets. Maybe the targets were too aggressive, maybe there are too few people, or maybe the product scope itself was the issue. It could also be our processes are impediments to success.

- People
- Processes
- Product scope

Figure 4.27 shows an organization tracking the gate reviews by month and shows the failures to pass the gate. All we see here is that we have some difficulty getting through the gates for projects. This graphic does not provide enough information to determine the reason. Maybe we are happy with this performance. At any rate, we will not know where the project constraints are if we do not have a view that lets us know there are areas for improvement.

We can dig a bit further by reviewing and categorizing (if this is not already done) the list of the metrics for each of the gates. Essentially we are identifying the gate specifics to an area we believe addresses some part of the project objective. For example, test plans support product quality. The list below provides some example areas:

- Reliability
- Product quality
- Project cost
- Product cost
- Feature content
- Maintenance costs
- Profitability

In Figure 4.28 example, we see a Pareto chart of the areas on which the gate items missed had an effect. Based on our categorization of the individual gate items, we believe those items missed most influence the quality of the product, with product cost and project costs being roughly equal. If we were to make progress in the areas of the gate items that impact product quality, we would expect to see the success rate of our gate passing to improve (provided we did not damage anything else in the process

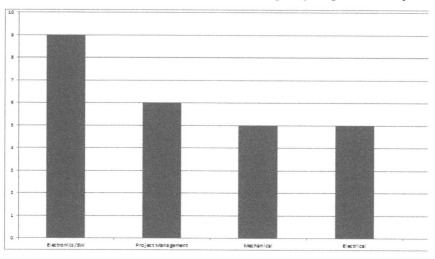

Figure 4.29 Failure to pass gate audits by department.

through unintended consequences). There is of course another alternative: "Is this gate item really needed?" It is possible that we are measuring the wrong things in the gate assessment.

We can break this down yet further and consider the areas within the company that were responsible for the specific gate item. In Figure 4.29, we see that of the failure to pass the gates, the majority resides in the electronics and software area followed closely by project management activities.

When we learn this information, we know where to apply our efforts to improve the outcome. For instance, we can start looking into why the electronics and software areas are problematic. Maybe we decide to create an Ishikawa diagram to better understand the problem with this area. We can gather other information such as:

- Rate of changes to requirements
- Stability of requirements
- Team load
- Processes within this part of the organization
- Skill level of the people within this part of the organization

We can look at other areas regarding gates as well. Let us consider an organization that has a number of phases in the product development process. This organization produces a number of levels of prototype parts on the way to a final production part.

- Level 1—mock ups—fit and shape
- Level 2—mock up hardware some level of functionality

	Project 1	Project 2	Project 3	Project 4	Project 5	Project 6	Project 7	Project 8	Project 9	Project 10	Project 11	Project 12
Total Fault reports	18	8	20	10	30	12	3	8	7	7	47	32
B01 phase	x	x	x	x	x	x	x	x	x	2	21	6
B02												1
C01 phase	2 x	x	1	0	15	12 x	x	x	x	3	9	
C02	3 x	x	x	1	x	x	x					
C03	x	x	x	x	4	x	x	x				
P01	12	3	16	10	10 x	x	1	1	2	15	1	
P02	1	0	1		x	x	x		1		2	0
P03		5	1		x		3	5	5			1
P04			1		x		x					12
P05							x					0
P06								2				11
Points												
1	0	0	5	0	7	5	0	0	2	0	1	3
10	15	5	3	3	1	1	0	3	3	2	16	21

Figure 4.30 Illustration of the failure rate when a particular organization skips some of its development phases.

- Level 3—full hardware feature—built off prototype line and tools—full features
- Level 4—full hardware built off production line and tools—full features

This company handles embedded hardware and software for the products. These definitions apply to the hardware and the software so we can see that some of these levels do not necessarily apply to the software development—specifically level 1. This company subtracts phases for some of the projects. For example, the project is deemed to be simple, only an adaptation to existing features, the project manager may decide to go from level 2 prototype to level 4. On the surface, this looks like a good way to cut time out of the schedule, and if the project were able to deliver product while skipping some of these material stages and maintain the quality of the product, this would be a right and fitting approach. Here is where we dig in and find out if this hypothesis is valid.

Though the data is limited we see every time the company tries to deliver a product (software or hardware) directly to production level, a number of redesign iterations are required to be performed on the product to meet the expected quality.

Not shown in Figure 4.30 is the effect on the project schedule when the project manager bet the entire project on a single, one-shot release of the product being suitable for production and the customer. The total quality project manager that pays attention to this data and converts it to information would know that a single-production proposed part (often called a "big bang" approach) is not likely to succeed based on the historical record. The project manager would then plan to make contingency allowances for the subsequent releases the historical record indicates would be required. For example, making sure we had room to push the schedule for subsequent product releases; making stakeholders aware of the probability of a single release working being risky at best and probably impossible. The project manager could also work with the sponsor to lower the quality targets, meaning the product could be launched with fewer features and with more errors to meet the expected delivery date. The project manager should also to acquire additional contingency funding for post-launch clean up of the problems found where no time was available to provide the required corrections. In the end, if the historical record indicates a single release does not work, there are only a few options available

- Understand why this strategy does not work and account for these issues

- Work within the confines of the historical record

- Ignore the record, do not adjust how the work gets done – use hope as the project management method.

Another instance shown in Figure 4.30 is when the organization removes the middle prototype parts phase in the same attempt to reduce the amount of time to get the work completed and meet a delivery date. In this case the historical record is also interesting. The test record shows that we still have the same result. There are multiple releases to clean up the problems found. In addition, we list some comments the people who were pressured to deliver as follows:

- Also, for harnessing, there is very little benefit for us to do a level 2 part if we are not going to build and test a truck before we have to do the next release. For instance we have a level 2 part released in the ABC project harnesses, but no truck builds have been planned until after we do the production release. Also for DEF project we level 2 prototype parts released harnesses and will be production releasing before any builds are planned. We feel this is not a real good use of our time and resources. Time needs to provide to adequately test and verify the functions. We cannot afford to take short cuts here if we expect to have clean introductions. We can clearly see this on any number of projects from the RRR introduction to the current CCC introduction.

- Schematic and harness designs take time and rushing a release can and will often lead to errors. We can look at projects such as RRR, which went into production with errors.

- The majority of our harnesses require packaging work, which needs to be completed before we can completely bundle our parts. We hear a lot of complaints about our parts not fitting, but the packaging group is not given enough time to properly design and provide us a packaging review.

These are some comments from one of the organization's line functions affected by this cutting short of required process steps taken in order to meet an arbitrary launch date. At present this, ad hoc approach, removal of parts of the process, does not meet all of the project objectives. A dissection of the issues that lead to these failures would be required to know if removing prototype iterations could work for the project.

How does the project manager meet the delivery in the face of unrealistic expectations? What happens when the date to deliver is an unrealistic demand? In our experience you do not provide your teams with the space for positive morale by pushing them into situations they know are failure bound or resemble the figurative "death march."

The use of overtime as the way to meet project milestones is counterproductive. There are costs to routinely pushing the people you count on to their limits with long days and weekend work. Generally, we see a short term boost in productivity that comes at the price of employee satisfaction. The project manager who believes he or she is receiving forty hours per week of effort on his or her project and only his or her project is probably incorrect in that assumption. Cutting the time to do the work is the same as identifying an inflated rate of hours spent working on the project activities. Either way, we expect these choices to be steps toward failure. To violate the rules with minimum risk you must know what breaking the rules puts at risk. If an organization believes its processes should be adjusted to improve throughput of the time to deliver, then it follows that they must develop an understanding of the objectives of each phase and the reason for the individual steps in that phase. In instances where we violate our own project protocols, skipping the use of prototype parts did not produce the desired results. That is not to say this strategy could not be successful if the reasons for the failures were known and we took mitigating actions. However, until the reasons for the failures are known and addressed, the probability this strategy will be successful is very slim.

B. White Book

We frequently hear from people of the uselessness of the white book. Like many activities, you get out what you put into it. If this is a check box to be able to close a project there is likely not much worth in the activity. First of all, experience suggests this activity happens only at the end of a project. This is too late to have any effect on the project that is presently under way. White book exercises would provide more immediate benefit if this review happened as part of the gate process, more closely resembling the agile retrospective approach, where we look back at what we have learned in the previous period. In this way, the white book is more than a post-mortem history of the project; rather, it identifies corrective actions or process alterations

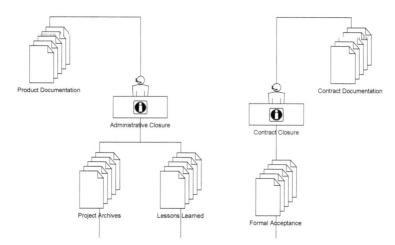

Figure 4.31 Closing the project compares the expected outcomes to the actual outcome.

we can adopt in the upcoming phases of the project. We can make use of the gate measures at these points to predict problem areas for the future gates of the specific project on which we are working. One of the benefits of the agile approach to project management is the mechanism in place to adapt quickly to the circumstances in which the project team finds itself.

We cannot count the number of times we have heard project members lament that they were never part of the white book generation. For the effort to be worthwhile, the team really must have some say as to what happened. We have seen instances where key players were not included in the white book, only to have their effort critiqued with little area for rebuttal or a contesting perspective.

C. Project Closure

Project closure is where we review contracts for closure. We compare what we have delivered to what was expected to be delivered (see Figure 4.31), as well as store the project documentation for future use. At this point the project is closed out with people being reassigned to new projects. The product will be moved to the maintenance phase taken up by a line organization. The money support for the project will be discontinued.

Here is the tricky part: when we deliver a product at the final stages, we usually have a good understanding of the cost of the product. We have a great understanding of the costs the project has incurred when we look over our shoulder. We will even know if we have delivered the product on time. The one thing we seldom if ever know, is the *real* quality of the product.

Quality as seen in the field, is a lagging indicator (i.e., it follows the behavior rather than predicting the behavior). Projects that take decisions to skip steps or downplay the risks can find themselves in a position that the delivered product quality is less than expected. The organization will likely learn this, months after the project delivery. In the case of long lead time products such as vehicles, or custom low volume products, it may take months to a year or more for a product to be put on the vehicle, and make its way to customers that could provide feedback. Then we find a product that is in maintenance phase that has problems because the project delivered a less than stellar product. Warranty dollars erode the product margins. The company has to find a way to fix the incomplete work of the project.

XIV. Exercises

- Create a level three Work Breakdown Structure for an embedded product.
- How does task variation impact the critical path of a project schedule? Provide a strategy for handling the critical path tasks versus the non-critical path tasks in terms of accounting for variation.
- What tasks are least impacted by task duration variation?
- What happens when non-critical path items show up on the critical path due to schedule changes and execution? How can this be anticipated?
- List 2 duration estimating techniques?
- Define a project with a number of gates. Identify the key deliverables and what each gate should address. You can use your industry's project life cycle model if needed.
- What is the reason behind a project white book? What level of team participation is appropriate? What happens when team members are excluded? What happens when the content of the white book is captured with a "positive spin"?
- List three brainstorming techniques? When is this approach least effective?
- What are the prerequisites to employing Earned Value Management tools?
- What are the obstacles to developing a time phased budget?
- What happens when you can't get the information you need to be successful in your project activity?
- What are the prerequisites to employing Earned Value Management tools?

Endnotes

1. James P. Lewis, *Project Planning Scheduling & Control* E3. New York City, NY: McGraw Hill, 2001.

2. Kim H. Pries, Jon M. Quigley. *Scrum Project Management*. Boca Raton, FL: CRC Press, 2011.

3. Project Smart. "Project Management Skills: Avoiding Management by Crisis." Stakeholder Management: Managing Expectations. Last modified January 1996. Accessed August 13, 2011. http://www.projectsmart.co.uk/stakeholder-management.html.

4.   Ting, Dan. "Quantitative Risk Analysis Step-By-Step." Last modified December 2002. PDF. Captured from http://www.sans.org/reading_room/ whitepapers/auditing/quantitative_risk-analysis-step-by-step_849 on 18 August 2011.

CHAPTER 5 – STATISTICS AND CONTROL

I. Rubric

	Novice	Sr. Novice	Journey-man	Sr. Jour-neyman	Master
x-bar R	x	x	x	x	x
x-bar S		x	x	x	x
Median			x	x	x
np				x	x
p				x	x
u				x	x
c				x	x
EWMA					x
CuSum					x

II. Questions to Ponder

- Do statistics and control provide any added value?

- Are statistical models too abstract or are they really down-to-earth?

- Why is the statistical model approach so seductive?

- What does it take to improve your organization's abilities with statistics and control?

- What positions in your organization should have the greatest capabilities regarding statistics? Do project managers really need to know statistics?

- Does the enterprise really need statistics?

- Would the enterprise pay attention to the statistics anyway? How would you get the organization to accept this level of control?

- Does statistical control have any marketing value?

- Why do we have so many types of control charts?

- Why are the statistical models different and yet the same (compare and contrast)?

- Is a statistical model/control chart just another way to keep the quality department busy?

- Is the ISO version better than the other models?

- Why can't we just "roll our own?"

III. Why Statistics and Control Are Important to the Project Manager

One of the purposes of statistical analysis lies in its ability to discern random variation from non-random (or "controllable") variation. Random variation is extremely difficult to control, although we have seen situations where variance could be diminished through rigorous use of designed experiments. It is much more common for practitioners to move the mean rather than "fix" the variance.

The TQM project manager will want to understand what factors he or she can control and which factors effectively lie outside the domain of project management. When this awareness manifests, project managers begin to have true control, because they are working with those factors that they can, indeed, influence.

Furthermore, the charts can provide a valuable visual indicator to management about what is really going on during the process. The most difficult part of the statistics and control chart approach is finding project material that is amenable to control charts. In our experience, project managers often treat each project as if it were so unique nothing can be derived from experience.

IV. TQM Project Manager Scenario

A. Situation

The enterprise produced a product with a marginal design that "expected" the values provided by component parts during prototype testing. Unfortunately, parts from other lots demonstrated different behaviors while still meeting the supplier's claimed tolerances.

B. Objective

The reliability engineer needed to calculate the expected fallout from this situation, given that some of the product had shipped with the marginal design.

C. Action

The reliability engineer had just enough information from the supplier about standard deviations and means to be able to make an assumption of a normal distribution, although unable to prove the distribution was correct, and produced an estimate of the number of failures.

D. Results

The product actually failed at about ten percent above the estimate, which is probably not so bad, given the assumptions and general lack of good, clean data.

E. Aftermath

The reliability engineer made numerous remonstrations regarding statistically oriented testing, which largely were ignored. Basically, one of the "Achilles heels" for testing is the lack of variation in component material. Of course, resilience should have been built into the design from the beginning.

V.   What Does Control Mean?

Control is somewhat of a misnomer with statistical process control (SPC), the primary tool of which is control charts. In most situations, we are measuring lagging data (although leading data should be used whenever feasible) and we make our decision after a counterproductive event occurs. When we refer to lagging data, we refer to the data that comes at a point in the process where it tells us what we did. This method is great for predicting what is happening now; however, the downside is that the event has already happened. In other words, it is too late for containment, we already built parts, and parts may have already arrived at our customer's receiving dock..

True process control is sometimes called "engineering process control" or EPC and uses gains to adjust the control values for the process under study.

VI. Project Risk and Management

We can measure projects with a standard set of metrics and these metrics include the following:

- Schedule variance (SV)

  - SV greater than 0 is good (ahead of schedule). The SV will be 0 at project completion because then all of the planned values will have been earned.

- Schedule performance index (SPI)

  - SPI greater than 1 is good (ahead of schedule).

  - Budget at completion (BAC): The total planned value (PV or BCWS) at the end of the project. If a project has a management reserve (MR), it is typically not included in the BAC, and respectively, in the performance measurement baseline.

- Cost variance (CV)

  - CV greater than 0 is good (under budget).

- Cost performance index (CPI)

  - CPI greater than 1 is good (under budget).
  - < 1 means that the cost of completing the work is higher than planned (bad).
  - = 1 means that the cost of completing the work is right on plan (good).
  - > 1 means that the cost of completing the work is less than planned (good or sometimes bad).

- Estimate at completion (EAC)

  - EAC is the manager's projection of total cost of the project at completion.

- Estimate to complete (ETC)

  - ETC is the estimate to complete the remaining work of the project.

The to-complete-performance-index (TCPI) provides a projection of the anticipated performance required to achieve either the BAC or the EAC.

Many other metrics are possible; however, these are fairly typical and they can be generated quickly using project management software such as Microsoft Project. With any metric where we have anticipated or expected values, we have the possibility of using a variables-based control chart.

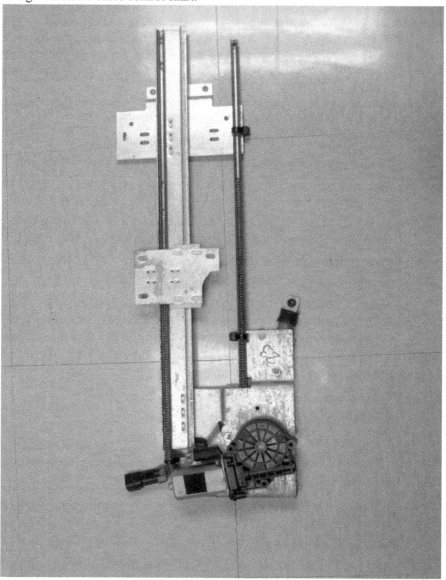

Figure 5.1 Typical sample test material for a subsystem on a commercial vehicle.

VII. Attributes Data

Attributes data is qualitative. This qualitative data can be counted, recorded, and analyzed; hence, it is often called "count" data. The count is always expressed as an integer (Figure 5.1). Typical items for count are non-conformities, non-conforming units, percent non-conforming, and so on. Subgroups for attributes frequently require 50 to 200 sample units per subgroup to provide meaningful information. Because of the large size of the subgroups and the type of data, most project managers will not use the attribute charts to analyze their metrics.

When it comes to the product however, we are talking a different story (see Figure 5.2). For us to understand the product capability we must evaluate more than a sample of one to determine the range of variation. We can calculate beforehand many of the engineering types attributes. However, when we are working with products from other

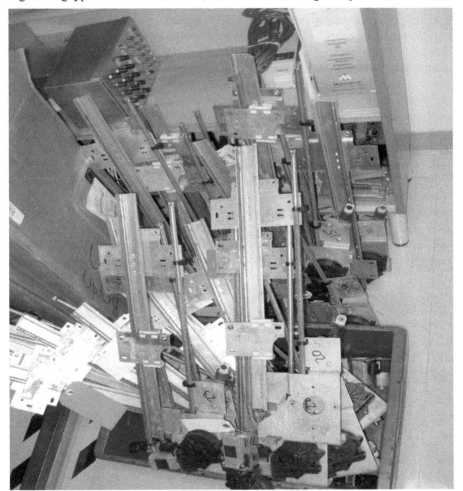

Figure 5.2 For statistical testing, we need to have a meaningful sample size.

suppliers or that have parts subject to their own manufacturing processes, we have the possibility of unknown variation. This unknown variation can have some dire consequences upon the end product and the cost of the quality of that product.

To understand the variation we have to look at a range of possible outcomes. In the case of the product, if we sample one window lift motor for example, we learn very little about the range of window lift motor performances. We may learn something about this single piece current consumption or the amount of lift force that is generated over a range of voltage and current supplied. However, we would not be able to make a reasonable assessment of the range of performance possibilities of the product. Neither can we glean the capability of the product—its behavior—when put into the customers' vehicles. For example: how much friction variation can be seen by the lift mechanism from the window glass guides? How does this perform from the first installation? How will it perform over the expected life of the product? We have a multitude of variations possible and not just in the performance of the product but the environmental exposure as well. Instead we sample some set of parts to understand the range of possible product performances. We will test the parts to a wide range of stimuli to assess the key attributes (motor torque) over time and environmental stimuli. We will learn this by taking key measurements of the product while it is undergoing the assorted test stimuli. We should measure after the stimuli as well to see if the performance of the product alters after the test stimuli. In this way we learn if there are long-term changes in the product performance after the test exposure.

If we use our imagination, we can devise tools that will help us accomplish the tasks we must. These tools are not always so elaborate. Consider a connector with more than 200 connection points to be populated. We may have a big job ahead of us if we deem it necessary to inspect the pins going into the connector or if we have to rework this part. The example below is how one department at a company improved their connection inspection needs for a specific connector. Though the solution the staff determined seemed to be an easy solution to construct, they decided to build a prototype of the product (see Figure 5.4) that they envisioned would hold the connector

Figure 5.3 Connector pin out fixture provides identification of the wires populated within the connector for both the male and female connector.

in place and identify the individual pins from the reverse side of the connector. The staff built the prototype part out of cardboard complete with labels for each connector pin by row and column producing a matrix of connection points. The prototype part could be produced quickly giving the responsible person time to work with the product

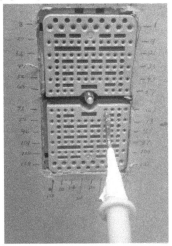

Figure 5.4 Connector inspection fixture built as a cardboard piece to prove concept.

to see if the concept would in fact make the job easier.

Once the cardboard part was built and proved to be capable, the team then turned to

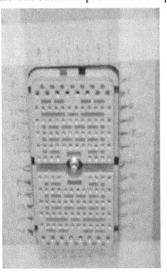

Figure 5.5 Closeup of connector pin out fixture for inserting and testing pins during point to point testing or to repin the connector.

make a more hardened part out of aluminum (see Figure 5.3 and Figure 5.5).

As luck would have it, this tool is also sufficient for troubleshooting the connector. The matrix of numbers corresponding to the pin-out for both the male and female ends of the connector facilitate troubleshooting of the connector both from the pin out perspective and from a connector failure.

VIII.   Variables Data

The classic variables[1] control chart is the X-bar R-chart, which is actually two charts (see Figure 5.6). Variable is normally expressed as a floating point or real value. Other variables control charts are the X-bar S, the median, and the individuals and moving range charts. Variable data is always quantitative. Variables control charts can have subgroups as small as individual units, although sampling allows a more common value like five to six units per sample.

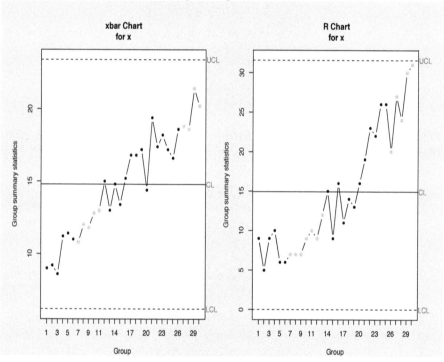

Figure 5.6 Xbar-R plots with anomalies.

IX. Statistical Process Control (SPC) in Use

A. Attribute Charts

We will provide no examples with attribute charts because they are much less applicable for the TQM project manager.

B. Variables Charts

Xbar-R Charts

The Xbar-R ($\overline{x}$-R) control chart is an archetype for all variables-type control charts. In essence, we collect data in sample groups, typically of five to ten pieces. We then plot the means of each of these "rational subgroups." We know from the Central Limit Theorem that the means of subgroups, when plotted, will trend toward a normal distribution. The decision to use subgroup means allowed Dr. Walter Shewhart to use the well-understood normal statistics as the basis for his control chart plots.

The dotted lines are control limits. If our product is "under control," then the values should remain within the control limits while still exhibiting random variation. That is, in fact what we see in this plot, taken from the R data set "pistonrings," which were sampled in subgroups of five pieces each.

Applicability to the Project Manager

While it is interesting to note that we have this powerful tool for our use, we might wonder what the relevance is to the project manager. Let's look at some possibilities:

- Make sure any pre-production samples are "under control" and understand what that means.

- If we have enough data regarding a standard item (process) that is realized in every project, we can plot these values using a special version of this control chart

- We can plot meeting attendance—we are not joking—of our team. We treat the team as a subgroup and the average of their arrival time versus the meeting time as our x-bar value.

C. Median

Why would our project manager care about the median? We use medians because they are more stable than means. In one case, we simulated the document configuration management process using the median instead of the mean and we were able to achieve a fairly accurate simulation.

D. Xbar-S

The Xbar-S chart uses the standard deviation as a measure of dispersion rather than the range. With modern calculational ability, we see no reason for not using this chart, which is effectively as simple as the Xbar-R.

E. More Advanced Charts

More advanced charts than Shewhart's original groupings for exist to deal with more advanced problems. They are not particularly difficult to use, although the resulting graph looks much less like the data because the data is transformed. We

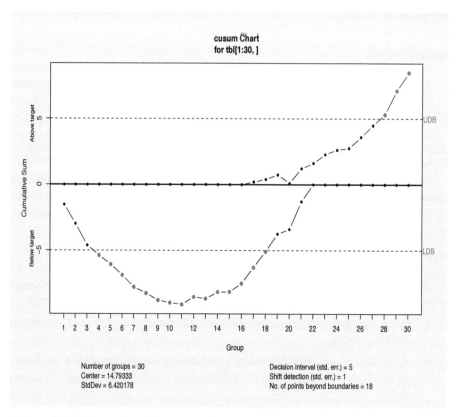

Figure 5.7 CuSum plot with anomalies.

discuss the exponential weighted moving average (EWMA), the moving average, and the accumulated sum of differences (CuSum).

CuSum

CuSums are another solution to the small change problem. They have been around since the mid-1950s. They are capable of detecting shifts in a process that is generally opaque to the Shewhart-style control chart.

Older versions of the CuSum chart use a control limit tool called a V-mask. The dimensions of the V-mask depend on the degree of sensitivity you might desire regarding the detection of the process shift as well as the confidence level (see Figure 5.7).

So why do we call it a CuSum? We call it a CuSum because the calculations are based on the accumulated sum of the differences. The first value is the difference *between the measured value and some target value.* This idea continues throughout the run of measurements. Differences can be negative, which affects the ongoing cumulative result. Negative data slows down the rate of accumulation but does not cause it to drop. We can use CuSum charts with rational subgroups (samples and means) or with individual values.

EWMA

One of the topics of concern in the use of control charts once a process is under a very high level of control is the ability to detect small shifts in process behavior. The exponential weighted moving average (EWMA) chart is a solution to this problem.

Mathematically, the EWMA formula is an abstract definition of a filter often used for noisy analog signals called an exponential lag filter. More recent values of data are given more "weight" and earlier values are given less "weight." This makes sense if we have a good reason for giving the greatest importance to the most recent data. Weighting the data farther back in time increases the smoothing on the filter and increases the lag between the nominal value and the filtered value, which, in some cases, may not be what we want.

Moving Average

Moving averages are typically used to smooth extremely noisy data. The more

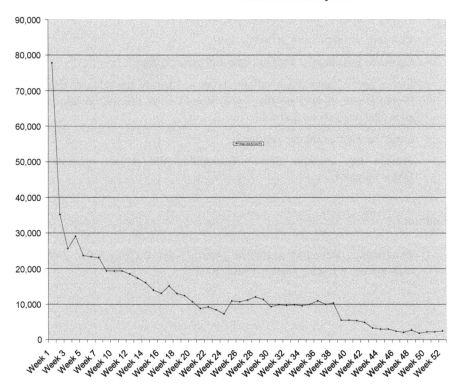

Figure 5.8 Notice the decline in failure rate as the product "settles down."

components to the moving average calculation, the greater the smoothing until the data becomes virtually unrecognizable (over smoothing). Similarly to what we do with stock market data, we can observe long-term trends with careful use of extreme smoothing.

Moving average charts can be used for individual or subgroup data because the average values determined are based on "artificial" subgroups to begin with. Generally, the weighting of a moving average chart (see Figure 5.8) is less sophisticated than that of the EWMA and, hence, this chart is probably less desirable than the EWMA. Furthermore, the EWMA is computationally more efficient, although this is not usually a concern in a PM environment with fast personal computers.

X.   Exercises

- Use any collected data and group through time in subgroups of five to ten items and take the mean of these values—you will see a normal distribution.

- Use the R statistical tool and any of the following packages: IQCC, qat (quality assurance toolkit), or qcc (quality control charts). Perform the same grouping as above but use the tool to plot the results.

- Try any other statistical package: Minitab, Statistica, SAS, SPSS, or other.

- Follow a stock price value with a CuSum chart.

- Follow a stock price value with an EWMA chart.

- Plot your weight over a period of time.

- Compare and contrast attribute data and variable data.

- Pick a part of your organization's process, identify the relevant data needed to acquire to understand that capability. Gather this information. Perform statistical analysis on that data.

- Describe what a running average is.

- Provide one example how understanding the project processes via T QM is valuable.

Endnotes

1. Zimmerman, Steven M. *Statistical Quality Control Using Excel, 2nd Edition.* Milwaukee, WI: ASQ Quality Press, 2003.

CHAPTER 6 – PROCESS ANALYSIS AND IMPROVEMENT

I. Rubric

	Novice	Sr. Novice	Journey-man	Sr. Jour-neyman	Master
SPI	x	x	x	x	x
CPI		x	x	x	x
WBS			x	x	x
SOW				x	x
Functional decomposition				x	x
Activity sequencing				x	x
Duration estimates				x	x
DFMEA					x
APQP					x

II. Questions to Ponder

- Do functional decompositions provide any added value?
- Do work breakdown structures provide any added value?
- Are hierarchical decompositions too abstract for real use by real people or are they really down-to-earth?
- Why are structured models so seductive?
- Does the enterprise really need scope control?
- Does the enterprise need change control for the processes?
- Do these various analysis documents have any marketing value?
- Why do we have so many methods for analyzing scope, risk, work, and functions?
- Why are the hierarchical breakdowns different and yet the same (compare and contrast)?
- Is a work breakdown structure just another way to make somebody some money?
- Who cares about formal cost centers?
- Is some version better than the other models?
- Why can't we just "roll our own?"

- What sort of analysis is possible if there is no established process?

III. Why Process Analysis and Improvement Are Important to the Project Manager

If we do not stand back occasionally and look at our process from both holistic and particular points of view, we are likely to end up with an evolutionary collection of outdated procedures that once served a purpose for a specific set of parameters, but which no longer meet our needs. Without critique of these procedures, we aren't able to adapt and refine the capabilities of our organization. Additionally, without an understanding of these capabilities, we find our estimates for schedules, budgets, and quality will be fraught with considerable risk.

One goal of process analysis is to come to some understanding of how the organization works. What does it really take to do the variety of functions within the organization? When it is said a particular activity takes two weeks, what does that really mean? Understanding the process variation improves the estimates and provides some context for those estimates. We learn the limitations of the processes and of the organization. Knowing the limitations provides us with the starting point to address the limitations we can—thus improving performance. We want to know what is going on in the process before we begin to make decisions to change the process. Once we know where we stand, we can begin to make improvements. If this description sounds like the define-measure-analyze-improve (DMAI) portions of the Six Sigma approach, we should not be surprised—Six Sigma is a rational approach to problem solving and enterprise improvement. Once we know what is going on, we can choose to: 1) live with the performance, 2) alter the existing process to improve performance, or 3) scrap the present process and create a new one that will better meet the needs of the organization.

IV. TQM Project Manager Scenario

A. Situation

An organization wishes to move from its present ad hoc method to capability maturity model-integrated (CMMI) level 2. However the organization has a culture that is in alignment with the ad hoc approach, which is the lowest level of the maturity model. The organization prefers the "can do" hero-oriented approach with little consideration for the historical data, preferring the "old college try" and those that do try to use historical data as evidence of true capability are dismissed as being naysayers and disregarded because they are "not team players." The organization also has no process management people to manage the development process. A group manager for one of the groups is assigned this project. This manager will also be required to maintain the line function responsibilities within the organization.

B. Objective

Bring the organization to CMMI level 2.

C. Action

Create a project to move the organization into this level. Identify key individuals both from the management area as well as those within the line organization that have product development competence. Each group within the department identifies requisite inputs, processes, and outputs.

D. Results

Unfortunately, the lack of focus on improving this area, which manifested itself when management assigned people who carry other loads within the organization made it difficult to move toward the objective quickly.

E. Aftermath

While the staff learned more about a formal development process, there was little incentive to move the organization toward this disciplined methodology. Ease of adapting—going with the flow—is highly prized within the corporation. Reaching this level within the time allocated from only one part of the entire enterprise was another detriment.

V.   Functional Decomposition

Functional decomposition applies for the most part to the process of analyzing functional relationships into their component parts (or deconstruction) such that the top-level function can be reconstructed from these parts. We execute this exercise primarily to determine the lower-level functions and their relation to high-level functions, including the topmost function. It should be clear that we are building a modular hierarchy that resembles the typical root-like appearance of a taxonomy.

We use the hierarchy as a tool to help manage the increased complexity yielded by the decomposition; however, we also need to be aware that any given component is likely to be less complex than the final product. We should not be overwhelmed by the concept of hierarchy—we could have used an egalitarian network model also or even a relational model (the resemblance to database modalities is deliberate since they must manage data [modules]).

We use the word "modules" for subcomponents of hierarchies. A module is usually a set of collaborative lower-level components that interact with the external subsystems using controlled connections, and by hiding selected features of their internals. The goal is to eliminate "side effects" caused by too much coupling between modules. The elimination of side effects applies to both hardware and software.

We recommend functional decomposition of requirements because it is fairly natural for human beings to analyze something this way and because it is relatively easy to understand. A network model can become extremely complicated as we begin to add nodes.

VI. Work Breakdown Structures

The work breakdown structure is a natural development from functional decomposition.

A. Thesis

The often overlooked and key activity in project management is the Work Breakdown Structure (WBS). To be able to deliver the goals or objectives of the project, it is imperative to develop knowledge of what we require to meet those goals. This tool is the WBS. The WBS is a key component to project execution as well as a standard project deliverable document, particularly on Department of Defense projects where it is normally a legal requirement. Insufficient time spent performing this activity can doom the project, which can devolve and strangle itself on its own tangle of confusion. Whenever we are in a project where last minute activities are identified, we probably see insufficient exertion given to generating the WBS. These forgotten items will result in cost over-runs as well as late deliveries and poor quality. Additionally, without the well-constructed WBS and subsequent estimates, tracking of the project duration, costs, and status are unknown or conjectured. We do not have a functioning "road map" to guide through scheduling and costing for the project.

The WBS is sometimes confused with a bill of material (BOM). The BOM is part of the delivery from a project and constitutes a component-level breakdown of the hardware of the product. Both are hierarchical, with upper levels (systems) decomposing into subsystem and components. That is where the similarities stop. The WBS is a hierarchical list of the activities and deliverables expected to be produced to deliver the project, not a component list for the final product.

B. General Description

The first step in generating a WBS is to define the scope of the project and divide the program or project into cost centers. This "cost center" terminology comes from the U.S. Department of Defense, because a government agency like DoD does not us profit centers per se. This essentially means we define the responsibilities for specific deliveries of the project.

A WBS for the project should be created as early as feasible during program/project development. The WBS provides the structure from which to base real estimates for the project. For each of the responsible areas, or cost centers, we will use the WBS as a record of the decomposition of higher order components into their more manageable parts—including the quality safeguarding activities. The smaller the resolution of the breakdown, the easier to estimate the duration and costs, and the less risk associated with the schedule and cost development. The WBS can be developed for each phase of the project life cycle or for the entire project. However, if the WBS is created for the entire project, the subsequently developed portions of the WBS will be fodder for future critiques at any gate reviews that may exist. At any rate, the WBS identifies the total work to be performed in a hierarchical format with increasing levels of detail.

C. Scope

A prerequisite to developing a WBS is knowledge of the scope, the objectives, and deliverable items for the project. Without knowing the entire scope, including documents to be delivered, the quality expected, and the actions to be taken to deliver that quality, we can anticipate many incomplete or non-existent tasks, found at the end of the project—and the ensuing mass scramble to cover those items. Typically, these missed tasks are obvious, and should have been expected. The worse case will be times when the discovery of less than expected quality will be found after the project's product has been launched upon your customer.

So how do we capture the project objectives and the work to be performed? We use documents such as a project charter or statement of work (SOW) for the project.

D. SCOPE and Statement of Work (SOW) and Project Charter

The scope of the project is often detailed within a SOW. We believe the SOW is one of the best tools to control the project.

Scope is often identified or constrained in a SOW. The SOW establishes the boundaries and activities of the project and spells out in substantial detail the work that is to be done, including all required standards listed (including the quality level expected) and work products, which are defined to include process support (for example, configuration management and project management).

The project charter, on the other hand, is a very high level document used in the early stages of the project to define an overview for management, a listing of team members, functional relationships, top-level cost, and estimated duration. In most cases, the SOW will have considerably more detail than the project charter.

E. WBS and Recyclability

Organizations often deliver similar projects (embedded, software, etc.) and they can reuse any WBS from previous projects as a starting point for the new project. On the downside, there is a risk of recycling earlier problems and not accounting for changes since the last use of the WBS. If we conducted a good post-mortem on previous WBS documents, then we should have already captured the major issues and recorded permanent corrective actions. Our project "white book" work will go a long way toward understanding the risks from the previous projects.

F. Generating the WBS

We can solicit expert opinion, follow industry practices, or borrow from standards and regulations. In some cases, the enterprise will have established processes. We also want to capture team member perspectives as well as identified risks, which may have an impact on the WBS; that is; we will instigate mitigating actions such as outsourcing, parallel, and duplication of activities. Outsourced activities will require WBS elements from the supplying and customer organizations.

G. Creating the Hierarchy of Tasks

Top level tasks represent areas of costing interest (for example, software development). The decomposition of tasks will follow the way in which the tasks are assembled or go together functionally once we have defined the top level cost centers.

Here is a military example (MIL-STD-881B) for electronics development:

- Prime Mission Product (PMP)
- Subsystems, from the first to the nth subsystem
- PMP Applications Software
- PMP System Software
- Integration, Assembly, Test, and Checkout
- Platform Integration
- Systems Engineering/Program Management
- System Test and Evaluation
- Development Test and Evaluation
- Operational Test and Evaluation
- Mock-ups
- Test and Evaluation Support
- Test Facilities
- Training
- Equipment
- Services
- Facilities
- Data
- Technical Publications
- Engineering Data
- Management Data
- Support Data
- Data Depository
- Peculiar Support Equipment (note: customized equipment)
- Test and Measurement Equipment
- Support and Handling Equipment
- Common Support Equipment
- Operational/Site Activation
- System Assembly, Installation, and Checkout on Site
- Contractor Technical Support
- Site Construction
- Site/Ship/Vehicle Conversion
- Industrial Facilities
- Construction/Conversion/Expansion
- Equipment Acquisition or Modernization
- Maintenance (Industrial Facilities)
- Initial Spares and Repair Parts

Note how the breakdown is logical and accounts for the complete project. MIL-STD-881 provides templates for major programs/projects to provide a good start to new programs.

The sub-tasks have progressively smaller durations and are the constituent tasks of upper level tasks.

H. Activity Sequencing

Each of the building blocks may have interactions and dependencies; for example, we must *design* hardware before we *build* hardware. The WBS structure allows for manipulation of the tasks to work through the dependencies and the associated risks. The WBS provides enough information to define all required tasks—the project manager will still use a network diagram to represent task dependencies.

I. Duration Estimates

The smallest size WBS elements have a reasonable chance at accurate estimation due to their small size (see Figure 6.1). The status can be binary (complete, incomplete). This approach has the advantage of eliminating the use of percentages to represent completion status, a technique which our experience shows to be overly optimistic and highly subjective. The small-element approach also makes for easier deployment of estimating techniques such as Program Evaluation and Review Technique (PERT) and Monte Carlo simulation.

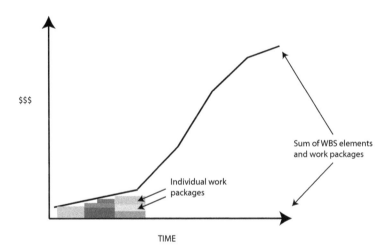

Figure 6.1 An illustration of how the work packages or individual WBS elements are in the accumulation of the budget for the project.

J. Time-Phased Budget

The time-phased budget will include the schedule and cost (usually in hours). This approach is necessary for earned value management (EVM), which includes the following metrics:

- Schedule performance index
- Cost performance index
- Cost variance
- Schedule variance

- Estimated budget to complete
- Estimates at completion

Figure 6.1 illustrates the accumulated budget for the project. The WBS elements make up the project budget. When the time (t) is beyond the WBS element, then the project is in duration overrun.

The smaller the task, the quicker it is for us to confirm the task is on schedule and the sooner it is for us to identify when the project is in an overrun condition (schedule or budget).

K. Scope Control

The WBS helps to simplify and empower scope control for the project manager. The rules are simple:

- Changes to scope change WBS
- Changes to product have an impact on the WBS
- Changes to project have an impact on the WBS
- Unaccounted for changes (not included in WBS) will not get lost, especially in costing because they require an explicit update of the WBS

These rules imply that any change to the WBS is a reflection of change in the project, which is precisely what we must do in order to make the WBS a living document and a useful tool.

L. Task Identification

Task identification is accomplished through a format know as the WBS dictionary, which—as dictionaries do—defines the meaning and properties of each element of the WBS. Of course, the task must be known beforehand so we can identify expectations, attributes, and quality levels for the task. We must also identify resources and processes required to generate the specific WBS element.

M. Quality Assurance

Tasks and descriptions of those tasks are used to generate quality assurance activities such as reviews, tests, and inspections. We can also perform a comparison of actual deliverables to the task quality description as a form of auditing—this action is often performed by some person or entity not delivering the task.

N. Task Sequencing

To properly identify sequencing, we must understand task dependencies. Additionally, tasks will relate to each other in the form of:

- Start-Finish
- Finish-Finish
- Finish-Start
- Start-Start

We can sometimes shuffle tasks in order to manage risks and improve on the schedule delivery date. If the shuffling is very complicated, we may need software support in the form of capacity resource planning or critical chain software.

O. How Far Do We Break It Down?

Based on experience, we suggest that hierarchical task sets should be broken down to the "atomic" level, which is the point at which breaking the element down any further makes no sense or becomes silly. This approach helps when using binary reporting (complete, incomplete). Project management software can calculate percentages for upper management based on the roll-up of the binary status of each task. More importantly, it is easy to detect when the project is executing outside of the expected rate of task closure.

P. WBS and Responsibility

We assigned WBS elements (tasks) by identifying the responsibility for each delivery/deliverable. We can do this by using a resource allocation matrix, which represents responsibilities and deliverables graphically by matching work with organization breakdown structure (OBS) shown at right angles to the tree/table that represents the WBS.

Q. Organizational Breakdown Structure (OBS)

An OBS is a similar tree structure to the WBS—effectively an organizational chart of human resources available to the cost centers of the WBS. We use cross-mapping with the WBS to provide a responsibility matrix. Clearly identifying who is responsible for what part of the project is important no matter the industry.

R. The WBS and Work Packages

Work packages are WBS elements. They can be a sub-task or a collection of related tasks. In some cases, the tool helps us to outsource another company's internal work group. Since the WBS requires substantial definition of each element, the requirements are unequivocally known.

S. The WBS and Outsourcing

Contract work can be outsourced initially with a SOW. Afterwards, we follow up with identification of the contract work breakdown structure (CWBS) for the outsourced activity; we derive this CWBS from the upper level project WBS. The tool helps to provide points for status updates and control. The fine resolution of the CWBS allows for quick determination about what to do when things don't go according to plan and provides for initiation of previously considered risk mitigation activities (we did consider contingency plans already, right?).

We are not off the hook just because this work is outsourced. We must identify milestones and monitor the progress of the supplier. Our earned value techniques can help. If we know what our tolerances are on the cost and schedule, we can calculate the schedule performance index and the cost performance metrics our supplier must meet to deliver our package on time at the cost expected. We establish control regions on the SPI and CPI chart with contingency action identified when the supplier breaches these identified levels. Better still, we are able to anticipate an imminent breach of the SPI and CPI based upon this monitoring and start our contingency actions as soon as we see that there is a very real probability of the breach.

T. WBS Provides a Baseline

The WBS gives us a baseline of activities to achieve the project targets. As we noted already, changes to project targets, or scope additions have an impact on the WBS. Each change can be reviewed for impact by comparing the original WBS to changes required, again providing for a high level of project control.

U. WBS Does / Doesn't

There are some things the WBS can and cannot do. For example, it doesn't:
• Clearly identify *task* dependencies
• Substitute for project follow-through
• Identify the project organization

The WBS does:
• Support scope identification/clarification
• Serve as a baseline for schedule generation
• Facilitate duration estimation
• Allow earned value management techniques
• Facilitate responsibility and accountabilities

V. Concluding Words on the WBS

Without task details for the project, success is largely luck and often improbable (the use of the "hope" method of project management). Additionally, the WBS prevents falling through the cracks by accounting for everything that must be done.

VII. Scope of Work

We use the WBS to help us manage the scope of the work for project.

A. Process Improvement Tools

Implement AIAG Advanced Product Quality Planning[1]

The advanced product quality planning (APQP)—a standard source for the manufacturing-oriented process control plan—approach provides a logical and rational program for product development, while remaining flexible enough to meet contingencies (see Figure 6.2). It can be used for embedded software development as well as for other industries. We suggest, given the industrial success of this approach and its variants, further deployment would benefit any industry for which it is a reasonable fit.

The APQP philosophy is that of an often concurrent waterfall that employs concurrency as desired. It is composed of a logical sequence of events (not just product development or manufacturing) which, in turn, are supported by a well-defined collection of tools. A strong ingredient of APQP is the focus on feedback: within the enterprise, with suppliers and customers. The feedback required by APQP allows for true control in the technical control system sense. The approach is also consistent with Shewhart Plan-Do-Check-Act (PDCA) cycle popularized by W. Edwards Deming and often called the Deming loop.

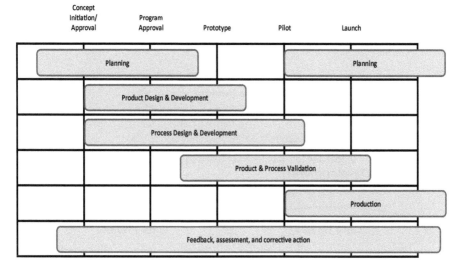

Figure 6.2 A graphical representation of the layered AIAG model for product and process development.

Like any system, APQP has some pluses and minuses. Some of the benefits of APQP reside in the:

- Rational process
- Allowance for concurrency (but not mandated)
- Well-defined list of minimal deliverable items (defines a minimum level of management oversight and intensity)
- Understood across the U.S. auto industry and among suppliers

Some of the inadequacies of APQP come from:

- The necessarily generic approach to product development
- The fact that the process itself needs a process failure mode and effects analysis
- Most commonly only one design solution is managed early in the process, which may be restrictive
- Early verification and validation are not emphasized sufficiently
- The feedback system not well-defined (the approach is not prescriptive)

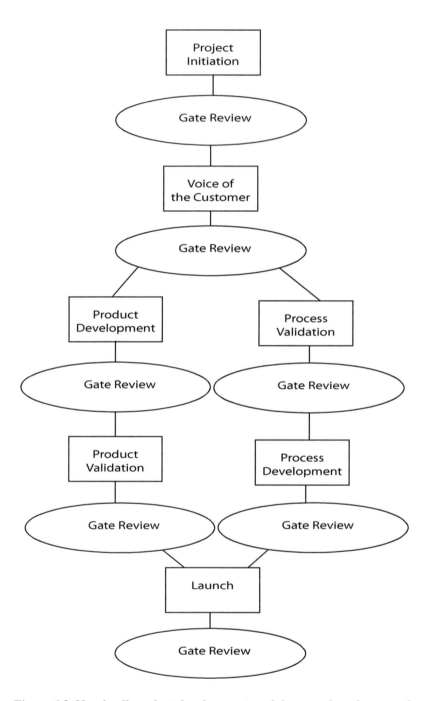

Figure 6.3 Nearly all product development models use a phased approach with numerous gates.

APQP Phases

APQP supports a minimum of five phases, to whit:

- Plan and define program
- Product design and development
- Process design and development
- Product and process verification and validation
- Feedback, assessment, and corrective action

The first four phases often occur as a staggered concurrent engineering approach. The last bullet should occur throughout the process.

The APQP phases can be used directly as project phases (see Figure 6.3), although we recommend a higher level of granularity than that provided by the AIAG document. The phases provide a basis for gate reviews or kill-points through the project life cycle. This approach facilitates detailed project planning and integration by both phases and functional areas of product and process development. Hence, we can use APQP to help us plan and define the entire development program.

Product Development

Let's say the marketing investigation and conceptualization phase of any project is already complete. Using APQP we would perform the following actions with respect to product development:

- Design verification (key product characteristics)

- Design reviews (hardware and software reviews)

- Prototype build and evaluations

- Drawings

- Specifications

- Support equipment requirements analysis

- Test/measurement equipment requirements

If we were designing an instrument cluster for example, we would begin the specification work detailing the functional and performance demands upon the hardware and the software. We would have design reviews of that documentation, and we would identify the key product characteristics and begin developing test plans around the design results.

We can use a range of product development tools to assist in completion of the product development actions (see Figure 6.4). Some of these tools consist of the following items:

- Simulation
- Component / Subsystem
- System
- Vehicle
- Design failure mode and effects analysis (DFMEA)
- Prototypes
- Design for manufacturability/assembly (DFMA)

- Design release notes
- Hardware revisions (unique revision level / part number)
- Software revisions
- Configuration management
- Basis of test configurations
- Change management
- Control changes to the product through development

While we recommend the toolset that comes with APQP, we don't recommend getting "hung up" on the tools but, rather, consider APQP as a process to help ensure control and quality through the duration of the development process.

Process Development

Analogous to the product approach, we also have a process design and development sequence which, again, can be expanded into many more actions than these:

- Process verification (key control characteristics)
- Packaging design
- Quality reviews
- Floor plan layout
- Process instructions
- Planning measurement system analysis

In our instrument cluster example, we would develop the material handling and manufacturing processes from start to finish including how the part will be shipped to the customer. We consider and identify the key control characteristic of the processes that produce the product to the desired quality.

As with product development, the process development sequence has its own set of tools:

- Preliminary process capability plan
- Process flow chart
- Characteristics matrix
- Process failure mode and effects analysis (PFMEA)
- Pre-launch control plan

Product and Process Verification and Validation

The APQP approach demands that both products and process be verified and validated. "Verification" generally refers to proving that the design of either the product or the process meets requirements. "Validation" may consist of similar actions, but validation typically occurs toward the latter portion of the project and it is oriented toward the satisfaction of customer needs. Many of the actions taken include, but are not limited to, the following:

- Pilot runs and run-at-rate
- Measurement system analyses
- Process capability studies
- Production part approval
- Test and field vehicles
- Production part approval process (PPAP)

- Design verification and plan and report (DVP&R)
- Packaging reports
- Production validation test reports

We recommend that the APQP practitioner institute product and process design verification as early in the process as is feasible. The validation phase should include testing to the design limits, pushing the product to the failure limit, and going all the way to the destruct limit when possible to characterize potential warranty issues. This is especially necessary when the development work has made use of standards in the requirements as standards do not necessarily reflect customer use of the product (see our article on product requirements `http://www.pddnet.com/article-understanding-real-demands-on/?terms=pries`).

In this phase, we confirm the instrument cluster design meets the targets and that the manufacturing processes are able to deliver the product at the required quality and volume of production.

Feedback, Assessment, and Corrective Action

As we noted earlier, the APQP approach emphasizes feedback and corrective action while remaining curiously non-prescriptive. Some of the facets of this part of APQP include:

- Variation control
- Failure reporting and corrective action system (FRACAS)
- Fault reporting (fault designator / identifier)
- Traceability of:
  - Fault
  - Status
  - Quick response

In the automotive world, a common approach to corrective action is the use of the eight disciplines (8D) tool, which incorporates emergency actions, containment actions, irreversible corrective actions, and verification for each of these phases to the overall corrective action.

What about concurrency? We also indicated that concurrency can be supported by the APQP approach.

Use in Industry

The APQP approach originated with Ford, Chrysler, and GM and has been deployed within nearly all automotive suppliers including off-road (e.g., Caterpillar or John Deere) and commercial vehicles (trucks of all categories—for example, Volvo or Navistar). The supplier management tools are formalized into a production part approval process.

The APQP approach has also evolved into the Hazard Analysis and Critical Control Point (HACCP) system which is used in the following industries:

- Food
- Pharmaceutical
- Medical

All of these industries make use of variations on the original APQP tools, such as failure mode and effect analyses.

Control Plans

The process control plan (PCP—not the drug!) is the very heart of the AIAG manufacturing approach, perhaps more than any other tool. We feel that the tool can be slightly modified to become a major benefit for the TQM project manager. Please note that AIAG has granted permission to refer to their documents, but the following text is our own and, while based on the AIAG process control plan (see Figure 6.4), is by no means a product of AIAG nor does it have their blessing—it is a tool that we have expanded to include the project process in our project factory model.

We structure the control plan with the following column headings:

- Part process number
- Process name / operation description
- Machine, device, jig, tools for manufacturing
- Characteristics
  - Number
  - Product
  - Process
- Special Char. Class
- Methods
  - Specification/tolerance in production/process
  - Evaluation measurement techniques
  - Sample size
  - Sample frequency
  - Control method
- Reaction plan

Part Process Number

The TQM project manager can take the process number directly from the time line tool he or she is using to manage the project.

Process Name / Operation Description

This field is the actual task from the project time line. As long as we have a one-to-one relation with the time line, we should have no difficulty keeping track of our tasks. We know of no tool at this time that will directly display a project time line in process control plan format.

Machine, Device, Jig, Tools for Manufacturing

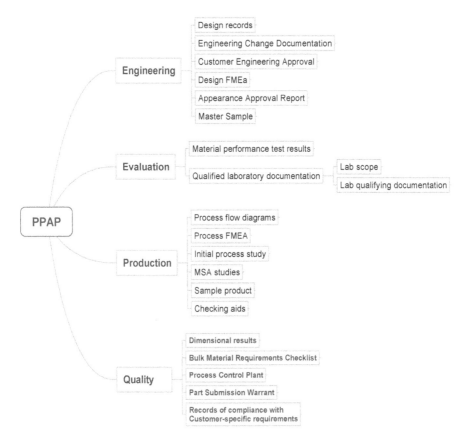

Figure 6.4 The AIAG PPAP structure provides a method for ensuring requirements are met.

This field bears modification since the heading is relatively irrelevant to the project process although it is completely relevant to the *manufacturing* process.

Characteristics–Number

We can give more information about our project task, including a special number, which we generally don't find necessary.

Characteristics–Product

If it makes sense, we can define some kind of information about the product we are in the process of developing. Often, we are more interested in the process than we are in the product, so this column can be left blank or eliminated completely if it is not relevant to a specific project.

Characteristics–Process

We can define the specific characteristics for this task. Once again, the project manager should remain utterly pragmatic with respect to inclusion of the various control plan fields.

Special Char. Class

This field can generally be eliminated.

Methods–Specification/ Tolerance of Product or Process

For a task, we specify acceptable completion dates. We can use this field for this information. If we are going to this level of detail, it might make sense to build a "macro" to convert from the project management software to the spreadsheet version of the process control plan.

Methods–Evaluation Measurement Technique

How will we measure our task? Most commonly, we will use the optimistic date, the expected date, and the pessimistic date as possible boundaries for acceptability.

Methods–Sample Size

We may choose to populate this field if we are testing product samples and we wish to document the sample size. Do not get wrapped up in the mythical number "30" that is supposedly so significant in statistics! Sample size is a much more complex issue that can't be solved with a simple rule of thumb.

Methods–Sample Frequency

What we just wrote in regard to sample size applies here also, which means, in many cases, the field will remain empty and that is just fine. The goal is for the tool to help the TQM project manager improve and risk-inoculate the project process, not to see how closely we can adhere to the model of a manufacturing assembly line.

Methods–Control Method

We may be using a statistical control technique such as control charts to help separate assignable causes from random variation. We use this field to document our means for accomplishing some level of control.

Reaction Plan

The reaction plan tells us what we are going to do when things do not go well for this particular task. We consider this part of the control plan to be perhaps the most important portion of the document.

The reaction plan as used in many process control plans usually involves an action, for example, such as "Inform supervisor of anomaly." This reaction is not particularly aggressive and probably represents filling out the control plan document perfunctorily rather than any kind of serious intent to provide for the inevitable failure of the system.

We have used the reaction plan field for contingency planning. We have seen few project managers spend the time to plan for contingencies during the early portions of the project. We know from experience that having a backup plan already in hand is a quick way to look the hero when things are going well.

If we apply the concept of failure mode and effects analysis (Chapter 7) to the project management process, we should already have potential solutions in place for each failure mode at each task. Yes, this approach involves a lot of work! On the other hand, knowing the next step or the alternative step goes a long way to bringing in the project under budget, ahead of schedule, with great quality.

As with other parts of APQP we have some benefits and defects to the control plan approach. The benefits of the control plan are the following:

- Concurrent creation with PFMEA

- Controls clearly identified

- Contingency plans (reaction plan) clearly identified

- Specification limits defined

- Sequence spelled out

- The defects of the control plan approach are the following:

    - Inadequate contingency planning

    - Poor tolerance specifications and failure to recognize importance of target value

    - Doesn't handle decision points gracefully

*Production Part Approval Process (PPAP)*3

As we indicated earlier, the supplier management portion of the APQP approach is formal. A PPAP submission has eighteen required documents, which include all design-oriented documents, all major process-oriented documents, appearance, and materials assessment.

The benefits of PPAP are various but one of the most important is that it represents the last chance for suppliers to review themselves before submitting results to customers—ultimately, being more important to the supplier than to the customer. It decidedly formalizes the release relationship from supplier to customer and it also standardizes the documentation required for the complete submission.

The defects of PPAP are the following:

- It can become a mere formality

- Slipshod work on component documents misses the point for both supplier and customer

- Often, customers don't review very well

- May stay in a condition called "interim PPAP" for years

Application of APQP to Embedded Development

The APQP approach can be easily adapted for embedded software development. Software development falls immediately under product design and development (if it is product software). Software verification falls under product verification and validation. It is less common to use embedded software for process design and development, although automated test equipment can be subject to the same design requirements as product software. Please note that we find the FMEA approach for software unsatisfactory due to the immediate exponentiation in product complexity; that is, only the architectural level of the software can be adequately handled by the FMEA2 tool. The software deliverables are not explicitly defined by APQP. The following table shows a potential embedded software sequence lined up with the more common APQP items (a sample of these) to show how the process meshes nicely with the more basic APQP requirements:

- Product design and development
- Embedded software sequence
- Process design and development
- Embedded software sequence
- Design goals
- Reliability/quality goals
- System requirement specification
- Preliminary BOM
- System requirements review
- Preliminary process flow chart
- System design specification
- Preliminary control plan
- System design review
- Software requirement specification
- Software requirements review
- Preliminary design description
- Preliminary design review
- Detailed design description

Design reviews

- Detailed design review
- Process flow
- Control plan
- Formal software release

- Product assurance plan
- Test design description
- Verification/validation
- Test equipment verification and validation
- Test readiness review
- Test readiness review
- Physical configuration audit
- Physical configuration audit
- Qualification review
- Production readiness review

When doing embedded development we would define additional deliverable items and process control under the APQP umbrella. We recommend a test, analyze, and fix (TAAF) approach throughout development (via repetitive product availability) to eliminate faults and to verify the defect status of software and hardware statistically (software defect appearance rates can often be modeled with a Rayleigh distribution).

Additional candidates for inclusion might be those spelled out by the Institute for Electrical and Electronics Engineers (IEEE) and include the following deliverable documents:

- Critical and preliminary design review
- Software configuration management plan
- Software configuration management plan review
- Software design description (SDD)
- Software quality assurance plan
- Software requirements specification (SRS)
- Software requirements review
- Software verification and validation plan
- Software verification and validation plan review
- User documentation review

The embedded developer could just as easily use a military approach or any other standardized model for software development. The benefit of these models is that they provide a structure for development, the formalisms of which provide for some level of control and, if all else fails, an audit trail for understanding the history and decisions made during the project.

At a minimum, the embedded deliverables during development should include requirements analysis documents, design documents (SDD and SRS), the results of design reviews (hardware and source code), the code (compiled—typically iterative), test plans/reports, the recommended architectural document, and, of course, product release documentation.

One might ask how this embedded software approach is really APQP? We insist that our approach represents APQP for software due to the presence of:

- Defined product and process development actions
- Specific output and input items
- Deliverables spelled out in process
- Verification/Validation
- Feedback and corrective action

By the time we reach the end of the development process, we expect to see embedded software in production. We recommend that it be formally released and that the software fall under formal configuration management system for production. Additionally, we would expect to see chip programming verification using checksums or a cyclic redundancy check (for electronic products). In-circuit test verification when feasible provides a good hardware check on printed circuit boards and we would expect to see functional in-line testing of subsystems before the product ships.

We believe it should be clear that APQP can be adapted and applied to other industries and systems. Beyond the ones we have mentioned, we could also deploy APQP to service industries (including process planning and development, process verification, and run at rate activities). APQP can support the launch of consumer products, contract manufacturing (non-automotive), and the education arena.

Implement a Test and Evaluation Master Plan (TEMP)[5]

This tool allows the project manager to improve the process by using progressive refinement for both the product and the testing. The beauty of this approach lies in the fact that it is planned from the very beginning. The general outline and idea derives from MIL-STD-499B (Draft) and we have found it to be a sound approach. We include a sample TEMP in appendix 2. We also provide an enhanced version call TIEMPO in appendix 3.

Here is a generic outline of a typical TEMP:

1. Program background
1.1. Mission description
1.2. System objective assessment
1.3. System description
1.4. Critical technical parameters
1.5. Maintenance concept
1.6. Training concept
1.7. System operational and support capability
1.8. System administration support
1.9. Data conversion and loading
2. Integrated test program summary
2.1. Integrated test program schedule
2.2. Evolutionary development
2.3. Management
3. Developmental test and evaluation (DT&E) outline

3.1. Developmental test and evaluation overview
3.2. Future DT&E
4. Operational test & evaluation (OT&E) outline
4.1. OT&E overview
4.2. Critical operational issues
4.3. Future OT&E
5. Test and evaluation resource summary
5.1. Test articles
5.2. Test sites and communications
5.3. Test support equipment
5.4. Threat representation
5.5. Test targets and expendables
5.6. Operational force test support
5.7. Simulations, models and testbeds
5.8. Special requirements
5.9. T&E funding requirements
5.10. Manpower/personnel training

This document provides for substantial up-front planning. The approach is particularly suitable for software development, particularly when we design our software like an onion. Our onion-software approach begins with a core that we can validate; afterwards, we keep adding layers with complete validation at the end of each layer. In this way, we can discern in most cases at what point we introduced flaws into the code. The same approach holds true to a lesser extent with the development of hardware.

One goal of the TEMP approach is to bring the verification and validation of the product to a higher level of concern, rather than being tacked on at the end of development as has been the case in many projects we have witnessed.

VIII.   Exercises

- Create a process control plan for the main thread of the project time line with special attention paid to the reaction plan.

- Create a process FMEA for the main thread of the project time line.

- Create a process for project change management including stakeholders.

- Show a time line that looks "sewn" because the main thread bounces between product development and process development.

- What would a short version of the statement of work look like?

- Discuss the level of detail used in a statement of work. What is important?

- Build a work breakdown structure for a wooden pencil.

- Build a work breakdown structure for a mechanical pencil.

- Build a work breakdown structure for a ballpoint pen.

- Link responsibility to the above work breakdown structure.

- Search the world wide web for Microsoft Excel examples that support various control charts and try them with the data we have already used.

Endnotes

1. Automotive Industry Action Group (AIAG). *Advanced Product Quality Planning and Control Plan, 2nd Edition.* Southfield, MI: AIAG, 2004.

2. Automotive Industry Action Group (AIAG). *Potential Failure Mode and Effects Analysis, 4th Edition.* Southfield, MI: AIAG, 2008.

3. Automotive Industry Action Group (AIAG). *Production Part Approval Process, 4th Edition.* Southfield, MI: AIAG, 2006.

4. Automotive Industry Action Group (AIAG). *Statistical Process Control, 2nd Edition.* Southfield, MI: AIAG, 2005.

5. Joint OSD/Services/Industry Working Group. *Military Standard 499B (draft). Systems Engineering.* Washington, DC: U.S. Department of Defense, 1993.

CHAPTER 7 – PROCESS CONTROL AND METRICS

I. Rubric

	Novice	Sr. Novice	Journey-man	Sr. Jour-neyman	Master
DFMEA	x	x	x	x	x
PFMEA		x	x	x	x
Configuration Control			x	x	x
Configuration Auditing				x	x
Configuration identification				x	x
Configuration Status Accounting				x	x
Production controls				x	x
Poka-yoke					x
Testing controls					x

II. Questions to Ponder

- Do process controls provide any added value?
- Are process controls too abstract for actual use or are they really down-to-earth?
- Why is the frequent addition of more controls so seductive?
- Does the enterprise really need process controls?
- Will a process control plan help any enterprise?
- Does our control expertise have any marketing value?
- Why do we have so many ways to do control plans?
- Why are the process controls different and yet the same (compare and contrast)?
- Is a process control plan just another way to keep the bureaucracy busy?
- Is any version better than the other models?
- Why can't we just "roll our own?"

III. Why Process Controls and Metrics Are Important to the Project Manager

The TQM project manager is the master of the project process. He or she is responsible for instituting whatever controls are necessary to drive the project to conclusion with minimal anomalies. Additionally, the TQM PM will want to oversee any process controls for the multitude of subgroups that deliver both product and process.

One of the most important controls for the TQM PM is configuration management, which allows the PM and the enterprise to define their product exactly and provide meaningful designations in the form of revision numbers and, in some cases, part numbers. Without configuration management, the PM may end up with a handful of nothing.

IV. TQM Project Manager Scenario

A. Situation

An automotive manufacturer secured some new business and began a design for a personal recreational vehicle. Formal configuration management was poor to nonexistent on both the hardware and the software sides of the house.

B. Objective

The initial objective was to deliver functioning prototypes as proof of concept, particularly given that the vehicle would be used in harsh environments.

C. Action

Design proceeded to the point where a nearly-complete hardware design existed (housing, gauges, etc.), the electronic design was fully functional, and the software possessed all specified features.

D. Results

The supplier sent a set of prototypes to the customer in which neither the hardware version nor the software versions were known. The supplier's senior salesman was on-site to demonstrate this new product. No prototype functioned *in any way*. The situation was maximally embarrassing.

E. Aftermath

While the supplier was able to follow up with working prototypes with known versions, the damage had been done. At some point thereafter, the customer dropped the supplier in favor of another supplier whose product was ugly but functional.

V.   Risk Management

A. The Forgotten Task

What do PMs almost never do? In our experience, we have rarely seen significant time spent on contingency planning; for example, preparing for expected anomalies, preparing for unexpected anomalies, control of slack time and dependencies, and quantification and contingency budgets as a part of the project planning activity. Even when team members willingly bring forth the risks they may see—we see project managers resenting the input or at the very minimum ignoring the information completely. In many cases, a new product will launch with major materials shortages and problem-ridden or late software.

Of course, nothing will help the project manager who chooses to ignore the information brought by team members. Neither will it help to make note of the risk but plan no moderating actions or following the risk symptom. It does little good to know the risk is possible, but not to plan contingency action or monitor for the potential risk occurring. However, one approach we can take to help reduce these nightmares is through the use of a document similar in concept to the failure modes and effects analysis (FMEA[1]) methodology. If we view the project timeline as a directed graph analogous to a production flow diagram, we can also visualize the sequence of the time line as the beginning of an automotive or HACCP-style control plan. One of the tools used to reduce risk in the production process is the process FMEA, which matches the process defined in the process control plan step for step, often identifying multiple failure modes for each step.

B. What Approach Can Help?

We recommend a modified version of the FMEA approach, tailored to the needs of project and program managers. We will model the time line as a control plan with minimal controls other than the typical toll gate reviews, and perhaps, team meetings. We know from personal experience that treating potential failures systematically can often forestall risky events completely. Even when the risk is not eliminated, the awareness of the potential for disaster allows the project manager to manage expectations of the stakeholders, not to mention preparing appropriate contingency plans for risk management. It is seldom a good idea to ignore the risk—hoping the risk never occurs. The better solution is to quantify the risk, understanding the probability and magnitude or severity and consciously either ignoring or assigning moderating actions and tracking via symptoms. Clearly, not all risks are equal in terms of consequences. Tracking the symptom and potential triggers provides us the clue that the risk is no longer a risk but potentially a certainty and we can engage our risk management plan.

C. What Does It Look Like?

Our approach uses a header section much like the automotive FMEA so that the document can be appropriately identified, team named, and other information added for tracking purposes. The main fields are

- Project identified
- Key (responsible) personnel
- Document registration
- Product / project name
- Revision control

Here is a partial sample of such a document:

We start by identifying potential risks to which the project can be subjected. This can be done individually and brought back into the team for compiling the total risks seen by the team (or any other contributors, for that matter). Some of these risks may be transferred outside of the project to other groups better able to manage these issues. For example, supplier issues might be referred to a company's procurement department with some notes added for follow-up. For those risks that are not transferred, a specific individual is designated with the task of monitoring the project for symptoms associated with this risk. The symptom means we are close to incurring the risk and if we have really performed a critique of the risk earlier in the project we have some clues to the root cause for the event. A single person is responsible for monitoring the risk and reports back to the team, or initiates the risk response actions identified.

One of the most significant fields is "Risk Description," where we explicitly identify the risk. In general, it is wise to include enough information that a casual reader can understand the risk status; that is, a clear, concise, and complete description of the potential issue. It is important at this stage that we do not include potential solutions, because the table has special fields for this.

We define other fields to be

- Severity
- Probability
- Controllability
- RPN, where
    - RPN = risk priority number
    - RPN=severity x probability x control, for example:
        - $S = 10, P = 7, C = 4$
        - RPN = 280
- Alternate version
- RPN= SS + PP +CC, for example:
    - $S = 10, P = 7, C = 4$
    - RPN = 1074

Once we have identified the risk and quantified it, we associate a dollar amount with this potential risk should it happen. If the risk were to occur, this estimate would be the amount of money that would probably be at stake.

D. Risk Quantification and Detection

The SEV, PROB, and CTRL fields quantify the amount of risk to which the project is exposed. The higher the number, the more risk to the project. This information is used to prioritize and generate action to mitigate or eliminate (transfer) the risk.

Also, we wish to identify the detection—how do you know the risk is imminent or has been encountered or is likely to be encountered. The responsible person or persons have an established completion date for the action as a stimulus to completion. If our actions are successful, we would expect to see the following changes to the fields

SEV

After mitigation, severity may be reduced. In many cases, the severity will remain the same but the other two factors will decrease.

Example of severity assessment values:

Description level	Value scale
Minor impact on cost schedule performance	1 to 2
Moderate impact on cost, schedule, performance	3 to 4
Significant impact on project baselines	5 to 6
Very significant impact on project baselines	7 to 8
Disastrous impact, probable project failure	9 to 10

PROB

The probability of the event should be reduced. Reducing this factor will affect the post-mitigation RPN. Example of probabilities to be used in the table:

1	10.00%	very unlikely
2	20.00%	
3	30.00%	somewhat unlikely
4	40.00%	
5	50.00%	50/50 chance
6	60.00%	
7	70.00%	highly likely
8	80.00%	
9	90.00%	nearly certain
10	100.00%	

CTRL

The control should have a reduced value if we have implemented one or more improved controls into the process. Of course, we are working under the assumption that adding a control will improve the situation—which is not always the case.

Example of controllability numbers:

Description level	Value scale
Essentially avoidable through selected risk mitigation	1 to 2
Highly controllable through organization or project actions	3 to 4
Moderately controllable through organization or project actions	5 to 6
Largely uncontrollable by the organization or the project	7 to 8
Uncontrollable by the organization or the project	9 to 10

Risk Priority Number (RPN)
The post-mitigation RPN should be reduced over the pre-mitigation RPN.
If this is not the case:

- We have to live with the risk (if RPN is not very high)
                    OR

- We have an issue that should be elevated to higher levels of management

Financial RISK
We may choose to sort our table on financial risk rather than severity to highlight significant financial challenges. The sum of all the financial risks is the contingency risk for the total project.

The trigger is a new concept to those acquainted with the FMEA approach to problem elimination. We could use, for example, the Schedule Performance Indicator

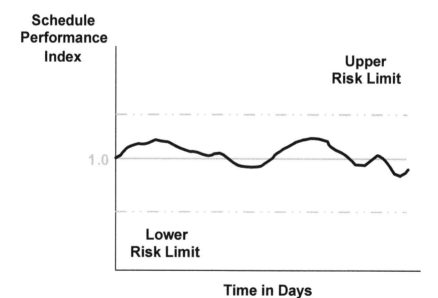

Figure 7.1 Schedule performance index with risk limits identified for severe action from the PM similar to a control diagram only not based upon control knowledge but acceptable risk levels or performance expectations.

as an index showing the efficiency of the time utilized on the project, as compared to the estimates for the project. Schedule performance indicator can be calculated using the following formula:

- SPI = Earned Value (EV) /Planned Value (PV)
            OR

- SPI = BCWP / BCWS

The formula mentioned above gives the efficiency of the project team in using the time allocated for the project.

SPI > 1 indicates project team is very efficient in using time allocated to project.
SPI < 1 indicates project team is less efficient in using time allocated to project.

When we know the performance expected from our supplier to meet the needs of our project, we can monitor that performance against the needs. When the supplier's performance starts to move outside the zone that our project deems acceptable, we can start mitigating actions. Figure 7.1 illustrates our tracking a supplier's performance against the project's operating expectation. These expectation levels are identified as the upper and lower risk levels in the graphic above. We monitor the SPI<1 because this will mean our project / supplier is executing below what is needed to achieve the project expectation portending a cost over-run.

That addresses the reason for the lower SPI limit but what about the upper limit? Why would we worry about a project that provides a great deal more efficiency than planned (SPI>1)? We can suggest a few reasons. The first reason—we may question the validity of the estimates upon which the SPI calculation is based. Maybe the estimates were unduly padded. It could also be that some of the activities that went into the estimation are being neglected—essentially cutting corners from what we expected. We can ask questions to determine if this is in fact the case. It could also be that the numbers have undergone some tampering. In any of these events, follow on questions and exploration will help determine if there is a reason for concern. We are surprised that tactics such as establishing control limits on a supplier's SPI or CPI do not seem to be very common in industry. Then again, we wonder why we infrequently see such things as tracking Gantt charts of the supplier.

E. Risk Response and Contingency Budgets

Each dollar at risk is multiplied by the probability of risk occurrence. This dollar amount per risk is added together to generate the total contingency budget for the project. For example: we have a risk that we estimate to be $200,000. If this risk has a 50% probability we would plan our contingency budget for this risk to be $100,000. We will do this for the risks that are the most severe and the risks where we may not have another suitable mitigating action.

When early attention regarding risk is not employed, then contingency budgets are a guess or are based upon the last project over-runs, or are a percentage of the total budget, random generated, or non-existent. When employing any of these techniques, we are hoping for the best result instead of planning to make the delivery and accounting for the risk.

F. How Do We Follow Up?

The risk status section should provide us with some follow-up notes on the result of actions taken, including our approach to risk handling. Risk handling includes the means by which we identify, evaluate, select monitor, and implement our choices to reduce or eliminate the risks we have previously identified. This approach includes the specifics on what we need to do, scheduling, responsibility, and budget. It is common to see the term risk mitigation, which is a subset of risk handling. The point here is that we must employ planning (anticipation) followed by execution (which, in turn, leads into follow through) in order to control our quality, schedule, and costs against plan. Some of the options we have for doing this are as follows:

- Risk control
    - Seek to reduce or mitigate the risks
    - Example: explicit identification with explicit actions
- Alternative design
    - Create a backup option that uses a lower risk approach
    - Example: new technology risks
- Alternative development process
    - Product is too complex and project to complex to use stage gate method
    - Example: Use a scrum approach
- Tradeoff analyses
    - Arrive at a balance of engineering requirements in the design of a system
    - Example: Pugh concept selection
- Early system design
    - Use of simulation in early system design
    - Example: digital mockup units to verify fit between associated parts
    - Example: hardware in the loop simulation of proposed function (data bus)
- Early prototyping
    - Build and test prototypes early in the system development
        - Use of simulation in early system design
        - Working models
        - Example: stereolithographic (SLA) models to verify fit of mechanical parts
- Incremental development
    - Design with the intent of upgrading system parts in the future

- Staged releases with known good releases
- Example: staged releases with planned test sequences and always-correct core design
- Use the concentric design method that always protects the core code if we are working with software
- Robust design
- Parameter design
- Tolerance design
  - Makes product insensitive to noise
  - Example: screwdriver head robust enough to be abused as a hammer
- Reviews, walk-throughs, and inspections
  - These three actions can be used to reduce or eliminate both the likelihood and potential penalties of actualized risks through evaluation of actual or planned events
  - Example: code inspections in software development
- Design of experiments
  - This engineering tool identifies critical design factors
  - Can be used in tandem with robust design
  - Example: combinatorial testing of multiple electronic inputs simultaneously
- Open systems
  - Carefully selected commercial specifications and standards whose use can result in lower risks
  - Open source software
  - Example: mature and relatively risk-free open source software like Ruby and Python
- Real world measurements
  - Carefully selected specifications and standards whose use can result in lower risks
  - Example: use of standards such as ISO for performance or exposure of the hardware
  - Example: perform actual measurements of the environment for the proposed system

The primary task for the project manager can be summed up with the word "anticipation." To anticipate challenges, the project manager must fill the function of boundary spanner and recruit someone (more likely multiple people) from within the project team to perform that function. Factual and objective (not overly optimistic and hopeful) assessment of the project environment is necessary to ensure the delivery to planned schedule and budget. In addition to anticipation, the project manager will add "execution" and "follow-through" to make a complete package for project success. So, in addition to the triad of quality-cost-schedule, we now also have anticipate-execute-follow up.

G. Final Words on FMEA

A time line or schedule is—to all intents—a process. We have wondered for years why organizations, which often tout their FMEA prowess, never use the process FMEA to analyze the project time line. We suggest that such preparation provides for ample risk management, provides for lessons learned as we improve in our contingency

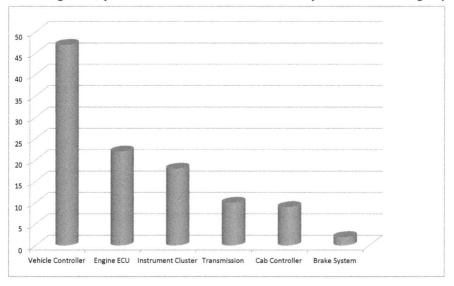

Figure 7.2 Pareto of configuration issues found during verification and test.

planning, and provides for subsequent project success. Anticipation is the key to great contingency planning. Anticipation is only as good, however, as the quality of effort and the imagination put into the upfront project preparation.

We also want to make sure that appropriate follow-through occurs. We do that by flagging items that need subsequent checking. We might use a dedicated project tool or a database to provide decision support.

We see multi-project management as one of the biggest risks in its own right, since we then must have a means for interleaving the tasks while understanding the state of our resources. Furthermore, task switching can incur the same kinds of penalties that occur when executing a process switch on a computer—to whit, delays, potential for error on return to task, and sheer complexity. We think it wise that any enterprise that is pushing multiprocessing/multithreading spend some time meditating on the benefits of unitasking. In fact, our experience indicates the benefits of agile project management such as Scrum is in significant part due to this unitasking and focused approach to project management.

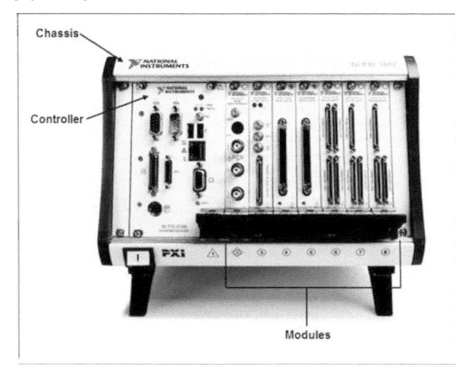

Figure 7.3 NI chassis from which modern testing occurs. The testing can be automated. The tool allows improvement in the repeatability and is faster than by hand or manually.

VI. Hazard Analysis and Critical Control Point Method

The basic principles for HACCP are spelled out in ISO 22000 and other documents. It is effectively an extension of the FMEA approach. The general procedure is as follows:

Principle 1: Conduct hazard analysis to determine hazards and identify the preventive measures the plan can apply to control these hazards.

Principle 2: Identify critical control points—a point, step, or procedure in a manufacturing process at which a control should be applied and, as a result, a hazard can be prevented, eliminated, or reduced.

Principle 3: Create critical limits for each critical control point—a critical limit is the maximum or minimum value to which a physical, biological, or chemical hazard must be controlled at a critical control point to prevent, eliminate, or reduce to an acceptable level.

Principle 4: Initiate critical control point monitoring requirements to ensure that the process is under control at each critical control point.

Principle 5: Generate corrective actions—actions taken when monitoring indicates a deviation from an established critical limit defined in the control point.

Principle 6: Implement procedures for ensuring the HACCP system is working as intended. Verification ensures the plan is working as intended. Verification must include "validation," the process of finding evidence for the accuracy of the HACCP system (e.g., scientific evidence for critical limitations). Note that this use of the word "validation" is different from that often seen in automotive manufacturers.

Principle 7: Define and initiate record-keeping.

Observe how this rational process is somewhat different from that of the FMEA process. We suggest this situation occurs because HACCP is the predominant analytical approach used in North American and European food, cosmetics, and drug industries.

VII. Scope

We can use the WBS and the statement of work (SOW) to control scope. We have

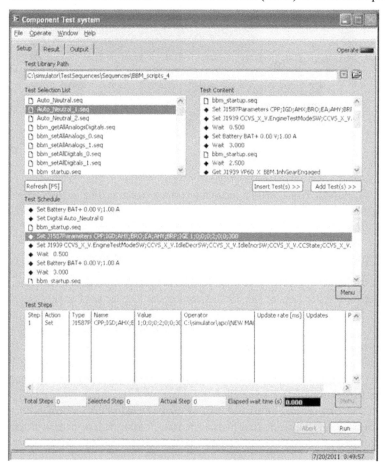

Figure 7.4 Screen shot from the NI test chassis test report for a vehicle module.

discussed the WBS extensively; remember, the WBS is largely an internal planning support document. The SOW, on the other hand, should be shared with the customer. The implementation of complete SOW documents is a total quality management improvement for any project manager.

The general structure of a SOW is as follows if we follow MIL-HDBK-245D *Handbook for Preparation of Statement of Work* (SOW):

1 Scope

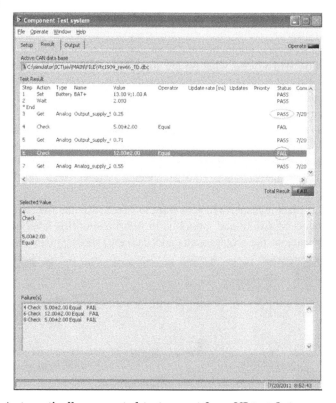

Figure 7.5 Automatically generated test report from NI test fixture.

2 Applicable documents

2.1 Department of Defense specifications (NOTE: these can be customer specifications!)

2.2 Department of Defense standards (NOTE: these can be standards appropriate to the industry)

2.3 Other publications

3 Requirements

3.1 General requirements

3.2 Technical objectives and goals

3.3 Specific requirements

3.3.1 Contractor services (NOTE: supplier and subcontractor services)

3.3.2 Integrated logistics support

3.3.3 Management systems requirements

3.3.4 Production planning for phase II

3.3.5 Reliability program

3.3.6 Maintainability program

The SOW is important to the project manager because it can serve as the standard for determining if the supplier meets the stated performance requirements. Please be aware that the document is sometimes called the Statement of Objectives (SOO) when the supplier/contractor creates the document based on the specifications. The structure, however, remains largely analogous to that shown above.

A good SOW will address what we are supposed to do and how we can prove we have done it. It is not a design control document, so we expect minimal commentary about the product itself. We expect the SOW to cover transactional activities—those that cover the relationship between supplier and customer.

The section of the SOW dealing with how we prove we did what we were supposed to do is often called "acceptance" or "qualification." On government projects, the project manager will ensure that the team demonstrates functionality with witnesses present. With civilian customers, the acceptance criteria may be defined in the customer specification.

The TQM project manager will also want to make sure that the supplier team has tested the product to failure and, possibly, to destruction. This level of testing goes beyond compliance to the requirements and increases the confidence in the product

Figure 7.6 Hardware in the loop simulator interfaces with the various components of the system via conditioned input and output signals.

or service.

VIII.   Communication

A. Voice

Voice is perhaps still the most powerful way to communicate, since we are really speaking about face-to-face communication. All parties can see body language, facial expressions, and hear nuances in the voice. Voice is also one of the most difficult to disregard.

B. Phone

The use of the phone is similar to voice, but we do not have body language (even with video like Skype), we do not have much in the way of facial expressions, and the electronic sound can sometimes dampen nuances. Saying "no" on the phone is easier than saying it face-to-face.

C. Voicemail

Voicemail is an extension of the phone. Because it can be erased, it can more easily be disregarded by the listener. Furthermore, the sender must exercise care, since he or she has now left a record of what was said. Voicemail, while asynchronous, is somewhat impersonal and can be dangerous to the sender.

D. Written

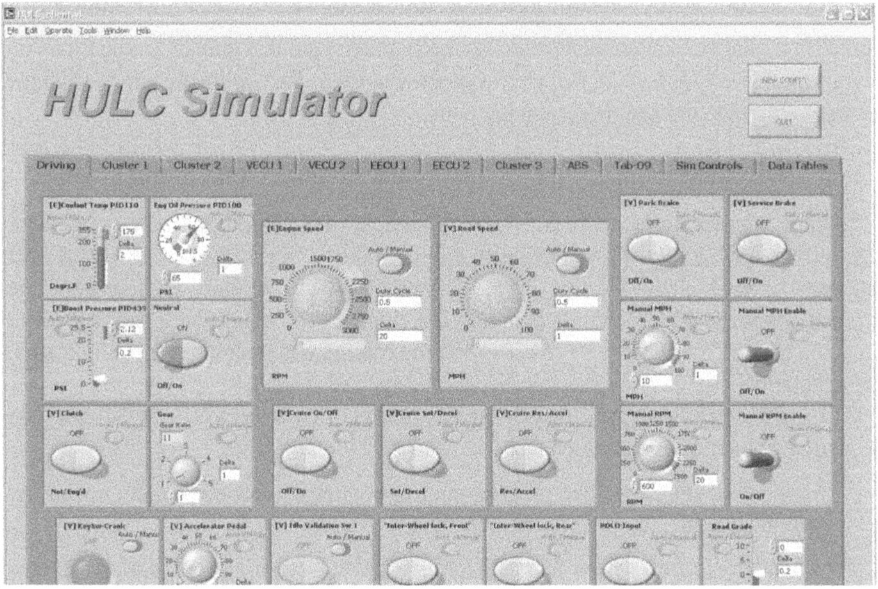

Figure 7.7 Hardware in the loop rigs are employed to simulate the system and the component interactions.

Written records must be used with care for the same reason we exercise care with voicemail—we have left evidence of our thoughts. Written material can be thrown away, although in business it makes more sense to dispose of written material securely through cross-cut shredding.

E. Email

Emails are often a substitute for voice communication. They are positive in that we can communicate asynchronously; they are negative in that we receive so many useless emails they stand a chance of getting lost in the noise.

We have used the technique of only messaging through the subject line in email— by the time they read the subject, they have already read the message. This approach keeps messages terse, as opposed to evidentiary messages designed to provide cover in case further action is taken (so-called CYA email).

F. Signage/Posters

Posters may be the weakest approach to communication. They often become visual noise. One of us asked five classes of high school students (65 students) whether they could remember the contents of any poster in the classroom they had been in for seven months—only one student could vaguely remember one poster. The classroom had seven or eight posters. While this is not a statistically meaningful survey, it does suggest that posters and signage become background rather than foreground quickly.

IX. Change Management

Change and configuration management are essential for any project management work. Total quality management tools can help understand the change implications on your project (see Figure 7.2). Before we go too far, let us first delineate what is change management and configuration management.

Change Management

Change management can be considered the input to the configuration management process. We have a request to make alterations to the project, process, or the product that must be evaluated. We lay out the details of the change and we determine the implications upon the project of taking on the change. At the end, we either accept or reject the change (see Figure 7.8). Accepting the change will then require configuration management.

There are metrics that are change management in orientation where TQM tools can be used to answer questions such as:

1. How often do particular projects undergo change (categorized by spending, technical areas, or some other hierarchy)?

2. Are there project types that are more subject to change (telematics systems versus instrument clusters)?

3. What is the typical impact in terms of cost and time to delivery?

4. Where (what customer or part of the company) do most of the changes originate?

5. How much time is spent with the typical change request evaluation?

6. How close are the estimated implications to the final impact of adopting the change (cost, time, product take rate, etc.)

An even longer time horizon approach can provide the project manager and even line managers with clues what processes within the organization could likely improve when placed under some scrutiny. For example, if we find that the time to make a decision to accept or deny the change is too long, we can turn our TQM tools toward that process and understand how the present process performs, and more importantly, where to alter and improve.

Configuration Management

Sound configuration management is critical to delivering a capable product—it is nearly impossible to evaluate what you have, especially if you know not what you have. Configuration management is not just a nice idea; it is a necessity in embedded development or, for that matter, any kind of product or process development. We suspect the reason for myriad project complaints about the quantity of changes to the product during development due to inadequate attention to this very important detail.

Experience is clear—the benefits of an optimally running configuration management program results in reduced erroneous fault reports that will streamline test times. We have also had the converse experience, where we saw much redundant work and reported failures due to incompatible system components. The impact of good (or poor) configuration management becomes even more pronounced if the product under test is actually a system or collection of components. The culmination of the development configuration management continues into manufacturing also. After all, it does not matter how well you designed the product, if you are unable to manufacture and deliver that design. Manufacturing firms with good configuration management systems control the part numbers and product releases. Even the production line software should fall under configuration management.

Consider, for example, the very probable scenario where the hardware has the required capabilities (such as communications support) while the software has no such a function yet available. The test engineer may consume many hours with the mismatch between hardware and software before he is aware that there is no such function to test in the software (see Figure 7.3, Figure 7.4, and Figure 7.5). Another example occurs when the test engineer reports a problem in a particular revision of software. There is a subsequent revision of software that provides a correction to that fault. The next software release exhibits the original fault once again. This could be a symptom of inadequate configuration management of the software builds.

Successful product development, in general, is completely dependent on robust configuration management, whether the product is software, firmware, hardware, or especially some combination of all three. Sending the customer the incorrect version of a product creates immediate dissatisfaction.

As we will see shortly, configuration management provides a known point upon which to control subsequent changes. When we know the state of the system at any point in time, we mitigate some of the risks with integration of the changes. We no longer think we know; we use the configuration management system to understand. This is done via the configuration baseline. When we make changes to the system, product, or process without this revision control point, we know little about the scope of any unintended consequences of that change.

A. Why Configuration Management

Configuration management systems facilitate delivery of coordinated software and hardware to produce a fully functional component or system. This is done by identifying features and functional content in advance of the delivery, for each specific software and hardware delivery. This includes synchronizing the software and hardware revisions where required. Additionally, configuration management provides a straightforward traceability of function and feature growth over specifications (see Figure 7.8). This subsequently creates a traceability point for product hardware and software revisions and finally testing. At any point during the process, we can clearly identify changes, execute pre-release containment, and identify compatible components within a system.

Wrestling with configuration management issues is another obstacle a project manager need not contend. Weak configuration management will lead to problems throughout the development process, from specifications through delivery and especially the testing.

B. Configuration Management and Project Management

Configuration management starts with the planning phase and, as such, project

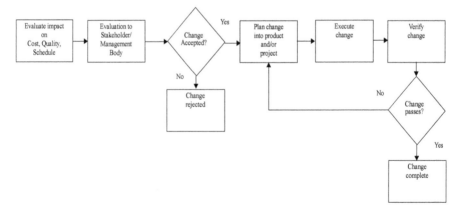

Figure 7.8 A simple change management process.

management staff should be aware of this need and address it. Some organizations already have a configuration management system in place that is well-documented. If you are not fortunate enough to be a project manager in one of those organizations, you must work with your development team to address this issue during the course of the project. The team can develop the product or system road map, which provides the part numbers and proposed introduction dates for the various software and hardware releases. To help with this goal, we suggest creating a formal configuration management plan. The requirements themselves should fall under this plan. Furthermore, all changes should receive cost and time quotations and be agreed upon by all parties.

Configuration management is a prerequisite to delivering robust software or hardware. It is necessary that we plan and coordinate the software and the hardware deliveries of functionality and the level of product refinement. In short, functionality (hardware and software), deliveries, testing, and production follow a master plan rather than hope and pandemonium.

Configuration management can be applied to specifications (documentation), models, simulation, hardware, software, the combination of hardware and software, and to system integration. That truth is that configuration management can be applied to just about anything where iterations need to be known and tracked. We may be able to capture important lessons from the following measures:

- Product baseline

- Product change management

- Number of product changes

- Time spent on product changes

- Cost impact of changes

- Product configuration (CMP)

- Test configurations (test coverage)

- Configuration audit

We can apply the TQM tools to the configuration management process as well, with appropriate attention to details and setting:

- How often do we have configuration management problems (audit performance statistics and Pareto)?

- Do our suppliers have a robust configuration management system for their build processes (do we see recurring problems)?

- Can we trace the present revision of a product through the iterations taken to get to this point?

- How much do we spend on our configuration management? How much do we spend upon configuration management failures?

- Check in and check out statistics.

For example, engine electronic control unit, cruise control rev 1.0 within a particular software revision.

IEEE Standard 10422 provides some guidance upon what is required to have a performing configuration management system. Specifically and of fundamental interest are the four tool levels, 1) basic tool set; 2) advanced tool set; 3) online tool set; 4) integrated tool set.

Basic Tool Set

The basic tool set consists of:

- Basic database management systems
- Report generators
- Means for maintaining separate dynamic and controlled libraries
- File system for managing the check-in and check-out of units for controlling compilations and capturing the resulting products

Advanced Tool Set

The advanced tool set consists of:

- Items from the basic tool set
- Source code control programs that will maintain version and revision history
- Compare programs for identifying (and help verify) changes
- Tools for building or generating executable code
- A documentation system (word processor) to enter and maintain specifications and associated user documentation files
- A system/software change request authorization tracking system that makes requests for changes machine readable

On-Line Tool Set

This set of tools includes:

- Generic tools of the advanced tool set integrated so they work from a common database
- A tracking and control system that brings generation, review, and approval of changes on-line
- Report generators working on-line with the common database, and a tracking system that enables the configuration management group to generate response to on-line queries of a general nature

Integrated Tool Set

The integrated tool set includes:

- On-line tools covering all functions
- An integrated engineering database with command built into the on-line engineering commands commonly used in designing and developing programs
- The integration of the commands with the on-line management commands for

building and promoting units and components

Software Revision Level

The software revision level information should include the following items:

- Complete with release notes

- Hardware revision level

- Complete with release notes

- Subassembly revision level in the case where we have firmware "burned" onto a chip

- Systems integration (phased feature release)

- Valid combinations of sub-systems

The authors of IEEE standard 1220 [a descendant of MIL-STD-499B (draft)] favor the master plan approach to systems engineering, providing an alternative to standard project management practices.

C. Configuration Management Areas

Configuration management applies to nearly every task within product development, particularly anywhere change is introduced and identification of the composition is required. Configuration management is applied to specifications (documentation of product and process), models, simulation, hardware, software, the combination of hardware and software, and to system integration. The truth is that configuration management can be applied to just about anything – wherever there is a need for control and traceability.

Any discussion of configuration management invariably will lead to the concept of a baseline. To baseline is to identify the product state at a given point in time. In a manufacturing facility, we might see the following approach to configuration management, namely:

- Product baseline

- Product change management

- Product configuration (configuration management plan)

- Test configurations (test coverage)

- Configuration audit

- Product production configuration

These items in the list apply to both software and hardware, for development and production. We can apply our TQM tools to help us understand the capability of our configuration management process and improve the process where we can. For example:

- Number of product changes

- Origin of product changes (internal, external, missing requirement, legal change)

- Time spent on product changes
- Change volume by customers
- Changes by project lifecycle
- Range of changes for historical projects
- Configuration non-conformities
- Cost impact of changes (per each change, and compared to starting point)
- Test configurations (test coverage)
- Area of the organization with the most configuration management issues

D. The Four Department of Defense Components

Military standard 973 and military handbook 61 spell out four requirements for any configuration management system:
1) Configuration identification
2) Configuration control
3) Configuration status accounting
4) Configuration auditing

Configuration Identification

To establish configuration identification, we must have the means to define a configuration item. In DoD software implementation, these are known as computer system configuration items (CSCIs or "siskies"). Generally, we pick an item and define the initial version or state of it as a baseline. This baseline will function very much as a baseline in a project management tool; namely, it allows us to know where we started and to detect and record change as the project and product development proceeds. The same approach applies to document management and hardware configuration management also.

Typically, we will associate a part number with the highest level of the configuration. The next level of configuration items will describe the feature content and apply a specific revision level to the individual features. We may even define further levels of refinement with the individual parameters that may apply to the configuration. At every stage in the product life cycle, configuration identification provides a process and product that is documentable and controllable. Even if we never used the other three components, this one alone would allow us to at least know what we have.

Configuration Control

Configuration control is the part of configuration management where we manage changes to the product. This ranges from planned revisions and updates to the hardware or software, to changes that have been requested and accepted in the course of the product development activities. These additional changes, in some cases, may necessitate a re-baseline of the product, although it is more typical that these "later adaptations" are not part of the baseline—allowing the customer and supplier to clearly view the impacts of the changes. It is desirable to have only one version in release at a time. Control will become complicated when more than one version is available, although we have seen some rare cases where multiple versions were being used. If we have multiple releases available we often will be required to manage some merge of these branches. No matter what form of control, but typically with part numbers, managing these multiple releases and subsequent processes such as testing and evaluation is going to be difficult. Management can also become complicated, with multiple component configurations or multiple iterations for the components for a system. This is especially valid when there is a mass of customer-customizable parameters. With motor vehicles, we often see attribute-based requirements (ABR), where order options drive changes to the parameters of a number of components. This can also happen via line sequencing, in which the parts are customized to the vehicle identification number (itself a form of configuration identification). This production complication can have significant impacts on verification activities. These production variations have to be accounted for during testing, which includes verifying those customer ordering systems that drive the component configurations.

Typical configuration control baselines might be the following:

- Developmental Baseline (DBL): the state of the delivered product through the iterations of the development process

- Allocated Baseline (ABL): the initially approved allocated configuration documentation, which is often allocated from a higher level or system

- Functional Baseline (FBL): the approved functional configuration documentation that adds verification to the mix

- Product Baseline (PBL): the approved product configuration documentation which generally includes a description of the acceptance testing and may also include the actual hardware and/or software

No matter the situation, a configuration baseline necessitates an agreed upon description of the attributes of a product and associated dates. At some point, this becomes the starting point for defining what constitutes downstream change. We would expect to see an approved and released document or documents (revision) for every specific version, the purpose of which is to provide a solid foundation for managing change. These baselines always include the currently approved and released configuration documentation and, with software, a released set of files making up a software version and related configuration documentation.

Configuration Status Accounting (CSA)

Configuration status accounting is used primarily for the reporting feature, although its significance is much broader. Under CSA, we record changes and update configurations when items change and we issue reports. When dealing with software we might audit the frequency of check-in/check-out to verify that the developers are protecting intellectual property by preserving new versions. We may audit the release documentation to confirm that the proposed or planned configuration has been delivered. Additionally, we might take a look at the count of changes to get an idea of the stability of a given release. Also, if we are dealing with software development, we can also store the status of our test results along with the software.

CSA can be supported by software (for example, the open source product called *subversion*) and it is definitely a component of product data management software, product lifecycle management software, and document control packages. However, it is also possible to use ubiquitous spreadsheet software. The point is to use it frequently as a kind of formative assessment, the feedback of which will allow the TQM PM to make informed decisions regarding product and process development as well as help to ensure the customer is protected. Use of the TQM tools to support these assessments is often overlooked.

Configuration Auditing

Configuration auditing has two primary actions: physical configuration and functional configuration, both of which will compare the configuration expected to what is delivered. A physical configuration audit compares existing documents to contracted or required documents and a functional configuration audit verifies functionality against requirements. The results are part of the release notes.

Hardware

Hardware configuration management is most commonly accomplished through the part numbering system and the associated bill of materials. The bills themselves can take on different structures; for example, modular, phantom, or one-level bills. It is not unreasonable to ask that the bills of materials themselves fall under configuration management control. This may not necessarily be the same configuration system as used in the development work of the product. We might also expect this idea to apply to the item master list; that is, the list of all components of all bills of material.

Software

With software, we are usually well-served using dedicated software configuration management tools; for example:

- Subversion
- Revision control system (RCS)
- Concurrent version system (CVS)
- Sourcesafe
- MKS *source integrity*

Configuration management programs must be able to lock out other users from making changes during an edit and provide some level of reporting. It should not be possible for two people to write simultaneously to the item under configuration control. These systems basically mechanize the software build process by defining what modules are included and enumerate the revision counts of the modules. Most "make" programs have a means of accessing the software configuration management system automatically. A list of typical programs is:

- Apache Ant
- CMake
- Configure script
- Fastmake
- Flowtracer
- GNU Automake
- imake
- Jam
- mk
- Premake
- qmake
- Rake
- SCons
- Waf
- Xconfig

Such tools are sometimes called "build automation tools." They are part of the development factory concept. These tools also help maintain the development of the software product as well as ensure consistent product-building through the life of the development.

Hardware and Software

There is hardware, software, and the combination, which is often referred to as "firmware." When we have firmware, we add another dimension to the configuration management mix. We need to have coordination with all three of these aspects within embedded projects. The firmware can undergo change through the first part of the development activity, but usually reaches some kind of steady state during the project. Firmware is often set up as an assembly part number with two subassemblies: the chip and the software—together they make the subassembly. For example:

- Subassembly X104AG573
  - Product Y508BBD99 Rev 4.2 software
  - Flash Microcontroller HX349855S

Configuration and System Made Up of Subsystems

Configuration management does not end at the hardware and software in complex systems. In addition to tracking these items, the system configurations, what parts constitute the systems, and compatibility issues between revisions of various components must be accounted. In these instances, there is a system configuration, which will consist of a number of individual component configurations. This will have a big impact upon the verification.

Configuration and Verification

Any testing performed on a configuration must be identified explicitly with the following information:

- Hardware release including subassemblies
- Software version
- Customizable parameters (where applicable)
- Developmental version or
- Released product version (they are not necessarily the same)
- System level configuration

The configuration items should be linked to the test cases and test documents. In fact, the test descriptions are prioritized by the hardware and software delivery schedule and functional content identified in the configuration management plan. Since change can happen even at this level, the documents themselves can also come under configuration management.

Verification is performed starting at the component level configurations, before the systems level configurations. Components that have a number of configurable parameters associated can take great benefit in automating both the configuration and the testing of those configurations. Automating these activities facilitates the confirmation of the numerous configurations via the subsequent testing.

Release Notes

Release notes are linked to the hardware configuration by part number with the content and known bugs identified. The release notes are also linked to software, again by part number, revision levels, software modules, functions/features, and known bugs. The revision level will reference back to the configuration management system. Additionally, release notes may provide notification of any deviations within the product. These are exceptions from the planned configuration and are dangerous. We will discuss deviations later in this article. Release notes don't only apply to the hardware, but apply to software aspects of the product as well. Software may not only have the part number on paper, but the part number will be part of the software itself with the ability to view. Release notes will report the same issues as the hardware release notes, including feature and revision levels as well as known bugs.

Another function of release notes is that they provide another level of documentation of changes occurring to the product. In general, they will normally provide a more detailed explanation than the one-liner typical of automated programs such as RCS and they become even more valuable when we uncover a problem in that particular version of the software.

Change Management

Change management is an umbrella term that contains configuration management, independent of source. Often the change is brought on by a customer request. Change can occur to a process that is actually a service and not a tangible product. Additionally, change can occur within the production process and it may have some impact upon the final product. Often customers expect this manufacturing change to change the product part number, as a way to track quality impacts of the process change. Change will be constant, no matter the source of the change; we must consider scope and subsequent configuration impacts. A well-defined configuration baseline must be present at the start of the project. It then becomes possible to plan future changes, integrating them into the future revisions with significant control.

Configuration Management and Revision Control

To manage the complexities of software, the configuration management tool should allow branching, merging, developmental release numbers, and released product release numbers (not same as developmental). Developmental configurations are often delineated by the use of special characters that would not otherwise be used during production. For example, the part number may be preceded or followed by the character "X," signifying "experimental." Sometimes, customers prefer to designate the release number instead of using the developmental release version number. That means the software configuration management software must be able to support multiple numeration schemes. Additionally, the configuration management tool must not allow for duplicate uses of a particular number. This is especially valid for same part numbers within the same product line.

Managing Released Products

Released products come under the same sort of controls as developmental products. The systems need to control the engineering release documentation, design change notifications, engineering change requests, and any similar change causing activity and documentation. This activity extends into the maintenance phase of the product. Just because a product is delivered, does not mean there is no longer a need for change management. Often, the part numbers are changed when there is any change that may have an impact upon the product quality. This provides some measure of traceability of change to subsequent quality impacts. Any automotive, commercial vehicle, or ISO-certified organization will have configuration management for released products to avoid contaminating the supply chain with nonconforming material.

Configuration Management and Outsourced Work

Configuration management rises in importance when contracting outsourced work or if the development team is distributed. Configuration management is really a communications and development synchronization tool. The distribution of the team has an impact on the results. It does not matter whether for outsourcing reasons or if the team is within one company but geographically distributed. Managing the configuration will be more important and critical to product success. This is particularly true with software development. In small, co-located teams, informal and frequent communication can partially augment or reduce the dependency upon a robust configuration management system, but not eliminate the need. The more distributed the development team, the more configuration management is a priority. We can use technology to help maintain document and item integrity. The distributed team can use existing software configuration management tools as well as databases and/or Microsoft Sharepoint.

Configuration and Systems Development

Configuration management takes on even greater importance when multiple subsystems are being put together to create an entire system. These multiple configurations make up a system configuration and multiple releases of configurations, which means all of the constituent parts, are staged and introduced in a meaningful order imposed by parts and resources dependencies. In complex and distributed systems development, this is paramount to systems integration testing. If the product is customer-adaptable, this idea extends to items such as those customizable product parameters (for example, those stored in non-volatile memory) that alter the product features to customer demand, increasing adaptability and customer contentment. All of this requires updates to the system configuration and tracking of the revision progression, and subsequent testing of those customer adaptation variations. Under these conditions, we would expect more branching and less merging of configurations.

The testing issues may require configuration management of original development software (e.g., compilers), equipment (development boards and systems), and processors (for firmware). Controlling all the pieces for some contracted amount of time becomes a non-trivial, but required, task. In the commercial vehicle industry, some OEM manufacturers support their products for up to twenty years.

Non-Conformities

Product non-conformities (ungrammatically called "non-conformances"), also known as deviations, are a written authorization granted before manufacturing a product. This document describes a product non-conformance that is accepted by the customer. This document allows us to release the product from meeting one or more requirements or it proposes another temporary solution to meet the functional demand (jumper wire to printed circuit board). These documents only work if they represent a temporary condition that is controlled by time or by count of product and is in some way differentiated from the other previous and subsequent revisions. Deviations are an explicit recognition of temporary modifications outside the bounds of the change control system only from a previously planned perspective. These deviations must be accounted for, and as such, they are a part of a configuration management system—often handled in the release notes for either software or hardware. As with all forms of configuration management, deviations require an identification method such as serialization, part number control, or some other marking.

Deviations not adequately accounted for and communicated are equivalent to lack of configuration control. They can cause great harm to a project and product development and usually the impact is not fully appreciated until the product is in the verification phase or released. For each deviation, it may be necessary to anticipate issues by assessing the sensitivity of various subsystems to the proposed fix. In some cases, this analysis becomes time-consuming and tedious and, when not performed, leads to catastrophic product failure.

Insufficient Configuration Management or Neglect

Failures in the configuration management system will result in a number of product failures and, of itself, can be considered to be a process and structural failure. One outcome is the inability to predict the impact of changes upon the project. Identification of development changes and product costing are part of cost recovery actions, which are designed to prevent runaway scope changes and margin erosion.

We may end up seeing non-functional components, subsystems, and systems. Testing may include combinations that were never planned to be tested or never should have been tested together. The same is true of the converse—the correct combinations may not get tested. The fact that the problem is a configuration management issue will likely not be found quickly. It will be after much time and resources are invested in determining why the system does not work – a very inefficient use of project resources. The problem is compounded, since testing is generally the last portion of the product delivery schedule. Duration over-runs on software and hardware development already affect the time available for testing. The spending of additional time and resources to solve problems that are not valid is a waste and reduces the probability of launching on time and within budget. We may also miss expected functions as well as see duplication of cost in order to test again.

We have also personally witnessed situations where a supplier shipped prototype parts with an unknown hardware version and an unknown software version, making traceability of any problems discovered to root cause difficult to impossible to achieve. It is easy to see why this supplier later lost the business. When the end product to the customer is configurable, these problems are transferred on to the customer, sometimes with no notice. If the volumes of the product are high, the issue may be found out after a number of customers and the product delivery pipeline are full of this errant product. At this point, we may see an expensive, time-consuming, and reputation-destroying product campaign or product recall.

Conclusion

We say that configuration management is indispensable to delivering quality products. Failure to manage the configuration leads to consuming time that need not be consumed in testing (system incompatibility, errant fault reports) as well as the very real possibility of sending the wrong item to a customer. Without proper configuration management, it is not unheard of to fix the wrong version of software, introducing yet more errors into the product. Any of these evils can be catastrophic to a customer/

supplier relationship, and it certainly will not improve the standing of your organization with the customer. Good configuration management always leaves a competent audit trail, and never is the recipient of customer complaints.

Configuration changes outside those that are planned are demonstrations of missing up-front work or missing or unstable requirements. TQM tools can be used to uncover these areas. Pareto analysis of configuration failures can provide clues as to the best place to focus efforts for corrections. Configuration management is an essential process within a project. The rate of changes, unaccounted-for changes, and errors in this key portion of a project inhibit the delivery to the cost, time, and quality an organization expects. The TQM tools help the organization constantly and continually improve.

Consider our project factory, we have the number of iterations we typically have in our development process. We can show the number of iterations we plan for a specific range of size of a project.

Good control of product configuration is essential to project management. Understanding the effectiveness of the change and configuration management capability of an organization allows the TQM project manager to assess the risks and plan the project in a way that improves the probability of success.

X.   Exercises

- Map your process and create a process FMEA (PFMEA) for this process.

- Make an argument for significant value part numbers (these are the part numbers where you can tell what it is by looking at the part numbers).

- Make an argument for random value part numbers (you can't tell what it is from the part number).

- Develop an efficient protocol for configuration identification.

- Read MIL-STD-973 and summarize the approach of the Department of Defense to configuration management.

- Read MIL-HDBK-61 and summarize the approach of the Department of Defense to configuration management.

- Create an efficient approach to MIL-STD-973 style configuration management.

- Explain why you want software development to fall under a software configuration management tool.

- Determine if you have a manufacturing resource planning (MRP) system or something like it and see if you can manage prototype part numbers in this system (many can't do this at all or very well).

- Create a protocol for shifting from MRO (maintenance, repair, and operations) purchased parts to MRP purchased parts (we often see a discontinuity in parts ordering during this shift).

- Evaluate the comparative and contrasting benefits/costs of using MRO purchasing or MRP buying.

- Difficult: compile a taxonomy of parts numeration schemes (a least five, with ten more desirable) and summarize the costs and benefits of each type.

- Difficult: choose a project time line that you already have for a small- to medium-sized project and restate the sequence of events in process control plan format (you may use the AIAG format).

- Contrast and compare the typical FMEA approach with FMECA (Failure Mode, Effects, and Criticality Analysis [MIL–STD–1629A]) and then HACCP (Hazard Analysis and Critical Control Point [ISO 22000 FSMS 2005]).

- Merge the concept of the FMEA with that of a process control plan and synthesize a new super-document.

- List probable documentation requirements for a typical project.

- Produce a protocol that specifies how much say a purchasing/procurement department or organization should have regarding acceptance of new products.

- Produce a specification that defines the steps necessary to avoid bad parts or bad designs when accepting a new product. Define whether you see a difference between commodity parts and specialized/customized parts.

- Compile a protocol that balances risk management with speed for incoming new components.

- Difficult: produce a complete program for reducing risk with new components, component changes, and other supplier changes.

- Difficult: produce a complete program for reducing risk with product releases, product changes, and customer demands and interference.

- Difficult: define an efficient method for tying an enterprise configuration management system on the supplier side with a different enterprise configuration management system on the customer side.

- Medium: if release of bad material to a customer is an "escape," what is the best way to prevent an escape? Define how you would do this improvement without simply adding more controls.

- Come up with some reasonable explanation why we don't have every component "mistake-proofed" (poka-yoke) and what recommendation you would make to improve this situation.

- Design a system that does not need quality inspections.

Endnotes

1. Automotive Industry Action Group (AIAG). *Potential Failure Mode and Effects Analysis, 4th Edition.* Southfield, MI: AIAG, 2008.

2. Institute for Electrical and Electronics Engineers. *ANSI/IEEE 1042-1987 IEEE Guide to Software Configuration Management.* New York, NY: IEEE, 1987.

CHAPTER 8 - INSPECTION AND QUALITY ASSURANCE

I. Rubric

	Novice	Sr. Novice	Journey-man	Sr. Jour-neyman	Master
Attribute inspection	x	x	x	x	x
Variables inspection		x	x	x	x
Double sample inspection			x	x	x
Continuous inspection				x	x
Sequential inspection				x	x
Skip lot inspection				x	x

II. Questions to Ponder

- Does inspection provide any added value?
- What is the "saddle point" for cost versus benefit for inspection?
- Why do we find inspection acceptable?
- Do we really need inspection of any kind?
- What is the way out from inspection, if any?
- Does inspection have any marketing value?
- Why do we have so many types of inspection?
- Why are the inspection models different and yet the same (compare and contrast)?
- Is inspection just another way to make somebody some money?
- Are the ISO standards better than the others?
- Can we rely on supplier inspection?
- Can we rely on customer inspection?
- Why can't we just "roll our own" inspection approach?

III. Why Inspection and QA Are Important to the Project Manager

We have seen some employees treat inspection as a sign of employer distrust—such is not the case. Inspection is a low-cost method for ascertaining the current or completion status of virtually any item, product, or service. While we recommend some sampling standards for large-scale incoming materials, inspections can be as simple as using a mutually agreed upon checklist.

The project manager should be highly involved with incoming material, particularly during the working model and prototype phases of a project. It is more difficult to set a supplier straight once we launch the product than it is to do so relatively early in the project. We make the choice between attribute and variables sampling plans based on our needs and what we consider to be critical values for the component. The project manager should also note that we can also apply sampling—to some extent— to services as well, particularly when we can either measure something or define an attribute of significance.

IV. TQM Project Manager Scenario

A.   Situation

Parts began to show fracture along the shaft where a metal part was pressed in to mate with a molded plastic housing. Initially, it was not obvious to the project manager that any change had occurred in his company's manufacturing line.

One of the tendencies in a customer dissatisfaction scenario is to try and blame our own supplier because this takes us "off the hook." Instead of doing this in this particular situation, we implemented 100% inspection of all incoming housing components as well as the metal part.

B.   Objective

Our objectives were immediate and significant:

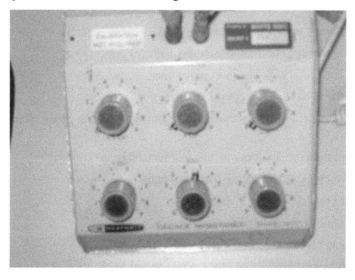

Figure 8.1 Decade box used for testing product response to variation on the resistive inputs of the product.

- Determine if the supplier caused the plastic housing issue
- Investigate the size of the metal components and the metal components supplier
- At a minimum, contain further broken parts
- Ascertain when and where the parts were breaking
- Determine if the manufacturing line had actually made an undocumented change

C.   Action

We implemented the 100% inspection as indicated. At the same time, our x-ray inspection devices indicated some movement of an internal component. We added material to prevent internal component shifting and added 100% x-ray inspection to the armamentarium. In addition, we upgraded production line testing to eliminate potentially weak product.

D.   Results

We were largely able to contain the broken part issue with improved inspection and testing. We saw a significant drop in failed parts, both immediate and long-term failures.

E.   Aftermath

We acquired knowledge about this particular product:

- 100% inspection is, at best, a stopgap since some material still failed
- The production process was actually at fault—an engineer had made an undocumented change to the metal to plastic insertion process
- The supplier was not at fault
- The customer was not at fault

The enterprise was also left with x-ray inspection and incoming inspection, even though neither item eliminated the problem. The customer was insufficiently sophisticated to understand why these approaches were minimally helpful once the issue was resolved.

V.   Inspection with Attributes

Inspection with attributes[1] means we are most likely looking at incoming supplier material (see Figure 8.2) and we are not *measuring* any scalar value (magnitude, variable, number with a decimal point). In some cases, we may have sample material displayed in a cabinet or pegboard with representatives of both acceptable and unacceptable material. Attribute inspection and sampling is often called "no/no-go" inspection precisely because we have no variables measurements (see Figure 8.1). Attribute assessment is usually quick, requiring just a glance, and the job is complete. The tradeoff is that we must examine a lot more material in order to make a decision.

The standard for this approach is ANSI/ASQ Z1.4-2008 *Sampling Procedures and*

Tables for Inspection by Attributes, which is an acceptance sampling system to be used for a stream of lots with an acceptance quality limit (AQL) specified. It provides a

Figure 8.2 An example of a product that would need to be inspected.

variety of plans to be applied for attributes inspection for percent nonconforming or non-conformities per 100 units. This standard is a much-updated version of the original MIL-STD-105E *Sampling Procedures and Tables for Inspection by Attributes*. Other military standards address failure sampling (1916) and continuous attribute sample (1235C). Sampling is a statistical approach that eliminates the necessity for looking at every part once we set our parameters: sample size, AQL, lot size, etc. One formula for sample size looks like:

$$\frac{4\sigma}{\sqrt{n}} = W$$

or

$$n = 16\sigma^2 / W^2$$

where "W" is the width of the confidence interval. "Sigma" is the standard deviation and "n" is the sample size. Note that "W" is sometimes represented by "d" and is the margin for error.

The acceptable quality limit (AQL) is the worst tolerable process mean, usually stated in terms of "percentage" or "ratio," that is treated as acceptable; hence the name. It is more reflective of a quality management decision to balance the cost of inspection against the cost of bad parts than it is any kind of presumed "acceptance."

An acceptable quality level is an inspection standard describing the maximum quantity of defects found acceptable during random sampling of an inspection (see Figure 8.3). While we may have defect taxonomies, the tables for this kind of inspection are based on *any* kind of defect. Buyers and sellers often negotiate an AQL value, based on the level of risk each party can live with. Again, we would like to emphasize the balance of costs considered during any inspection decision. Clearly, we will choose a more rigorous table when we have safety issues. If we are charging a premium for freedom from cosmetic flaws, we would also want to use an extremely rigorous sampling scheme.

One hundred percent inspections can be problematic, especially if we are dealing with visual inspection by a human being. The human attention span, based on experience, often runs about fifteen to twenty minutes at best—suggesting we

Sample	13.8V 20A (lbf at stall)	10V (lbf at stall)	8V (lbf at stall)	Notes
1	55	42	33	
2	61	45	35	stuck brush found at disassembly
3	49	37	27	
4	78	65	51	unused part, old design
5	45	36	27	unused part, new design, sample 1
6	46	33	27	unused part, new design, sample 2
7				sample number not used
8				sample number not used
9				sample number not used
10	57	44	34	
11	61	47	34	
12	0			dead, stuck brush, when rotated began to work ok
13	0			dead, stuck brush, when rotated began to work ok
14	56	44	32	
15	64	47	36	
16	0			dead, when disassembled and brush freed, works ok
17	55			
18	0			stuck brush found at disassembly
19	57			
20	N/A			Motor partially removed from assy when received. Motor runs ok. Sounds a little noisy
21	0			Not disassembled
22	57			
23	N/A			Motor partially removed from assy when received. Motor runs ok.

Figure 8.3 Demonstration of window motor performance over a range of units.

must replace our visual inspectors every 15-20 minutes. One alternative is the use of automated optical inspection (AOI), particularly suitable for some kinds of inspections of printed circuit boards (and also expensive!). Obviously, the robot never gets tired or loses attention like a human being.

VI. Inspection with Variables

Inspection with variables[2] is not the antithesis of attribute sampling but, rather, an alternative way of looking at parts. Here we use the improved MIL-STD-414 called ANSI/ASQ Z1.9-2008 *Sampling Procedures and Tables for Inspection by Variables*. As mentioned in the attribute sampling section, we are measuring something when we use the variables mode of sampling plan. Measurement generally consumes more time and is one of the reasons for the popularity of the attribute plans. However, we generally can usually harvest more information when we use the variables mode, whether for sampling, control charts, designed experiments, etc. The point here is that we need to use judgment.

Just as with the attribute sampling scenarios, we make a management decision about acceptable quality with variables also. In the case of variables, however, we must specify tolerance intervals. We also can use much smaller sample sizes when using variables, because it is easier to make a decision when we have numerical values.

VII. Skip Lot Inspection

We can skip lots[3] when we have a relatively trustworthy supplier, particularly one who has a sophisticated check on their own outgoing parts. The skip lot inspection and the continuous sampling plan have similarities, particularly given that they are both attempts to provide a reasonable amount of safety while attempting to reduce the time and cost of inspecting parts.

Skip lot inspection means that only a portion of the received lots are inspected. This method for sampling allows for cost-savings in terms of time and effort and eventually, money. Skip lot inspection should only be used when we know that the quality of the received product is very good.

A skip lot sampling plan is implemented as follows:

- Choose a single sampling plan by specifying the alpha and beta risks

- Start with normal lot-by-lot inspection, using the reference plan chosen in the first bullet

- When a predetermined number, i, of consecutive lots has been accepted, switch to inspecting only a fraction f of the lots. The selection of that fraction is random.

- When a lot is rejected return to normal inspection procedures of single sampling

Skip lot is a relatively coarse approach to saving money while still doing some spot checking.

VIII.   Continuous Sampling Plans

Continuous sampling plans[3] are not as coarse as skip lot plans. The continuous sampling plan (also known as "CSP-1") is used for continuous production—we inspect each unit as we manufacture it. The most common use of this sampling plan is for product flowing in assembly-line (simulated process flow). The sampling plan also requires a relatively undifferentiated production system. Each unit should be produced with the same requirements under stable conditions of production; that is to say, the product must be under statistical control. Perturbations should be used to terminate this sampling method; for example, change of materials supplier, tooling changes, or a significant stoppage of production.

The procedure is related to that for skip lots:

- Start with 100% inspection of the produced units consecutively and continue this inspection until a predetermined i units in sequence are defect-free

- When i units in succession are shown to be defect-free, stop the 100% inspection, and inspect only a predetermined fraction f of the production, picking individual sample units one at a time from production flow of production, so as to retain an unbiased sample

- If any sample unit is found to be defective, return to 100% inspection of sequenced units and continue until i units in sequence are found to be defect-free

- Correct or replace, with good units all defective units found

Continuous sample plans tend to work well (they are efficient) when we have really bad lots or very good lots. Obviously, good lots are the preferred choice.

IX. Dodge-Romig

The Dodge-Romig[3] plans for acceptance sampling were developed by Harold F. Dodge and Harry G. Romig. Four sets of tables appeared in 1940:

- Single sampling lot tolerance tables

- Double sampling lot tolerance tables

- Single sampling average outgoing quality limit tables

- Double sampling average outgoing quality limit tables

One item that sets these plans apart from the ANSI/ASQ standards is the focus on the lot tolerance percent defective (LTPD) mode rather than AQL. Again, while not necessarily better, it provides us with another tool to help make decisions during the progress of a project.

X.   First Article Inspection

First article inspection means we look at the first items that come in from our supplier. This approach allows us to inform the supplier promptly if we detect anomalies in the parts. The problem with this approach is that we only look at the first articles—which is not particularly valuable if we have moved through our project and we are seeing wear on a soft tool.

Suppliers generally submit a first article inspection sample when any of the following occur:

- The first time material is provided

- A change in design

- A change in manufacturing source(s), process(es), inspection method(s), location of manufacture, tooling, materials, computer numerically controlled (CNC) programming or a significant natural or man-made event (for example, the tsunami in Japan in 2011)

- It has been some predetermined time since the last inspection of first article material

First article material should be manufactured with production tooling, full production processing, and the package should include all design data, particularly if a design change has occurred.

XI. What Is a Meaningful Sample?

A meaningful sample is any sample sufficiently large to tell us what we want to know without being so large we are defeating the cost and time benefits of sampling. We know, for example, that good census sampling is actually more accurate than a raw count because it can be done quickly enough we don't have thousands of births and deaths modifying the data during the count. Do not rely on the magical number "thirty," which is merely the point at which the t-distribution converges to a normal distribution.

XII. Failure Types

A. Type 1 Failures

Type 1 failures are also known as "producer's risk" or alpha failures. These occur when we let something fail that should have been declared a good part. In some cases, particularly when we are dealing with a safety-significant part like a seat-belt sensor, we may assume a certain amount of type 1 failures rather than taking the chance of sending a bad part to a customer and ending up with liability litigation. Type 1 failures are relatively easy to assess because we can always examine the parts we have marked as unacceptable.

B. Type 2 Failures

Type 2 failures are also known as "consumer's risk" or beta failures. These occur when we let something pass that should have been declared a bad part. Type 2 failures are problematic since they occur at the customer site and we may never get an accurate count of all the parts. In essence, type 2 failures are a kind of failure we don't want to exist; hence, the option of permitting some modicum of type 1 failures is an alternative.

XIII.   Inspections and Project Management

Aside from material inspections, documentation can also be inspected. We can inspect our (or our suppliers') work breakdown structure. We can inspect their statement of work as well. Project scope documentation, especially when revised, is an area of interest as well. We have experienced on more than one occasion how a change in the project scope—though thought to be communicated well, went wrong—was found out only after the product went through the factory and, in many cases, delivered to the customer. We can inspect how the project obtains input such as time reporting against those WBS's and subsequently the earned value management analysis made. Essentially any documentation that drives the project and is subject to change can be reviewed. Any process deemed necessary for the project can be inspected as well. We do this to determine if we are following the stated process, as well as make some assessment as to whether the process is actually meeting the needs of the project. The TQM tools can help us understand the results of these inspections.

We are not just limited to inspection of material or of project documentation. If we are developing a product or service, we can inspect the documentation for that product. This inspection can be in the form of requirements, specifications, code reviews and design reviews. Essentially any documentation we use for the product or service we can critique to make sure it is as clear as we can make it.

XIV.   Exercises

- Explain why you would do 100% visual inspection when it appears to have so little real value.

- If you have inspection standards available (Z1.4 or Z1.9 or even MIL-STD-109), select an inspection mode and explain your selection.

- Construct a method for preventing type 2 failures.

- Explain (compare and contrast) the difference between quality assurance and quality control.

- State a well-reasoned argument for why we do not inspect every piece.

- Generate an essay explaining your approach to inspecting small commodity parts (for example, surface-mount resistors).

- Categorize the types of inspection (see if you can find some which we did not elucidate in this chapter) and explain in tabular format the benefits and costs of each approach.

- Analyze your own situation and determine when it is advisable to tighten up or loosen the inspection requirements (note that the standards provide for this situation).

- Justify using an attribute sampling plan instead of a variables-based sampling plan.

- Analyze a mass production situation (for example, surface mount soldering of printed circuit boards) and justify the cost of an automated optical inspection system.

- Compile a list of alternatives to an automated optical inspection system.

- Evaluate an x-ray inspection system. What are the limitations of this kind of system?

- Map a process flow and indicate the points where an inspection would make sense and indicate which kind you would choose.

- Create a method for eliminating inspection completely.

- Determine if it is possible to have "zero quality control" through the use of mistake-proofing.

- Not all inspection is visual. Describe five other ways to inspect material without using the visual approach.

- Design a rubric method for assessing incoming material. Do we accept some level of flawed material?

- Propose a visual method that simplifies inspection for line operators.

- Design an inspection approach for a service.

- Indicate how you would verify the inspection methods of a supplier.

- Make an argument for the value of first article inspection.

- Make an argument against the value of first article inspection.

- Recall a time when you did not perform first article inspection. What were the consequences of that decision?

- Are there project management components that should be put under inspection scrutiny?

- Define the costs/negatives of using first article inspection.

- Difficult: should the inspection technique chosen vary with the level of wear on the production tooling? How would you define the point (cusp) for change? Will inspection work at all? What other ways do we have to determine the current suitability of a tool?

- Perform a cost analysis showing how a supplier can assume some level of type 1 failures and reduce type 2 failures at our plant.

- As a project manager, you need to define how much you need to know in order to run your project—how much inspection capability do you need? Who can you trust?

- Write a protocol for the inspection of new material.

- Explain whether or not inspection is a valid control.

- Compose an explanation for how to handle the fact that the human attention span is roughly 15-20 minutes long. How can you manage visual inspection if this is the case?

Endnotes

1. ANSI/ASQ. *Z1.4-2008, Sampling Procedures and Tables for Inspection by Attributes*. Milwaukee, WI: ASQ Quality Press, 2008.

2. ANSI/ASQ. *Z1.9-2008, Sampling Procedures and Tables for Inspection by Variables For Percent Nonconforming*. Milwaukee, WI: ASQ Quality Press, 2008.

3. Stephens, Kenneth S. *The Handbook of Applied Acceptance Sampling: Plans, Procedures, and Principles*. Milwaukee, WI: ASQ Quality Press, 2001.

CHAPTER 9 – TRACKING METRICS

I. Rubric

	Novice	Sr. Novice	Journey-man	Sr. Jour-neyman	Master
Milestones	x	x	x	x	x
Floaters		x	x	x	x
Median			x	x	x
Slack				x	x
Critical path				x	x
Meeting data				x	x
Retest data				x	x
Reliability prediction					x
Slack man-agement					x

II. Questions to Ponder

- Why do metrics have value?
- How many metrics do we need to assess?
- Can the use of metrics introduce distortions in our comprehension of that which we are measuring? (Attention bias)
- How do we implement a metrics program without offending our employees, who may fear reductions in force?
- Should we implement a balanced scorecard?
- Are symbolic representations (e.g., red-yellow-green or smiley faces) necessarily bad or good? What is the best choice?
- What about the use of Chernoff faces as a representation?
- How do we sample?
- If we use statistics, what does a continuous probability distribution function really mean?
- If we use statistics, what does a discrete probability distribution do for us?
- Which kind of probability distribution more closely matches "reality?"
- If we are reporting defects, do we close the defect report when the engineers claimed it is corrected or after we prove it through testing?

- How do we apply PM practices to metrics and why?
- How do we apply metrics to PM practices and why?
- How do we assess value with regard to metrics?

III. Why Statistics and Control Are Important to the Project Manager

Control charts and the associated statistics provide the project manager and his or her project quality support team with the tools to assess that state of any given process:

- They can determine if the process is in statistical control
- They can assess the level of random variation
- They may provide us with ideas for how to reduce the variance
- They may be able to shift the mean to a more amenable value

Simply knowing that the process is "in control" is a positive step from the very beginning because it indicates that our process is not the result of complete randomness—that we do, in fact, have some measure of control over the results.

IV. TQM Project Manager Scenario

A. Situation

A recent project, now closed, launches a new highly visible product to your manufacturing facility. There are significant failures of the product witnessed where the product is integrated into the vehicle. These failures cause considerable material re-handling and costs in money and time for the manufacturing facility. The target failure rate (parts per million) was much lower than the actual performance.

B. Objective

Drop the failure rate for the product at the manufacturing facility as quickly as possible to the target parts per million.

C. Action

We identified team members at the supplier, design, and our manufacturing facility. We gathered firsthand accounts of the failures at our manufacturing facility. This included visits to our manufacturing facility with the supplier to understand how the product was handled. We reviewed all failures reported by our manufacturing organization with the supplier and kept a running list of the failures. We gathered weekly to discuss these failures, assign action items, and follow up. As we gathered more information on the failure symptoms, we developed a Pareto chart of the failures to prioritize the order in which we address the failures.

D. Results

We dropped the failure rate to one quarter of the original failures witnessed. We also found out that the target parts per million couldn't be attained. There were components within the product (Bourdon tube air gauges) that had an individual failure rate as high as the total allowed parts per million and there were at least two of these gauges on every product and in 30% of the cases there would be three of these gauges. Still there was considerable reduction in the failures at the manufacturing plant from 20,000 ppm to 2,500 ppm.

E.   Aftermath

The right people collaborating can produce exceptional results with moderate effort. Pareto and cost analysis made it possible to eliminate the bourdon tube air gauges in the subsequent design, at which time the rest of the organization followed our lead and removed their bourdon tube gauges from their vehicles as well.

V.   Tracking Metrics

Quality metrics are but one category of metrics a project manager may choose to use. In general the purpose of metrics is to allow for detection of change, whether the resulting information is positive or negative. Of course, the project manager should ensure that the metrics chosen have meaning to the project. It is also possible to measure a whole gamut of variables and attributes that do not inform us about the state of the project of product.

A. Project Quality Metrics

We have written about project metrics in other chapters of this book and we certainly want to include these in the category of project quality metrics. However, we are more interested in this particular venue with metrics that indicate our project itself is healthy. Examples of such metrics might be

- Milestones missed/(milestones missed + milestones achieved)
- Milestones ahead/(milestones missed + milestones achieved + milestones ahead)
- Slack time remaining
- Documentation about changes in critical path, if any
- The same metrics applied to subprojects
- The number of "floaters" in the project schedule (floaters are tasks without dependencies)
- Number of meetings
- Average and standard deviation for meeting length
- Meeting attendance Pareto chart
- Condition of discontinuity between prototype material and MRP-purchased material

Milestones Missed/(Milestones Missed + Milestones Achieved)

Milestones are figurative "markers" we put in place in our project schedules to serve at least two functions: 1) to provide a point for retrospective reflection on events-to-date and 2) to recalibrate the rest of the project schedule if that becomes necessary. If our milestones are set too far apart, then we will not properly understand our own project status, we will not communicate it to upper management, and we will not communicate the situation to our customer (perhaps the worst offense of this particular triad of iniquity).

In our experience, milestones should be no more than one month apart, even if we have to create what appear to be arbitrary names for some of these milestones. We have used the monthly retrospective concept with the scrum approach and found it adequate for both project and line management.

Milestones Ahead/(Milestones Missed + Milestones Achieved + Milestones Ahead)

We want to track milestones ahead as well as those missed, since either situation provides us with an indication of our project status. If we are ahead of schedule, we might assume we are doing well; however, consistently coming in ahead of schedule may be an indicator of less than competent scheduling or even of a padded schedule. We are well aware of the conservative adage of "underpromise, overdeliver," but using a heavily padded schedule may backfire with regard to customer satisfaction.

Any kind of visual indicator we can concoct for any of these indicators can serve as an early warning system. We are not interested in providing more "busy work" for the enterprising TQM project manager; however, we want to ensure that anomalies, good or bad, are visible quickly and easily.

Slack Time Remaining

Slack is the amount of time that a task in a project can be delayed without causing any delays to:

- Downstream tasks
- End-of-project date

The control of slack is one of the most important activities for a project manager, because the amount of slack gives us a strong indication of whether we will meet our project schedule commitments and may provide an anticipatory indicator of impending scheduling problems. It is incumbent, then, that the TQM-oriented project manager cherish and protect the slack throughout the project. Slack is almost like a savings account of time for the TQM PM. Without slack our project team is on a death march and schedule success is not very probable.

Documentation about Changes in Critical Path, if Any

The critical path is the longest, contiguous, and slackless path through the schedule network for the project. If we have a critical path, it will inform us about the earliest possible completion date. Note that the critical path is the *longest* path, but the *shortest* possible completion. We have heard many people over the years get this concept completely backwards.

In essence, we never really want to be in a critical path situation, where any delay in the critical path delays the entire project. As we indicated in the section on slack, we want to protect our bank of time so that we have the time when we need it. We do this by controlling slack and front-loading the project as much as we can.

Also note that some project management support software will show multiple critical paths if allowed to do so. These multiple paths can be misleading—we really want to know the true critical path. If we consider subprojects to be quasi-independent, then we can assess the critical path situation for them as well, particularly if they will have an impact on the main schedule.

The Same Metrics Applied to Subprojects

Milestones, slack, and critical path should be measured for all subprojects. We should use caution with project management software in order to be sure that it properly implements and represents the information we really need to know. For example, we might want to investigate the existence of a "slack" report.

We should also be aware that the subproject that develops a critical path may ultimately delay a project if the situation becomes severe. That is why the PM needs indicators, much like a pilot has an array of gauges providing aircraft status.

The Number of "Floaters" in the Project Schedule

Floaters are tasks without dependencies. The question the TQM PM should ask is "why aren't we executing these tasks immediately?" If, in fact, we are not executing a floating task because we do not have resources, then–in reality–we have a resource-based dependency and we should link the task to the appropriate upstream task that rectifies the resource problem.

One of us used to audit project time lines to see how many floaters were present in the schedule. We found this to be a moderately successful method for determining the aptitude of a project manager. Some of them never did understand why floaters were an issue.

Also, we would at least expect a floater to be connected to the project kickoff activity, which is often the first task in the schedule. If not, we could then ask "why wasn't this task done *before* the project started?"

Number of Meetings

Meetings are generally cost centers because so many of them provide no value. If we are deliberately using a scrum approach to project management, we will have daily meetings; however, this factor is simply part of the approach and the meetings are short.

We have seen enterprises where the weekly meeting went on for at least an hour of project schedule review over the entirety of the remaining project. We suggest that the

PM set a standard planning horizon that makes some sense and see to it that all players have a copy of the project schedule. The PM should start the meeting promptly, drive the meeting to an expeditious completion with agenda control, and follow through with meeting minutes that are a masterwork of concision and clarity.

Median and Standard Deviation Values For Meeting Duration

The TQM PM will keep close track of meeting durations, which after he or she collects enough samples (say ten), he or she can calculate the median value and standard deviation to provide estimates of central tendency and dispersion. If we have good agenda control, we should see minimal dispersion (standard deviation) and a relatively short median value. We use the median instead of the more common average because the median is less sensitive to outlying values. If we do have a noticeable number of outliers, we can also calculate the mean (average) and compare it to the median duration. The main idea of this metric is to avoid cost impact by controlling the meeting times and thereby assuring ourselves we are most likely adding some value.

Meeting Attendance Pareto Chart

The meeting attendance Pareto chart helps us to implement some accountability with regard to attendance. We can either use the names of the individuals who are supposed to routinely attend these meetings or we can use their department names if we wish to be more discreet. When the PM projects this information on a projection screen during a milestone retrospective, it often becomes apparent that the departmental problems with the project are caused by the non-attendees from those departments.

One of the most common non-attenders will be the production engineers because they are often kept busy managing problems on the production lines. Unfortunately, production line issues really do not make a good excuse for delaying a project because manufacturing had no clue as to what was going on.

Condition of Discontinuity between Prototype Material and MRP-Purchased Material

The shift from using MRO (maintenance, repair, and operations) purchasing to MRP (manufacturing resource planning) purchasing will often produce a supply discontinuity that causes line shutdowns during the initial launch of the product. The purchasing (procurement) department will typically use MRO purchasing to buy prototype material in small quantities "on the fly." With MRP purchasing, we are using customer demand to drive much larger quantities of material and the entire activity is largely computer driven.

Why not use MRP purchasing from the start of material purchases? The reason lies with the order quantity and lead time mechanism built into the software. In our experience, purchasing managers are reluctant to use small order quantities in the system because the purchase price increases, often significantly. We suspect any forward-thinking enterprise can deal with this issue without penalizing the purchasing manager for a temporary purchase price variance (PPV) that is less than desirable.

We have suggested elsewhere that the project manager allow for one-piece order quantities at the beginning of the launch and then switch to economical order quantities when the inevitable launch chaos subsides. The downside is that we will not see good margins for a few weeks. The upside lies with significant customer satisfaction as well as reduced risk with suppliers when we make an early change in the product.

B. Product Quality Metrics

Product quality metrics are important because they help determine whether the product is acceptable for release to the customer. At no point will the wise project manager give product testing and assessment short shrift. In our experience, crashed test schedules generally lead to customer dissatisfaction and a product that is launched with an already tarnished reputation. Typical metrics for this section might be:

- Original test schedule versus actual test schedule
- Rate of execution of test cases
- Number of retests (especially with software)
- Test case growth
- Reliability growth
- Number of major and minor design changes (this may be okay if we have an evolutionary launch process)
- Software defect prevention program in place
- Full configuration management throughout the project and post-launch
- Suppliers meeting quality requirements for their parts
- Original test schedule versus actual test schedule

Number of Retests (Especially with Software)

Retests are like manufacturing rework, they consume resources without adding extra value. Having said that, we need to be aware that some development models provide for test-analyze-and-fix (TAAF) as a legitimate approach to development. The goal for the TQM PM is to see to it that the retest level doesn't become an excuse for delays or for sloppy craftsmanship. The TQM project manager should pay attention to the retests for signs of previous failures making their presences known a second time. When you see previously solved problems recurring, you can bet there are process issues at that supplier. This could be in the change and configuration management systems or within the build processes of the company. The three main modes for testing, especially with software, are as follows:

- Test-Find-Test (TFT): we identify failure modes but we do not implement the fixes until after the consummation of testing.

- Test-Analyze-and-Fix (TAAF): we implement our fixes during the test after any failure modes have been identified and we have established the remedies. We can stop the testing while we remedy the known issues or we can continue to test. Testing continues with the updated product design.

- Test-Analyze-and-Fix with Delays (TAAFD): we implement some fixes during the test while we delay other remedies until the fulfillment of the test activity.

Test Case Growth

Test case growth during the creation of a new product is not unusual—nay, we should expect it as we learn more about our product. We found that with a moderately complex electronic product, we found an empirical breakpoint in quality at about 10,000 software test cases.

The TQM PM must remain cognizant that test time may increase with the increase in test cases. Under no circumstances should the PM attempt to reduce testing time. Eliminating testing is a surefire method for introducing substantial customer dissatisfaction.

Reliability Growth

Reliability growth occurs as we redesign the product to eliminate known time-dependent quality problems. The international standard for reliability growth is IEC 61164:2004.

Number of Major and Minor Design Changes

Design changes can be costly to both budget and schedule; however, (this may be okay if we have an evolutionary launch process). Mature PMs will generally estimate some amount of redesign as the design team better understands the behavior of the product, particularly after some modicum of testing has occurred.

We did one study of a selection of products to see how often the printed circuit board (PCB) had changed and how many changes occurred to the drawings (causing tooling repurchase or modifications). With one product, we could see at least ten redesigns of the printed circuit, which we considered to be excessive, particularly given the fact that the designers could simulate most of the schematic with the appropriate software.

Software Defect Prevention Program in Place

We have a software defect prevention program in place when our developers review software "lessons learned" on a regular basis (say, weekly). This approach can bring new developers up to speed and remind old developers of ancient sins. The development can't and shouldn't expect the testing team to be able to find every flaw in the software.

Full Configuration Management throughout the Project and Post-Launch

If the TQM PM does not have complete configuration management, the PM has nothing. Configuration management is the means by which we inform ourselves and our customers about the constituents of our product. MIL-STD-973 defines four components for any real configuration management system:

- Configuration control, which is often conflated with configuration management
- Configuration status accounting, wherein we provide reports to tell ourselves the status of our configurations
- Configuration identification in which we define all the components of our products
- Configuration auditing, which is composed of physical configuration audits (for the paperwork) and functional configuration audits (for the behavior of the product)

Suppliers Meeting Quality Requirements for Their Parts

Supplier quality can be a touchy issue for the TQM PM. Unfortunately, the PM needs to keep close watch on supplier quality metrics to ensure no degradation to the product through supplier misfires or malfeasance. In addition, the PM must be able to audit the supplier if such a step becomes necessary.

VI. Product Quality over Time

A. Reliability

One of the most significant problems with reliability is that we really can't say much about reliability without data on product returns, which is the most sound data with regard to true analysis.

Reliability Prediction[1]

Over the years, one of the holy grails of product development has been the need to predict the probable life of the product. Any technique we have seen ends up being an estimate based on a model that may or may not be meaningful.

One approach is the so-called "parts count" method, which is really the old military approach that assumes an average behavior for each type of electronic component and also assumes the design has serial reliability (no redundancy). Over the years, we have found this method to generate estimates that are upwards of four times too conservative, leading to extra cost in the product.

The other predominant method for reliability prediction involves using a physical model like the temperature-based Arrhenius equation, which involves substantial use of assumptions and, in some cases, is little better than the parts count approach. One of the most significant factors in the Arrhenius equation is the activation energy that allows the undesired event to occur. To choose an activation energy, we usually survey the literature, leading to substantial variation in potential activation energies. Perhaps the best approach here is to provide both the customer and us with best- and worst-case scenarios.

We recommend a reliability growth approach without any attempt to predict some number that is potentially void of meaning. At least with reliability growth, we are able to demonstrate improvement in the product as the development process continues. We can also use highly accelerated life testing (HALT) cautiously and with assumptions clearly defined. HALT allows early detection of potential weaknesses in the product and elimination of these before product launch.

VII. Project Quality over Time

The ethical TQM PM does not ever want to be in the situation where he or she is telling the customer the product is defective, too expensive, or late immediately before product launch. We have found the best approach is the quick and honest approach and most customers seem to like this behavior as well.

VIII.   Exercises

- Brainstorm a list of metrics that make sense for your enterprise.

- How would we determine which factors are significant? What is the appropriate technique for analysis?

- Check your project management software tool if you are using one—does it have a method for calculating and displaying the standard project management metrics?

- Consider using paired indicators—what would your paired indicators be? (Paired indicators keep each other "honest;" for example, lines of software code versus number of software errors per line).

- Meditate on potential distortions to understanding introduced by the very same metrics you are using to illuminate the project.

- What are the assumptions underlying your choices of metrics?

- How many of the discipline-centric metrics will you review? For example, will you look at a number of software test cases?

- Which cost metrics tell you all is well?

- Which cost metrics tell you something is horribly wrong with the project?

- Do you have historical data, so you can compile longitudinal metrics about typical and/or similar projects? What are the best metrics for longitudinal analysis?

- Which statistics make sense for analyzing longitudinal data? Describe the appropriate statistics for a project?

  - Describe the statistics for a well-defined and controlled project.

  - Describe the statistics for a poorly defined and out-of-control project.

- Can you simulate your project? Define a simulation solution.

- How would you simulate the "rest of the project" remaining after wherever and whenever you are located in the current project? Describe completely your simulation approach (actor-based or discrete event or other).

- What are the pitfalls of simulating project results? List them.

- Explain the statistical assumptions underlying any probability distributions you may use in your simulations.

- Consider the mean and the variance of a probability distribution and explain which one will tell you more about your situation.

- Compile a list of potential sources for historical project information.

- Choose four standard metrics and describe how you would use them to explain the status of the project to very-high-level management.

- Define whether "percentage complete" is a meaningful term in project management.

- Create a project dashboard with what you think are the four most important metrics. Is it good enough?

- Create a project dashboard with what you think are the eight most important metrics. Is it any better than the four-metric dashboard?

- Consider a balanced scorecard approach. What does this dashboard look like?

- Explain how you would synthesize your metrics into an analysis and development of enterprise strategy.

Endnotes

1. Blischke, Wallace R. and D.N. Prabhakar Murthy. *Reliability: Modeling, Prediction, and Optimization*. New York, NY: John Wiley & Sons, 2000.

CHAPTER 10 – OTHER SUPPORTING INITIATIVES

I. Rubric

	Novice	Sr. Novice	Journey-man	Sr. Jour-neyman	Master
CMM	x	x	x	x	x
CMMI		x	x	x	x
TMM			x	x	
TMMI				x	x
FAA-MM					x

II. Questions to Ponder

- How does an enterprise coordinate the multitude of initiatives to produce a desired outcome?
- Do maturity models provide any added value?
- How would you determine which model would work for your organization?
- Are maturity models too abstract or are they really down-to-earth?
- Why is the maturity model approach so seductive?
- Does the enterprise really need a formal audit?
- If our organization transforms itself such that it achieves one of the "higher" levels, have we really accomplished anything?
- Does the maturity model designation have any marketing value?
- Why do we have so many maturity models?
- Why are the maturity models different and yet the same (compare and contrast)?
- Is a maturity model audit just another way to make somebody some money?
- Is the ISO version better than the other models?
- Why can't we just make our "home grown?"
- Is there benefit to certification to a maturity model and level for the organization? Is business more easily acquired?
- Do our profit margins become more repeatable?

III. Why Maturity Models Are Important to the Project Manager

The TQM project manager can use maturity models to assess all or parts of his or her organization. Each model represents a path from ad hoc randomness to self-regulating improvement. All of these models except the approach of Philip Crosby derived from the original capability maturity model (CMM) developed by the Software Engineering Institute in Pittsburgh, Pennsylvania in the 1980s. While the original CMM was highly software development-oriented, each of these models represents a different viewpoint on improvement.

Maturity models provide a means for the TQM project manager as well as the enterprise to assess the putative maturity of their operations.

The initial actions in the project go far in securing the success. Scope identification and supplier selection are primary of these. At least one intent of the maturity models is to identify the level of capability of an organization based upon some recognized best practices. If you are a project manager and are looking with your purchasing organization for a supplier, you would want to know the capability of that organization to deliver the scope of the project. Maturity models can help provide some insight into that supplier's capability or more importantly, the weaknesses that the project manager may be called upon to mitigate. For example, imagine a supplier that was certified to level 2 CMMI. We know that to achieve this level the project management and configuration management practices have to be capable. We can also infer that the verification ability of the organization may be missing as this is part of level 3 CMMI certification. We would then ask questions around this area to understand whether in fact the organization was capable but not certified or not certified because the organization is not capable. We can then choose another supplier or we can choose some actions to mitigate the risks. For example, we could identify metrics that would let us know how the supplier is performing during the project execution and monitor these measurements closely.

For organizations that are not certified to a particular maturity model, understanding of a select model that meets your organization's (or supplier's) needs, provides the purchasing and project office with enough information either to ask questions to understand the supplier's capability, or find an expert in the area that can assist in quantifying the supplier's capability. Again, we use this information to manage the risks associated with the project and product development from a process capability.

For project managers that manage projects internal to the organization; for example, this individual works for a company that develops embedded products for a particular industry, knowledge of a maturity model provides some measure of structure upon which to base decisions. In this case, the maturity models, if considered rational, provide support for the project manager to guide the project. A knowledgeable project manager will know when the action parts of the task list pose undue risk to the project deliverables. It is good to know the rules and know the consequences and risks to breaking those rules before the rules are broken. A well-armed project manager will be able to ferret out the risks due to lack of understanding of the reason for some processes or what is considered to be a competent process. The project manager is then in a position to ensure the project has suitable processes to deliver and the information provided by the team is not inflated or overly optimistic puffery.

IV. TQM Project Manager Scenario

A. Situation

In the mid-1990s, the organization pursued projects using functional managers rather than dedicated project managers. The result was inattention to customer needs as the functional managers attempted to pursue both their functional responsibilities as well as their project requirements.

B. Objective

The goal was to develop the project management office (PMO) and let the functional managers return to their original responsibilities.

C. Action

The enterprise chose to engage a consultant to conduct a CMMI audit to determine the maturity of the organization as well as assist in the transition to a PMO.

D. Results

The PMO was successfully created and exists as of this writing. The overall enterprise has improved in maturity and the PMO itself has demonstrated robustness through some major structural changes in the enterprise.

E. Aftermath

The PMO became not only a functional management entity in its own right, it also became a training ground for new project managers.

V.   Capability Maturity Models

Capability maturity models are extremely seductive in their design. They represent a variation on Purgatory (not a joke), where the participant enters at the lowest level as a sinner needing cleansing and exits at the top of the seven-storey mountain into Paradise. What could be better than that?

All maturity models bear a family resemblance, with the most famous probably being the Software Engineering Institute's capability maturity model, designed to enhance software development and redolent with substantial and meaningful research to support their claims.

The TQM project manager should know about these for a variety of reasons; for example:

- It might be wise to apply appropriate models to different functions in the organization
- The systems engineering model is related directly to project management
- At least two project management maturity models have existed
- They are not a bad decision, although we might have some qualms about the consultant/auditing industry that has built up around the concept. The maturity level 5 process areas of CMMI are as follows:
  - Organizational innovation and deployment
  - Causal analysis and resolution

A. Philip Crosby Quality Maturity Grid

Philip Crosby was a plant manager who worked for ITT during ITT's manufacturing days. Notice a little bit of tongue in cheek, particularly the column headings (Philip Crosby, Quality is Free, 1979).

	Stage 1 Uncertainty	Stage 2 Awakening	Stage 3 Enlighten-ment	Stage 4 Wisdom	Stage 5 Certainty
Management understanding and attitude	No compre-hension of quality as a management tool. Tend to blame quality department for "quality problems."	Recognizing that quality management may be of value but not willing to pro-vide money or time to make it happen.	While going through qual-ity improve-ment program learn more about quality management; becoming supportive and helpful.	Participating. Understand absolutes of quality man-agement. Rec-ognize their personal role in continuing emphasis.	Consider quality man-agement an essential part of company system.
Quality organi-zation status	Quality is hidden in manufacturing or engineering departments. Inspection probably not part of organization. Emphasis on appraisal and sorting.	A stronger quality leader is appointed but main em-phasis is still on appraisal and moving the product. Still part of manufacturing or other.	Quality department reports to top management, all appraisal is incorporated and manager has role in management of company.	Quality manager is an officer of company; effective status reporting and preventa-tive action. Involved with consumer affairs and special assign-ments.	Quality man-ager on board of directors. Prevention is main concern. Quality is a thought leader.
Problem handling	Problems are fought as they occur; no resolution; inadequate definition; lots of yelling and accusations.	Teams are set up to attack major problems. Long-range solutions are not solicited.	Corrective action com-munication established. Problems are faced openly and resolved in an orderly way.	Problems are identified early in their development. All functions are open to suggestion and improvement.	Except in the most unusual cases, problems are prevented.
Cost of quality as % of sales	Reported: unknown Actual: 20%	Reported: 3% Actual: 18%	Reported: 8% Actual: 12%	Reported: 6.5% Actual: 8%	Reported: 2.5% Actual: 2.5%
Quality improvement actions	No organized activities. No understanding of such activi-ties.	Trying obvious "motivational" short-range efforts.	Implementa-tion of the 14-step program with thorough understanding and establish-ment of each step.	Continuing the 14-step program and starting Make Certain	Quality improvement is a normal and continued activity.

Summation of company quality posture.	"We don't know why we have problems with quality."	"Is it absolutely necessary to always have problems with quality?"	"Through management commitment and quality improvement we are identifying and resolving our problems."	"Defect prevention is a routine part of our operation."	"We know why we do not have problems with quality."

B. CMM

CMM

The table that follows shows the final set of categories for version 1.1 of the CMM[10]. The Software Engineering Institute (SEI) was mutating this idea into the CMM-integrated or CMMI.

Level	Key Process Areas
Level 1 - Initial	Often called "ad hoc" in other models
Level 2 - Repeatable	Requirements Management Software Project Planning Software Project Tracking & Oversight Software Subcontract Management Software Quality Assurance Software Configuration Management
Level 3 - Defined	Organization Process Focus Organization Process Definition Training Program Integrated Software Management Software Product Engineering Intergroup Coordination Peer Review
Level 4 - Managed	Quantitative Process Management Software Quality Management
Level 5 - Optimizing	Defect Prevention Technology Change Management Process Change Management

C. CMMI

The maturity level 2 process areas of CMMI[5] are as follows:
• Requirements Management
• Project Planning
• Project Monitoring and Control
• Supplier Agreement Management
• Measurement and Analysis
• Process and Product Quality Assurance
• Configuration Management

We suspect that organizations that can achieve at best evaluations that are less than level 3 are at risk. All of the practices up through level 3 are basic good practices that every organization should already be executing. The "Defined" maturity level 3

process areas of CMMI are as follows:
- Requirements Development
- Technical Solution
- Product Integration
- Verification
- Validation
- Organizational Process Focus
- Organizational Process Definition
- Organizational Training
- Integrated Project Management for IPPD
- Risk Management
- Integrated Teaming
- Decision Analysis and Resolution
- Organizational Environment for Integration

The "Quantitatively Managed" maturity level 4 process areas of CMMI are as follows:
- Organizational Process Performance
- Quantitative Project Management

The maturity level 5 process areas of CMMI are as follows:
- Organizational Innovation and Deployment
- Causal Analysis and Resolution

D. Education Capability Maturity Model

The education capability maturity model[1] can also be applied to the training activity within an enterprise. One of the points we are making in this chapter is that a maturity model of some sort exists for just about any activity or program of which one can conceive.

Level	Focus	E-CMM
Initial		
Repeatable	Project management establishment	1. Educational requirement 2. Degree program planning 3. Degree program monitoring and control 4. Solution provider management 5. Educational quality assurance 6. Faculty hiring program
Defined	Product and process quality measure	1. System approach of institution 2. Integrated program management 3. Documented process management 4. Intellectual property management 5. Faculty training 6. Student-support process
Managed	Engineering process: Use infrastructure	1. Institutional process performance 2. Educational quality management 3. Quantitative process management

Level	Focus	E-CMM
Optimizing	Continuous Process Improvement	1. Process change management 2. Technology change management 3. Total faculty involvement 4. Documented Feedback 5. Defect prevention

E. EIA-731 Approach

EIA-731[6] does a fine job of incrementally improving each description as we rise upwards in capability. The approach is somewhat different than that of the Software Engineering Institute, which generally has different tasks accomplished at different levels rather than improvements on existing areas.

	Capability	Process	Non-Process
0	Initial	• Practices are not performed • General failure to perform activities • No easily identifiable work products • No proof tasks are accomplished	• Activities and work products have little effectiveness or value • No assurance of success • Information is difficult to identify • Driving force for activities is indeterminate • No assurance of complexity management • No focus on the principles of systems engineering
1	Performed	• Specific practices are performed • Activities are done informally • Non-rigorous plans and tracking • Dependency on "heroes" • Work products are in evidence • General recognition of need for activity	• Activities are marginally effective and work products are of marginal utility • Information is ad hoc • Activities are driven only by immediate contractual or customer requirements • SE focus limited

	Capability	Process	Non-Process
2	Managed	• Specific practices are performed, and performance is characterized by the level 2 generic practices • Policies define need for activities • Processes are program specific • Activities are planned, tracked, measured, and verified • Corrective actions are taken to assure the program specific process is followed • Work products are reviewed for adequacy • Defects are removed from work products • Work products are controlled	• Activities are adequately effective and work products are of adequate utility • Key information managed • Activities driven by customer and stakeholder needs in a suitable manner • SE focus is requirements through design

	Capability	Process	Non-Process
3	Defined	• Specific practices are performed, and performance is characterized by the level 3 generic practices • Processes are well defined • The organization has a standard systems engineering process • Tailoring guidelines exist for the standard systems engineering process • The standard systems engineering process is tailored and used by each program • Tailoring is reviewed and approved • Customer feedback is obtained • Data are collected on the performance of the tailored process • Qualitative process improvement is performed on both standard and tailored processes	• Activities are significantly effective and work products are of significant utility • Consistent program success • Information is managed and integrated • Activities driven by benefit to program • SE focus is requirements through operation

	Capability	Process	Non-Process
4	Measured	• Specific practices are performed, and performance is characterized by the level 4 generic practices • Metrics are derived from data on the tailored process • The tailored process is quantitatively understood • Performance of the tailored process can be predicted • Tailored process induced defects are identified • Measurable quality goals are established for systems engineering work products • Causal analyses are performed for the tailored process • Tailored processes are quantitatively improved • Standard process continues to be qualitatively improved	• Activities are measurably effective and work products are of measurably significant utility • All information fully integrated • Activities driven by systems engineering benefit • SE focus on all phases of product life cycle
5	Optimizing	• Specific practices are performed, and performance is characterized by the level 5 generic practices • Process effectiveness goals are established for the program based upon business objectives • Causal analyses are performed for the standard process • Standard processes are quantitatively improved • Improvements to the standard process are flowed down into each tailored process	• Activities are effectively balanced and work products effectively provide their intended utility • Activities driven by systems engineering and organizational benefit • Complexity management is fully scalable • SE focus is product life cycle and strategic applications

This section defines each of the nineteen focus areas, divided into three categories, which make up the EIA SECM. Each FA segment consists of a general description of the FA. The practices within each FA are organized into five levels of systems engineering capability.

The numbering of each FA indicates the category to which it belongs, as follows:

TC 1.0 Systems Engineering Technical Category

FA 1.1 Define Stakeholder and System Level Requirements
FA 1.2 Define Technical Problem
FA 1.3 Define Solution
FA 1.4 Assess and Select
FA 1.5 Integrate System
FA 1.6 Verify System
FA 1.7 Validate System

TC 2.0 Systems Engineering Management Category

FA 2.1 Plan and Organize
FA 2.2 Monitor and Control
FA 2.3 Integrate Disciplines
FA 2.4 Coordinate with Suppliers
FA 2.5 Manage Risk
FA 2.6 Manage Data
FA 2.7 Manage Configurations
FA 2.8 Ensure Quality

TC 3.0 Systems Engineering Environment Category

FA 3.1 Define and Improve the Systems Engineering Process
FA 3.2 Manage Competency
FA 3.3 Manage Technology
FA 3.4 Manage Systems Engineering Support Environment

F. Design Maturity Model

The design maturity model[2] is taken from Betterproductdesign.net. This table is the design execution summary.

	Level 1	Level 2	Level 3	Level 4
Market research & analysis	Prejudice or 'gut-feel'	'Gut-feel' calibrated by experience	Marketing-led research	Full team involvement
Investigating user needs	Rely on anecdote and opinion	User opinions sometimes sought	'Voice of customer' a standard process	Different methods used as appropriate
Product specification	A poorly defined wish list	Incompatible market and technical specs	A single testable specification	Unambiguous USPs

Concept genera-tion	Go with the first idea	Engineering led	Cross-functional involvement	Radical ideas encouraged
Concept selection	There is only one concept	Chosen by the chairman's wife	Use a standard checklist	All stakeholders involved
Ergonomic design	Little consider-ation of usability	Engineers design the user interface	Early specialist involvement	Total 'user experi-ence' design
Product platform planning	Most of our prod-ucts are totally different	Some modular-ity - but not 'by design'	Planned reuse of technology	Platform-based strategy
Prototyping to reduce market risks	'Trust me - it'll sell'	Occasional user testing	Always test with users	Modelling is 'a way of life'
Prototyping to reduce technical risks	'Trust me - it'll work'	Pre-production prototypes	All risky elements prototyped	Modelling is 'a way of life'
Design for manu-facturing	Over the wall	Ad-hoc manufac-turing involve-ment	Regular design reviews	Formal DFA / DFM techniques

This table is the design management summary:

	Level 1	Level 2	Level 3	Level 4
Culture & envi-ronment	No 'playing' at all	Creativity kept 'under the desk'	Some managed 'soft time'	Creativity expect-ed and rewarded
Product develop-ment process	No process	A process exists, but ...	Process used and understood	Continuous im-provement
Teamwork	Functional rivalry	Lightweight proj-ect management	Heavyweight proj-ect management	Autonomous project teams
Specialist design involvement	'Silent design'	Brought in late to 'tart up' the product	Early specialist input	Strategic input

The table that follows is a presentation of the design activity "Investigating User Needs:"

Investigating user needs "Use of a range of methods to assess and disseminate the requirements and motivations of users / customers"			
Level 1	Level 2	Level 3	Level 4
• Rely on anecdote from user contacts • Not enough data to interpret or disseminate • Not required by the NPD process, so it typically isn't done • Engineer or marketer is the 'expert'	• A few users may be asked • Unstructured data collection • No formal interpretation of data - occasional 'market reports' • Ad-hoc process - no standard methods	• A representative cross section of users asked • Typically questionnaire/ interview based 'voice of customer exercise' • Outputs formally reported • Standard approach mandated in the NPD process	• All internal and external stakeholders involved • A range of qualitative and quantitative methods used • A single report synthesising all inputs into a coherent set of customer requirements

G. FAA

The FAA[7] model for maturity is complex but, nonetheless, represents a rational approach to scaled improvement. It does, however, follow a similar pattern to most of the other maturity models.

CAPABILITY LEVEL 0: INCOMPLETE

At this level we have not achieved one or more of the process area goals of the process area.

CAPABILITY LEVEL 1: PERFORMED

We anticipate the process achieves the goals of the process area and we have a set of generic practices:

1. Identify our work scope—we must identify the scope of the work we will perform and the work products/services we will produce and communicate this information to those executing the work.

2. Perform the process—Perform a process that implements the base practices of the process area to provide work products and/or services to a customer.

CAPABILITY LEVEL 2: MANAGED: PLANNED AND TRACKED

We institute our process as a managed (planned and tracked) process. We have a set of generic practices:

1. Establish Organizational Policy. Establish and maintain an organizational policy for performing the process.

2. Document the Process. Document the process for performing the practices of the process area.

3. Plan the Process. Establish and maintain a plan to accomplish the objectives of the process.

4. Provide Adequate Resources. Provide resources that are adequate for performing the process as planned. Note that this practice is relatively unusual in the maturity model world, yet makes complete sense.

5. Assign Responsibility. Establish responsibility, authority, and commitment for performing the process.

6. We should ensure skill and knowledge by ensuring that the staff executing the process has the requisite skills and knowledge.

7. We establish work product requirements by establishing and maintaining requirements on work products/services that result from execution of the process.

8. We consistently use and manage the process by using our documented plans, standards, processes, or procedures in implementing and managing (planning and tracking) the process.

9. We manage work products by placing clearly identified work products from the process under formal configuration management. Again, please note that we emphasize configuration management throughout this book.

10. We objectively assess compliance including adherence of the performed process to the documented process (as-is versus as-espoused).

11. We objectively verify work product to established requirements.

12. We measure execution and results against the plan.

13. We review the activities, status, and results of the process with executive management.

14. We take corrective action to address problems (failure reporting and corrective actions system = FRACAS).

15. We coordinate and communicate staff and stakeholders.

CAPABILITY LEVEL 3: DEFINED

We establish our process as a defined process and we have a set of generic practices:

1. We create and maintain a set of standard processes (SOP) for the enterprise, including guidelines for tailoring.

2. We create and use a *defined* process, designed to meet specific business objectives, tailored from the SOPs of the enterprise; in short, we have a specification that spells out the process exactly.

3. We collect and use work products, measures, measurement results, and

improvement information to improve the standard and defined processes—as with ISO-9000, we have records.

CAPABILITY LEVEL 4: QUANTITATIVELY MANAGED

We institute the process as a quantitatively managed process and we have a set of generic practices:

1. We select measures necessary to meet our business objectives and bring processes relevant to those measures under statistical process control (control chart usage); in short, the overwhelming bulk of the quantitative management is based on the very same tool that we recommend to TQM project managers.

CAPABILITY LEVEL 5: OPTIMIZING

We institute the process as an optimizing process.
We have a set of generic practices:

- We pursue improvement to the performance of statistically managed processes based on business objectives, innovation, and removal of common problems.

H. TMM

TMM[3, 4] was the first stab at a maturity model for testing, predominantly software testing.

Level 1 - Initial

Testing is a chaotic process—

- Ill-defined, effectively debugging

- Tests are developed in an ad hoc way after we produce code

- Testing and debugging are interleaved and iterated to get the bugs out

- The objective of testing is to show that the software works rather than looking for any and all anomalies

- We have no quality assurance/control for software product releases

- There is a lack of resources, tools, and properly trained staff

- This type of organization would be on level 1 of the capability maturity model (CMM) developed by the Software Engineering Institute

- There are no maturity goals at this level

Level 2 - Phase Definition

Testing is separated from debugging and is defined as a phase that follows coding—

- It is a planned activity
- Test planning at level 2 may occur after coding for reasons related to the immaturity of the test process. For example, at level 2 there is the perception that all testing is execution-based and dependent on the code, and therefore it should be planned only when the code is complete
- The primary goal of testing at this level of maturity is to show that the software meets its specifications. Basic testing techniques and methods are in place. Many quality problems at this TMM level occur because test planning occurs late in the software life cycle
- In addition, defects propagate into the code from the requirements and design phases, as there are no review programs that address this important issue
- Post-code, execution-based testing is still considered the primary testing activity

Level 3 - Integration

Testing is no longer a phase that follows coding; it is integrated into the entire software life cycle. Organizations can build on the test planning skills they have acquired at level 2. Unlike level 2, planning for testing at TMM level 3 begins at the requirements phase and continues throughout the life cycle supported by a version of the V-model.

- Test objectives are established with respect to the requirements based on user and client needs and are used for test case design and success criteria
- There is a test organization, and testing is recognized as a professional activity
- There is a technical training organization with a testing focus
- Basic tools support key testing activities
- Although organizations at this level begin to realize the important role of reviews in quality control, there is no formal review program, and reviews do not yet take place across the lifecycle
- A test measurement program has not yet been established to qualify process and product attributes

Level 4 - Management and Measurement

Testing is a measured and quantified process

- Reviews at all phases of the development process are now recognized as testing and quality control activities
- Software products are tested for quality attributes such as reliability, usability, and maintainability

- Test cases from all projects are collected and recorded in a test case database to support test case reuse and regression testing

- Defects are logged and given a severity level

- Deficiencies in the test process are now often due to the lack of a defect prevention philosophy and the mediocre state of automated support for the collection, analysis, and dissemination of test-related metrics.

Level 5 - Optimization, Defect Prevention, and Quality Control

Because of the infrastructure provided by the attainment of maturity goals at levels 1 through 4 of the TMM, the testing process is now said to be defined and managed and its cost and effectiveness can be monitored. At Level 5

- We have mechanisms that fine-tune and continuously improve testing

- Defect prevention and quality control are practiced

- The testing process is driven by statistical sampling, measurements of confidence levels, trustworthiness, and reliability

- There is an established procedure to select and evaluate testing tools

- Automated tools totally support the running and rerunning of test cases, providing support for test case design, maintenance of test-related items, defect collection and analysis, and the collection, analysis, and application of test-related metrics

I. TMMi

TMMi[11] is the integrated version of TMM, much like CMMI is the integrated version of CMM. In effect, we see an evolution of the initial concept into a more sophisticated approach and with the reins handed over to an oversight committee with their own web site.

Level 1 Initial

At TMMi level 1, testing is a chaotic, undefined process and is often considered a subset of debugging. The enterprise usually does not provide a stable environment to support the processes. In addition, the following characteristics often apply:

- Reliance on heroism and non-stop firefighting

- Tests are developed ad hoc following coding

- Testing and debugging are tightly coupled in iterative loops as the testers desperately endeavor to remove defects

- The objective of testing at this level is to show that the software works instead of the more appropriate attitude of testing to find out where the software fails

- Products are released with inadequate product integrity

- Product risks are poorly understood

- The product will generally exhibit field problems
- Within the test group there is a lack of resources

Process areas are undefined. In short, everything we might expect from an "immature" organization is realized.

Level 2 Managed

At TMMi level 2, testing evolves into a managed process—clearly separated from debugging. The process discipline reflected by maturity level 2 helps to ensure that existing practices are retained during times of stress. However, testing is still perceived by many stakeholders as being a project phase that *follows* coding. In addition, we might expect to see these features:

- A company-wide test strategy is created
- Formal test plans are also developed
- Product risk assessment follows a rational procedure
- Documented requirements are used in tandem with risk management techniques
- Test plans define required testing is required, times, durations, test steps, and personnel
- Commitments are established with stakeholders and revised as needed
- Testing is monitored and controlled to ensure it is compliant and corrective actions occur following procedural anomalies.
- The status of the work products and the delivery of testing services are visible to management through the use of a testing configuration management scheme
- Test design techniques are applied for deriving and selecting test cases from requirements
- Testing still arrives late in the development life cycle

At this level, testing is multi-tiered: we have component, integration, system, and acceptance test levels, following the familiar V model. For each identified test level there are specific testing objectives defined in the organization-wide or program-wide test strategy. Testing and debugging are differentiated.

The process areas at TMMi level 2 are:

1. Test Policy and Strategy
2. Test Planning
3. Test Monitoring and Control
4. Test Design and Execution
5. Test Environment

Level 3 Defined

At TMMi level 3, testing is no longer confined to a phase that follows coding. It is fully integrated into the development life cycle and the associated milestones. Test planning is done at an early project stage, e.g., during the requirements phase, and is documented in a master test plan. The development of a master test plan builds on the test planning skills and commitments acquired at TMMi level 2. The organization's set of standard test processes, which is the basis for maturity level 3, is established and improved over time. A test organization and a specific test training program exist, and testing is perceived as being a profession. Test process improvement is fully institutionalized as part of the test organization's accepted practices.

Organizations at level 3 understand the importance of reviews in quality control; a formal review program is implemented although not yet fully linked to the dynamic testing process. Reviews take place across the life cycle. Test professionals are involved in reviews of requirements specifications. While the test designs at TMMi level 2 focus mainly on functionality testing, test designs and test techniques are expanded at level 3 to include nonfunctional testing, e.g., usability and/or reliability, depending on the business objectives.

The process areas at TMMi level 3 are:

1. Test Organization

2. Test Training Program

3. Test Lifecycle and Integration

4. Non-Functional Testing

5. Peer Reviews

Level 4 Measured

Achieving the goals of TMMi level 2 and 3 has the benefits of putting into place a technical, managerial, and staffing infrastructure capable of thorough testing and providing support for test process improvement. With this infrastructure in place, testing can become a quantitative process to encourage continuous improvement. In TMMi level 4 organizations, testing is a thoroughly defined, well-founded, and measurable process. Testing is perceived as evaluation; it consists of all lifecycle activities concerned with checking products and related work products. Note that this can be expanded to include hardware testing and product-line testing.

An organization-wide test measurement program will be put into place that can be used to evaluate the quality of the testing process, to assess productivity, and to monitor improvements. Measures are incorporated into the organization's measurement repository to support fact-based decision making. A test measurement program also supports predictions relating to test performance and cost. At this point, we are testing the testers and we are mature enough to realize that every time we conduct a test on a product we are also conducting a test on the test.

With respect to product quality, the presence of a measurement program allows an organization to implement a product quality evaluation process by defining quality needs, quality attributes, and quality metrics. Work products are evaluated using quantitative criteria for quality attributes such as reliability, usability, and maintainability. Product quality is understood in quantitative terms and is managed to the defined objectives throughout the life cycle.

Reviews and inspections are considered to be part of the test process and are used to measure product quality early in the life cycle and to formally control quality gates. Peer reviews as a defect detection technique are transformed into a product quality measurement technique in line with the process area product quality evaluation.

TMMi level 4 also covers establishing a coordinated test approach between peer reviews (static testing) and dynamic testing and the usage of peer review results and data to optimize the test approach with both aiming at making testing more effective and more efficient. Peer reviews are now fully integrated with the dynamic testing process, e.g., part of the test strategy, test plan, and test approach.

The process areas at TMMi level 4 are:

1. Test Measurement

2. Product Quality Evaluation

3. Advanced Peer Reviews

Level 5 Optimization

The achievement of all previous test improvement goals at levels 1 through 4 of TMMi has created an organizational infrastructure for testing that supports a completely defined and measured process. At TMMi maturity level 5, an organization is capable of continually improving its processes based on a quantitative understanding of statistically controlled processes. Improving test process performance is carried out through incremental and innovative process and technological improvements. The testing methods and techniques are optimized and there is a continuous focus on fine-tuning and process improvement. An optimized test process, as defined by the TMMi is one that is:

- Managed, defined, measured, efficient, and effective

- Statistically controlled and predictable

- Focused on defect prevention

- Supported by automation when it is deemed an effective use of resources

- Able to support technology transfer from the industry to the organization

- Able to support re-use of test assets

- Focused on process change to achieve continuous improvement

The defect prevention process area is established to identify and analyze common causes of defects across the development life cycle and define actions to prevent similar defects from occurring in the future. Outliers to test process performance, as identified as part of process quality control, are analyzed to address their causes as part of defect prevention.

The test process is now statistically managed by means of the quality control process area. Statistical sampling, measurements of confidence levels, trustworthiness, and reliability drive the test process. The test process is characterized by sampling-based quality measurements.

Process areas at TMMi level 5 are:

1. Defect Prevention

2. Quality Control

3. Test Process Optimization

J. ISO 15504/SPICE

ISO 15504 and SPICE represent the European/ISO implementation of a maturity model derived from the Software Engineering Institute's CMM and CMMI models, but with a twist all their own.

Another variant is the so-called AutoSPICE, with special applications to the automotive industry.

K. Learning Management Maturity Model

Lessons learned and the learning organization ideas have been around for years, but they have proven difficult to implement and sustain—that is part of what the Learning Management Maturity Model is about[9]. Our own experience indicates simply finding software to store lessons learned in a way that is readily accessible to both inexperienced and experienced employees is a challenge on its own.

In essence, when we forget what we just experienced and the corrective action that may have taken place, we effectively learn nothing from the event. One goal of a learning organization is to institutionalize the learning process in such a way that these moments are not lost to subsequent generations of employees. One way to store this information is in the failure mode and effects analysis documents, since they are ostensibly for the purpose of preventing failure modes in the first place. Of course, a new, raw employee may not understand this particular approach and we are back at the beginning. We have recommended modular FMEAs for years with little success. In a modular FMEA, we pick a subcomponent (e.g., stepper motors) and analyze and capture everything we have learned about stepper motors. We want to capture information with what we know, what we want to know, and what we have already learned from experience.

We know our learning system is not working when we see the same errors surface repeatedly. One of us calls this the "stupidity loop;" a situation that often occurs as employees are fired or drift away. Witless termination of experienced middle managers can also cause this kind of unacceptable repetition.

This approach has been proposed by THINQ Learning Solutions Inc.

Ad hoc	• Many incomplete, informal approaches for managing learning • Unpredictable learning outcomes • Little organizational support for learning and development • Mix of manual and automated system • Departmental LMS(s) in place but not consistent or connected • Commercial off-the-shelf (COTS) learning content being utilized
Managed learning	• Enterprise LMS in place (centralized or interconnected) • Common terminology and nomenclature • Common, repeatable processes • Simple, standards-based integration with learning content • Use of common tools and techniques for key learning management processes • Learning plans in place for basic jobs and activities of the workforce • Organization efficiently planning, managing, integrating, and controlling learning activities • Repository of learning results (i.e., grades, costs, feedback, status) maintained and utilized • Compliance and certifications managed electronically • Measurement now an integral part of learning management • More predictable learning outcomes

Competency-driven	• Senior management support for learning management • Competency models in place to build a proficient workforce • Competency-based learning and skill assessments in use to align learning against developmental needs of the organization • Learning modalities (live, self-paced) blended for increased efficiencies • Consistent use of tools and techniques for learning management processes • LCMS providing central repository for content development and delivery • Universal, assumed interoperability between content and LMS • Prescriptive and self-initiated learning occurring • Collaboration and mentoring reinforcing knowledge transfer • 360-degree feedback instruments in place for skill and performance measurement
Integrated performance	• Active senior management support for integration of business planning and learning/performance initiatives • Business goals aligned with work activities • Interactive dialog among workforce a consistent part of activity • Management and coaching • Developmental planning occurring in relation to accomplishment of work activities • Learning and knowledge management systems beginning to integrate with enterprise portal technologies • Results of learning and work performance measured and correlated against key performance indicators

Optimized workforce	• Flexible, learning, and performance-centric organization structure • Improvements to the learning and performance management environment actively encouraged • Daily work and learning activities directly linked to business priorities • Shared understanding and appreciation throughout workforce of the factors and influences affecting the business • "Connected" organization sharing knowledge and content assets with key components of its extended enterprise • Just-in-time blended learning and performance support tools increasing skill proficiency and organizational performance

L. Berkeley Project Management Maturity Model

The purpose of the Berkeley Project Management Process Maturity Model[8] is to support and measure increased maturity by a systematic and incremental approach. It measures, locates, and compares an organization's current project management maturity level. The model generalizes across industries, whereas other maturity models have specific audiences like software development or new product development, security, or services.

MATURITY LEVEL	KEY PROJECT MANAGEMENT PROCESSES
Level 5 (Sustained Stage)	• PM processes are continuously improved • PM processes are fully understand • PM data are optimized and sustained
Level 4 (Integrated Stage)	• Multiple project management (program management) • PM data and processes are integrated • PM processes data are quantitatively analyzed, measured, and stored
Level 3 (Managed Stage)	• Formal project planning and control system is managed
	• Formal PM data are managed
Level 2 (Defined Stage)	• Informal PM processes are defined • Informal PM problems are identified • Informal PM data are collected
Level 1 (Ad-Hoc Stage)	• No pm processes or practices are consistently available

Major organization characteristics at each Berkeley level:

MATURITY LEVEL	MAJOR ORGANIZATIONAL CHARACTERISTICS
Level 5 (Sustained Stage)	• Project-driven organization • Dynamic, energetic, and fluid organization • Continuous improvement of pm processes and practices
Level 4 (Integrated Stage)	• Strong teamwork • Formal pm training for project team
Level 3 (Managed Stage)	• Team oriented (medium) • Informal training of pm skills and practices
Level 2 (Defined Stage)	• Team oriented (weak) • Organizations posses strengths in doing similar work
Level 1 (Ad-Hoc Stage)	• Functionally isolated • Lack of senior management support • Project success depends on individual efforts

M. Scrum and Agile

What is the scrum approach to projects? The scrum approach is a simple productivity technique derived from software development modalities such as extreme programming and agile software development. We found that a scrum implementation for line management led to an increase in the tempo of accomplishment, a decrease in steady state project lists, and improved communication.

The scrum approach provides some interesting opportunities for the TQM project manager. For example:

- Increased project velocity

- Improved folks on near-time horizon tasks

- Shortened meetings

- Graphical representation of progress

- Ability to use a variation of a lean tool called kanban

In short, scrum deserves a look from any project manager who wants to accelerate the project time line. They must understand, though, they will often see employees balk at the "new way."

Let's take a look at the basic requirements to implement a scrum approach:

- A team

- A facilitator for the team called the Scrum Master

- A product backlog list (the list of all things we need to do)

- Constant customer or stakeholder communication and involvement

- A sprint backlog list (the list of all things we are going to do immediately)
- Burndown chart (showing how we consume the hours allotted to the tasks)
- Daily scrum meetings (short meetings to answer three questions)
  - What did you accomplish yesterday?
  - What are you working on today?
  - What obstacles confront you?

What we describe above may seem somewhat simplistic and, indeed, it is. For example, we recommend in our new book from Taylor and Francis's CRC Press *Scrum Project Management*, that the scrum user begin by using the standard project management activities such as defining scope, developing a statement of work, and, most importantly, creating a work breakdown structure. Additionally, the book shows how this technique born out of technical projects will work wonderfully for entrepreneurial endeavors as well.

Using the WBS

The work breakdown structure (WBS) is the heart of project management and it is so important it has a U.S. Department of Defense military handbook (MIL-HDBK-881x) associated with it. Here are the main topics associated with the military handbook:

1. Integration, assembly, test, and checkout efforts
2. Systems engineering and program management
3. Training
4. Equipment
5. Services
6. Facilities
7. Data
8. Technical publications
9. Engineering data
10. Management data
11. Support data
12. Data depository
13. System test and evaluation
14. Development test and evaluation
15. Operational test and evaluation
16. Mock-ups
17. Test and evaluation support
18. Test facilities

19. Peculiar support equipment (items not currently in inventory and must be developed)

20. Test and measurement equipment

21. Support and handling equipment

22. Common support equipment (items currently in inventory)

23. Operational and site activation

24. System assembly, installation, and activation

25. Checkout on Site

26. Contractor technical support

27. Site construction

28. Site/ship/vehicle conversion (obviously military and defined as what must be done to accommodate the product—on the civilian side we would look for opportunities for reuse)

29. Industrial facilities

30. Construction/conversion/expansion

31. Equipment acquisition or modernization

32. Maintenance (industrial facilities)

33. Initial spares and repair parts

Work Breakdown Structure Is a Direct Reflection of Requirements

With this approach, the voice of the customer is the driving mechanism for the scope of work, which, in turn, drives the requirements. We don't care if the requirements come from external sources or if they are internally derived. When requirements change, the work breakdown structure must change, because the work breakdown structure is precisely a functional decomposition of top-level deliverable elements. Once we have a visible structure, updating, re-planning, as well as re-estimating cost, and duration become simplified because all elements are visible.

The work breakdown structure is important to scrum project management because the cost centers are always derived from project deliverable elements (so much so that it is easy to develop templates for the work breakdown structure). The work breakdown structure provides the product backlog for the subsequent sprints and distributes the work to cost centers or other sprint teams. The concept works because products are composed of systems which, in turn, are composed of subsystems and then components and so on. If we start with a top-level assembly as the first or second level on the work breakdown structure, we can easily break the product down into "atomic" level tasks.

The same approach will apply if we are dealing with other deliverables such as internal specifications, models, failure mode and effects analyses (FMEA), and the total round of documents that any formal quality system requires.

Modifying Work Breakdown Structure to Reflect Changing Requirements

Tracking updates to the project scope or changing deliverables to meet requirements is where many projects go astray, including scrum projects. Lack of change management or incompetent configuration control makes it difficult to compare what we have with our expectations and needs. With scrum, we derive the product backlog directly from the work breakdown structure. The work breakdown structure is not simply an action item list. The work breakdown structure is a formal document designed to support cost and schedule reporting (Earned Value Management) as part of a contract; we can derive our action item lists, schedule, and budgets from the work breakdown structure.

How Deep Should the Work Breakdown Structure Go?

We will deconstruct the work breakdown structure as far as we need to go such that we can put items into our product backlog planning document with minimal effort. This is another area where projects go astray with missing items and misunderstood or nonexistent dependencies between tasks. This is not the case with the scrum approach, as we are focused on the immediate goal. If we have an especially short planning horizon, as is used in our scrum project management approach, then we must have tasks that can be accomplished during that period. We call this highly-detailed analysis "'atomic'" decomposition because we are decomposing the higher-level tasks until further decomposition no longer adds value. When we complete this task, we will have a list of "atoms" that become part of our other planning documents. Once we have these "atoms," we are ready to go! We now take the "atomic" tasks and use these to populate the product backlog. If we have set up our breakdown correctly, we should not need to ever list the higher-order tasks—completing the "atomic" tasks in appropriate order will automatically result in completion of the higher-order task.

Setting Up the Scrum Sprint

We select meaningful tasks from the product backlog to populate the sprint backlog. These tasks can be low-hanging fruit that we think we can do quickly or, more importantly, they can be accomplished in priority order so long as we remember our dependencies. A dependency occurs when one task is dependent on the completion of another task. A typical sprint will last from two weeks to four weeks.

The sprint list is quasi-sacred. That means the sprint team should only consider breaking the sprint if a dire emergency occurs and they have a higher-level champion who is willing to override the sprint. Otherwise, the goal is to complete our tasks while tracking them with a burndown chart. The burndown chart will show us progress against plan (much like an earned value management chart) and may reveal that we bit off too much to chew or that the team is the target of interruptions from other parts of the enterprise. In that event, portions of the sprint backlog may be eliminated from the present sprint and postponed to a subsequent sprint. Likewise, if the sprint is accomplishing more then expected, the opportunity will be seized with the addition of components from the product backlog.

Daily Sprint Meetings

The daily sprint meetings are where the status of the project is communicated. In this meeting we ask:

- What did we do yesterday?

- What are we doing today?

- What are the "bottlenecks" and "road blocks?"

The scrum master will facilitate the meeting. The burn down chart will be reviewed and the areas of risk and constraint will be openly discussed.

Sprint Retrospective and Planning

At the end of the sprint, we take time to review what we have done, to see what:

- We did well

- We could do better

This meeting should be brief but thorough. We expect two-week retrospectives to be about half an hour and four week retrospectives to scale to an hour. At the end of the retrospective, we plan for the next sprint as a team.

Since scrum is a high-intensity technique with accelerated tempo, we do not want our meeting schedules to violate this ideal. The meetings should be organized well enough that we are not wasting the time of our team or teams. We will know that we have achieved this goal when the complaints about the meetings largely disappear.

Scaling Up Scrum

We can scale our scrum approach to larger development processes by creating the scrum of scrums. Basically, the scrum master (leader) from a scrum team at some level becomes the team member at the next higher level if this approach makes sense. If this choice does not make sense, then we either elect a team member to represent at the higher level or use some kind of round robin approach so that every team member receives a chance to represent the group.

Scaling Scrum Down

What is the pomodoro technique? The pomodoro technique is a personal productivity implementation of scrum. Pomodoro, as one might expect, is similar but different. We do the following:

1. Get a small clock—a kitchen timer does this well (pomodoro is a kitchen timer that looks like a tomato)

2. Make a list of all things to do (product backlog)

3. Select a list for today (sprint backlog)

4. Prioritize the tasks

5. Set the clock for 25 minutes

6. Work on top priority task without break for 25 minutes (sprint)

7. Take a 3-5 minute break at end of pomodoro

8. Continue same task if not done on next 25 minute pomodoro

9. Record each pomodoro with an "X" on today's list (burndown chart…well, sort of)

Experience with the scrum technique shows that it increases tempo, allowing for focused achievement and a counter-attack on the myth of multiprocessing. You can download some more comprehensive instructions for pomodoro at http://www. pomodorotechnique.com. It is a PDF file of between 40 and 50 pages in length.

Some Thoughts on Scrum

We have used the scrum approach in a line management setting. We found no difficulties scaling the process to meet our needs. Some areas that were less than satisfactory were the burndown charts (kind of complicated) and the full-fledged work breakdown structure. On the other hand, the team enjoyed the improvement in the steady-state list of projects they were working on and the daily scrum meetings improved communication to the point where different departments were achieving some level of cross-fertilization of capabilities.

Interestingly, we were unable to keep the team focused long-term on the scrum approach in spite of the success at reducing backlogs. It seemed that some of the managers actually enjoyed fire fighting and the feeling they were saving the enterprise with their daring management skills, a bit like firefighters that set fires for the "rush" they get when they put them out!

VI. Exercises

- Explain with contrast and compare how a scrum burn down chart is similar/ dissimilar to a standard project management Gantt chart.

- Make an argument for or against the statement "Scrum is a waterfall approach, just more quickly reviewed."

- Here are the seven deadly sins (seven levels of purgatory):

  - *luxuria (lechery/lust)*

  - *gula (gluttony)*

  - *avaritia (avarice/greed)*

  - *acedia (acedia/discouragement/sloth)*

  - *ira (wrath)*

  - *invidia (envy)*

  - *superbia (pride)*

  - List seven (or more) deadly sins you have seen in project management

- Given a list of project management sins, explain how a maturity model can help to rectify the identified issues.

- Make an argument for or against the use of maturity models. Be specific.

- Just to be fair, here is a list of the seven cardinal virtues and the Latin names:

  - Chastity   Castitas
  - Temperance   Temperantia
  - Charity   Caritas
  - Diligence   Industria
  - Patience   Patientia
  - Kindness   Humanitas
  - Humility   Humilitas

  - Explain how these virtues can be incorporated into project management.

- Create your own list of virtues that assist in the management of projects.

- Brainstorm every defect you can associate with the maturity model approach.

- Write a well-reasoned essay about whether you believe the work is done when we have reached the highest levels of a maturity model.

- List some defects of the scrum approach to project management.

- List some benefits of the scrum approach to project management.

- Come up with ten ways to improve the scrum approach.

- If daily reporting seems to improve completion, explain why even faster reporting might have diminishing returns.

- Project: create a maturity model for the scrum approach!

- Major project: synthesize the levels of all the maturity models we have listed here and any others you can find. List your choices for candidate levels and tasks and support your choices with well-reasoned arguments.

- Explain why maturity models are an exercise in futility.

- Explain why maturity models are not an exercise in futility.

- Subjective/intuitive: describe how you as a project manager can find joy and exultation in the management of a project, come what may.

Endnotes

1. Baig, Moazzam Baig, Sidra Basharat, Manzil-e-Maqsood. *A Maturity Model For Quality Improvement In Higher Education.* Lahore, Pakistan: National University of Computer and Emerging Sciences, 2007.

2. BetterProductDesign.net. Design Maturity. BetterProductDesign.net/Design_Maturity.htm (accessed May 6, 2003).

3. Burnstein, Ilene, Taratip Suwannasart, and C.R. Carlson. *Developing a Testing*

Maturity Model: Part 1. Chicago, IL: Illinois Institute of Technology, 1996. http://kopustas.elen.ktu.lt/~rsei/PT/Developing a Testing Maturity Model Part I - Aug 1996.htm. (Accessed June 4, 2006).

4. Burnstein, Ilene, Taratip Suwannasart, and C.R. Carlson. *Developing a Testing Maturity Model: Part 2*. Chicago, IL: Illinois Institute of Technology, 1996. http://kopustas.elen.ktu.lt/~rsei/PT/Developing a Testing Maturity Model, Part II.htm. (Accessed June 4, 2006).

5. CMMI Product Team. *CMMI® for Development, Version 1.2*. Pittsburgh, PA: Software Engineering Institute, 2006.

6. Electronic Industries Alliance. *Systems Engineering Capability Model, EIA 731.1*. Arlington, VA: Electronic Industries Alliance, 2002.

7. Ibrahim, Linda, Bill Bradford, David Cole, Larry LaBruyere, Heidi Leinneweber, Dave Piszczek, Natalie Reed, Mike Rymond, Dennis Smith, Michael Virga, and Curt Wells. *The Federal Aviation Administration Integrated Capability Maturity Model (FAA-iCMM), Version 2.0, An Integrated Capability Maturity Model for Enterprise-wide Improvement*. Washington, DC: Federal Aviation Administration, 2001.

8. Kwak, Y.H. and Ibbs, C.W. (2000) "Berkeley Project Management Maturity Model: Measuring the Value of Project Management." *2000 IEEE EMS International Engineering Management Conference*, Albuquerque, New Mexico, Aug 13-15, 2000, pp. 1-5.

9. Moore, Christopher. T*he Learning Management Maturity Model, version 1, revision 2*. Baltimore, MD: Thinq Learning Solutions, Inc., 2002.

10. Paulk, Mark C., Bill Curtis, Mary Beth Chrissis, and Charles V. Weber. *Capability Maturity Model for Software, Version 1.1*. Pittsburgh, PA: Software Engineering Institute, 1996.

11. van Veenendaal, Erik, ed. *Test Maturity Model integration (TMMi), version 3.1*. Dublin, Ireland: TMMi Foundation, 2010.

APPENDIX 1 – CHANGE MANAGEMENT

Change and configuration management are critical for any project management work because they allow us to apply some level of control to product and process modifications. Total quality management tools can help understand the change implications on your project. Before we go too far, let us first delineate what is change management and configuration management.

I.   Change Management

Change management can be considered the input to the configuration management process. We have a request to make alterations to the project, process, or the product that must be evaluated.   We lay out the details of the change and we determine the implications upon the project of taking on the change. At the end, we either accept or reject the change. Accepting the change will then require configuration management.

There are metrics that are change management in orientation where TQM tools can be used to answer questions such as:

1. How often do particular projects undergo change (categorized by spending, technical areas, or some other hierarchy)?

2. Are there project types that are more subject to change (telematics systems versus instrument cluster)?

3. What is the typical impact in terms of cost and time to delivery?

4. Where (what customer or part of the company) do most of the changes originate?

5. How much time is spent with the typical change request evaluation?

6. How close are the estimated implications to the final impact of adopting the change (cost, time, product take rate, etc.)

An even longer planning horizon can provide the project manager and also line managers with clues about which processes within the organization could improve when scrutinized. For example, if we find that the time to make a decision to accept or deny the change is too long, we can turn our TQM tools toward that process and understand how the present process performs and, more importantly, where to alter and improve the process.

II.   Configuration Management

Experience suggests that an optimally running configuration management program will reduce erroneous fault reports and will also streamline test times. Consider, for example, the very probable scenario where the hardware has the required capabilities (such as communications support) while the software has as yet no such function. The test engineer may consume many hours with the mismatch between hardware and software before he is aware that he can find no such function to test in the software. Another example occurs when the test engineer reports a problem in a particular revision of software. Suppose we receive a subsequent revision of software that provides a correction to that fault. The next software release exhibits the original fault again. This situation could represent a symptom of inadequate configuration management of the software builds, since we would anticipate that the fault would disappear once corrected. Unfortunately, if we don't control our configuration, we will not really know what we are testing.

In general, any enterprise that has change to product or process is completely dependent on robust configuration management, whether the product is software, firmware, or hardware, or even the processes that deliver those items. Sending the customer the incorrect version of a product is a quick way to become a "de-sourced" supplier; that is, to lose business due to configurational incompetence.

As we will see shortly, configuration management provides a known point on which to control subsequent changes. When we know the state of the system at any point in time, we mitigate some of the risks that occur with integration of the changes. We no longer *think* we know; instead, we use the configuration management system to understand our alterations. We do this via configuration baselines. When we make changes to the system, product, or process without this revision control point, we know little about the scope of any unintended consequences of that change.

We must keep track of the configuration of our systems even when those systems don't include software. The graphic above is of a collection of parts. Those parts are:

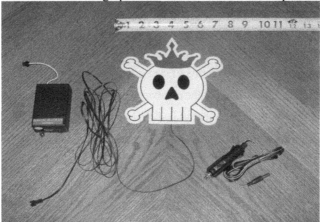

Figure A1.1 The complete kit of electroluminescent decal for automotive windshield power supply, interface connector and harness.

- An inverter
- A wire harness
- A plug-in adapter for automotive power point
- An electroluminescent graphic

Each of these parts makes up the system. Each of these parts was constructed to deliver the functionality. We show how this looks in a car below where the system is installed in a vehicle—an illuminated graphic attached to the rear window of a car. Each of these parts can be modified. We would keep track of these changes and continue to ensure the various parts work together to deliver the appropriate collection of features. If we alter any of the constituent parts, we will update those part numbers

Figure A1.2 Product night view in car.

and attributes changes we made to the product. We will use this to delineate various embodiments of the system. We make sure we keep the system intact and functioning as we plan. We can also talk to the customers and the manufacturing team and speak the same language when it comes to the definition of the system incarnations. As an added bonus, we have some measure of traceability from our previous actions and any

Figure A1.3 Illuminated graphic in the car from a distance.

performance issues with the product that occur after the changes should be readily discernible.

Configuration management systems help to deliver coordinated software and hardware. They do this by easily identifying features and functional content within a particular union of software and hardware. Not only that, we can have straightforward traceability of function and feature growth over specification revisions as well as over content—hardware and software—revisions and delivery. Throughout the process, we can always clearly identify changes, execute pre-release containment, and identify compatible components within a system.

In order to deliver robust software or hardware, configuration management is necessary to allow for the plan and coordination of the software and hardware functionality. In short, functionality, deliveries, testing, and production follow a master plan rather than ad hoc pandemonium. With appropriate planning we will always know the following items:

- Features and feature revision level
- Software revision level
- Hardware revision level
- Subassembly revision level in the case where we have firmware "burned" onto a chip
- Systems integration (phased feature release)

Also important will be the ability to trace problems found (eventually, and not necessarily during testing) to some combination of component parts of the product. With effective configuration management, problems in this area become less probable and those that do arise can be quickly solved. Effective configuration management makes it possible to focus on the parts that are not performing well. For example, consider a product that has undergone a number of changes, each of which has gone through our verification work but somehow made it into the field. If we pursued this product with sufficient configuration management, we would be able to isolate the specific configuration of the product in which the problem arises.

IEEE standard 1220 favors the master plan approach to system engineering, providing an alternative to standard project management practices. Configuration management is a component of such a master plan.

Configuration management can be applied to specifications (documentation), models, simulation, hardware, software, the combination of hardware and software, and to system integration. The truth is that configuration management can be applied to just about anything where iterations need to be known and tracked.

- Product baseline
- Product change management
- Number of product changes
- Time spent on product changes
- Cost impact of changes
- Product configuration (CMP)
- Test configurations (test coverage)
- Configuration audit

We can apply the TQM tools to the configuration management process as well.

With appropriate attention to details and settings:

- How often do we have configuration management problems (audit performance statistics and Pareto)?

- Do our suppliers have a robust configuration management system for their build processes (do we see recurring problems)?

- Can we trace the present revision of a product through the iterations taken to get to this point?

- How much do we spend on our configuration management? How much do we spend upon configuration management failures?

- Do we have check-in and check-out statistics?

A. IEEE Council

IEEE standard 1042 provides some guidance upon what is required to have a performing configuration management system. Specifically and of significant interest are the four tool levels: 1) basic tool set, 2) advanced tool set, 3) online tool set, and 4) integrated tool set

Basic Tool Set

The basic tool set consists of:

- Database management systems

- Report generators

- A means for maintaining separate dynamic and controlled libraries

- A file system for managing the check-in and check-out of units for controlling compilations and capturing the resulting products

Advanced Tool Set

The advanced tool set consists of:

- Items from the basic tool set

- Source code control programs that will maintain version and revision history

- The ability to compare programs for identifying (and help verify) changes

- Tools for building or generating executable code

- A documentation system (word processor) to enter and maintain specifications and associated user documentation files

- A system / software change request authorization tracking system that makes requests for changes machine readable

On-Line Tool Set

This set of tools includes:

* Generic tools of the advanced tool set integrated so they work from a common database

* A tracking and control system that brings generation, review, and approval of changes online

* Report generators working on-line with the common database, and a tracking system that enables the configuration management group to generate response to on-line queries of a general nature

Integrated Tool Set

The integrated tool set includes:

* On-line tools covering all functions

* An integrated engineering database with command built into the on-line engineering commands commonly used in designing and developing programs

* The integration of the commands with the on-line management commands for building and promoting units and components

B. Military

Military Standard 973 and Military Handbook 61 spell out four requirements for any configuration management system: 1) configuration identification; 2) configuration control; 3) configuration status accounting; and 4) configuration auditing. We will review each of these areas in the following sections.

Configuration Identification

To establish configuration identification, we must have the means to define a configuration item. In DoD software implementation, these are known as computer system configuration items (CSCIs or "siskies"). Generally, we pick an item and define the initial version of it as a baseline. This baseline will function very much as a base-line in a project management tool; namely, it allows us to know where we started and to detect and record change as the project or product development proceeds.

In many cases, we will define a part number, describe the feature content, apply a specific function and revision level, and we may even define further level of refinement. At every stage, configuration identification provides a process and product that is documentable and controllable.

Configuration Control

Configuration control is the part of configuration management where we supervise changes to the configuration of the product, whether it is software or hardware. In some cases, we may re-baseline the product. In general, we usually have only one version in release at a time. Control can become complicated during transitions when more than one version may be available; in these cases, we can control our versions with part numbers. Management can also become complicated with multiple component configurations for a system, particularly in the age of mass customization of products. With motor vehicles, we often see attribute-based requirement or line sequencing, in which the parts are customized to the vehicle identification number (itself a form of configuration identification). This production complication has ramifications for the verification activities. Specifically, these production variations have to be accounted for in the testing activities with alternative configurations of test cases.

Typical configuration control baselines might be the following:

- Allocated Baseline (ABL). The initially approved allocated configuration documentation, which is often allocated from a higher level or system.

- Functional Baseline (FBL). The approved functional configuration documentation that adds verification to the mix.

- Product Baseline (PBL). The approved product configuration documentation which generally includes a description of the acceptance testing and may also include the actual hardware and/or software.

In all cases, a configuration baseline involves an agreed upon description of the attributes of a product, at a specific point during development, which becomes the starting point for defining change. There should be an approved and released document or documents (revision) for every specific version, the purpose of which is to provide a solid foundation for managing change. These baselines always include the currently approved and released configuration documentation, and with software, a released set of files making up a software version and related configuration documentation.

Configuration Status Accounting (CSA)

Configuration status accounting is used primarily for the reporting feature, although its significance is much broader. Under CSA, we record changes and update configurations when items change and we issue reports. When dealing with software we might audit the frequency of check-in/check-out to verify that the developers are protecting intellectual property. We may audit the release documentation to confirm that the proposed or planned configuration has been delivered. Additionally, we might take a look at the count of changes to get an idea of the stability of a given release.

CSA can be supported by software (for example, the open source product Subversion) and it is definitely a component of product data management software, product life cycle management software, and document control packages. However, it is also possible to use spreadsheet software.

Configuration Auditing

Configuration auditing has two primary actions: for physical configuration and for functional configuration, both of which will compare the configuration expected to what is delivered. A physical configuration audit compares existing documents to contracted or required documents and a functional configuration audit verifies functionality against requirements. The results are part of the release notes.

Hardware

Hardware configuration management is most commonly accomplished through the part number system and the associated bill of materials. The bills themselves can take on different structures; for example, modular, phantom, or one-level bills. It is not unreasonable to ask that the bills of materials themselves fall under configuration management control.

Software

With software, we usually are well-served using dedicated software configuration management tools; for example:

- Subversion
- Revision control system (RCS)
- Concurrent version system (CVS)

All of these programs lock out other users from making changes during an edit and provide some level of reporting. They basically mechanize the software build process by defining what modules are included and what revision of the modules. Most "make" programs have a means of accessing the software configuration management system automatically.

Configuration and Verification

Any testing performed on a configuration must be identified explicitly with the following information:

1. Hardware release including subassemblies
2. Software version
3. Developmental version or
4. Released product version (they are not necessarily the same)

The configuration items should be linked to the test cases and test documents. The same is true for the specific requirements. A link between requirement and test cases is also part of the configuration management process. Of course, the documents themselves can also come under configuration management.

Release Notes

Working in concert with configuration management are release notes. Release notes are the means by which the development team communicates with the downstream users of the product. We document known limitations of the product, incomplete functionality, and changes that were approved and developed for the release. These notes are broken down by hardware (when there is a hardware release) and software. Understanding the effectiveness the change and configuration management capability of an organization allows the TQM project manager to assess the risks and plan the project in a way that improves the probability of success.

APPENDIX 2 – TEMP EXAMPLE

NOTE: at the time the original version of this document was created, many items were undefined and were so marked. You will see them in this appendix very much as they were in the original version. We made an effort to conceal the identities of the corporations involved. A TEMP is a test and evaluation master plan.

I. Overview

Beginning in 1998, Company A began a process that was to lead to the Modular Gauge System (MGS), a replacement of instrumentation for their then current heavy-duty line of trucks. Customer and supplier are working in concert on this project.

This TEMP applies to the MGS system, including at least the following:

- Data concentrator unit (DCU)
- Optional content unit (OCU)
- Gauges
- Speedometer
- Tachometer
- 2-inch gauges

This TEMP will describe MGS, Phase II.

A. Mission Description

The purpose of the modular gauge system is to take what has been learned from and earlier project and develop the in-cab electronics and communications systems for the customer's medium-duty truck line with potential application to the heavy-duty line as well. The supplier is responsible for the electronic gauge cluster, all buttons (switches) in the form of cluster add-ons or "b-panel" add-ons, the electrical system controller, and the power distribution module. Further descriptions of the system can be found in the MGS system specification.

B. System Objective Assessment

Truck in-cab subsystems and engine compartment systems are exposed to a host of environmental threats as well as anomalies on the data busses. Any subsystem may be exposed to electromagnetic interference as well as be guilty of supplying its own emissions. Therefore the MGS subsystems must be tested for

- Temperature effects
- Humidity effects
- Combined temperature/humidity effects
- Electromagnetic interference and EM compliance (EMC)
- Electrostatic discharge (ESD)
- Randomly oscillating signals (crank)

- Under-voltage and over-voltage
- Complete software testing

C. System Description

The DCU/OCU is an electronic assembly that provides multiple analog and switched input interfaces to read the status of various user switches and sensors. Additional features include one on board public SAE J1708 serial data link interface for performing electronic control of a gauge cluster with an optional digital display.

The gauge package consists of individual electronic assemblies that provide an arbitrary number of gauge functions; in general, each gauge performs one major function and has one LED. The speedometer has an odometer display and the tachometer has a multi-purpose LCD with a push-button to activate different features.

All components of the MGS system communicate using a public J1708 bus with the J1587 protocol.

Key MGS System Core Capability Features and Subsystems

The following are key features:

- Transducer modules are used wherever it makes sense to do so
- Additional analog inputs are used on the DCU
- Stepper motor-driven gauges to improve sweep appearance, reliability, and form factor
- LED telltale lights for reliability
- 2-inch gauges use micro-controller with UART (no "bit-banging")
- Upgrade-able software through flash memory on DCU

Interfaces with Existing or Planned Systems

Interfaces for the various parts of this system are defined in the following documents:

- J1708/J1587 Interface for MGS

Critical System Characteristics

- Upgradability
- System can be upgraded using a service tool
- Parameters can be modified to change the behavior of the product
- Standards
- System will use the SAE J1587 standard for system-wide communication
- Reliability
- System failure modes controlled (tool of choice = FMEA)

- Maintainability
- Design feature
- Serviceability
- Design feature
- Parts availability
- Customer service issue
- Dealer services
- Customer service issue
- Lifecycle costs
- Total cost of operation must be a consideration. If product has a low initial price but does not reach reliability goals, the real price goes up
- Low initial price
- Standard consideration
- Durability
- Life testing
- Power-train performance
- Driver environment
- Human factors
- Maneuverability
- Visibility
- Cab roominess
- Human factors
- Entry/egress
- Human factors
- Improved fit and finish
- Customer in-vehicle testing
- Weight
- Customer in-vehicle testing
- Ground clearance
- Customer in-vehicle testing

D. Critical Technical Parameters

Critical technical parameters for MGS can be defined as those measurable critical system characteristics, including software, that when achieved, support the attainment of the measures of effectiveness and suitability. The table in this section lists known critical parameters (and it will be updated on a continuing basis for the duration of the development portion of this project). For each software package (SWP), a specified number of parameters will be evaluated.

- Critical technical parameter
- Qualification
- Lines of code versus bug count
- Paired indicator over life of development and code maintenance for SWP's 1-4
- Durability, reliability
- Life testing
- Suitability
- Developmental test and evaluation

E. Maintenance Concept

The MGS maintenance concept consists of the supplier support for hardware and software in accordance with the contracted two-level support strategy (on-site, off-site). Hardware and software maintenance for prototypes will be provided by the supplier.

F. Training Concept

The supplier will provide internal training on an as-needed basis. Supplier maintains an open-line with customer with respect to phone "walkthroughs" and other training support activities for customer personnel.

G. System Operational and Support Capability

For developmental test and evaluation, the primary center of functions and capabilities will be located the supplier location in NoNombre, Mexico. For operational test and evaluation, the primary center for functions and capabilities will be located at the customer Technical Center in BigCity, State, with secondary support from the supplier.

H. System Administration Support

During the development phase, system administration will be performed by the supplier's MGS project organization. During the operational phase, system administration will transition to the customer technical center and company A.

I.   Data Conversion and Loading

Type of data
Disposition of data

Textual
Microsoft Word for Windows format
MIL-STD when available, then
IEEE when available, then
SAE
Spreadsheet
Microsoft Excel
Database
Microsoft Access
Presentation
Microsoft Powerpoint
J1587/J1708 data
Eaton Jtools

II.   Integrated Test Program Summary

A. Integrated Test Program Schedule

Integrated time sequencing of the critical test and evaluation phases are displayed in the time line in Appendix A. This schedule will be updated on a regular basis to include the most current information on critical events such as project milestones, major reviews, major deliveries, developmental test and evaluation, and operational test and evaluation.

B. Evolutionary Development

The lifecycle model for this project reflects evolutionary development; that is, at every given milestone based on a SWP, the customer will possess a package that represents a functional prototype.

Scope

The schedule encompasses all event profiles from acquisition, through developmental test and evaluation, operational test and evaluation, and deployment of the system. As noted previously, this system will be developed as incremental hardware/software blocks, or packages. As each package evolves, it is integrated with all previous levels until the full system is developed, tested, and deployed. The SWP's are defined in the developmental test and evaluation and operational test and evaluation sections of this document. Each SWP will experience developmental testing, primarily in the supplier facility and secondarily in the customer technical center. As described in the operational test and evaluation section of this document and a separate operational test and evaluation description, operational testing will commence as early as is practically possible. Product configuration baselines will be established for each SWP and each SWP will be subject to a functional configuration audit before delivery to customer.

C. Management

Key Organizational Responsibilities

Supplier will take the lead for the overall development, testing, evaluation, and fielding of the MGS system. PM customer and supplier PM MGS, as system codevelopers for the MGS system, will certify the readiness of the MGS system to undergo operational test and evaluation. The test integrated product team (IPT) will ensure that the requirements are included in the formulation of the basic operational test and evaluation resource, planning, and execution documents. Organizational responsibilities for the conduct of the MGS system program are provided in the MGS system program management documentation (MGS SEMP). Key T&E program responsibilities include:

Program manager—PM MGS is responsible for the overall control and direction of the test program and serves as the Test Integrated Product Team (IPT) coordinator. The IPT coordinator is the single point of contact in the MGS system PMO for all matters related to the planning, conduct, schedule, and budgeting of test and evaluation. PM MGS oversees the verification and validation (V and V).

Independent operational tester—at their discretion, customer will designate specific customers as independent operational testers.

Test Site—Each test site may provide representation as an associate member to the IPT and will review the TEMP and other test documentation (in general, cooperative assessment between the northwest and TexTown). In addition the sites will provide resources and assistance required for testing including: test personnel, facilities, and assistance in identification/collection of test data.

Initial Operational Capability (IOC)

IOC will be achieved at the first attainment of the capability to employ effectively the MGS system of approved specific characteristics, and which is manned or operated by a trained, equipped, and supported test team.

For the MGS system, the following definitions apply to the process of establishing IOC.

IOC certification: Statement that service believes that the program, upon successful completion of IOTE, will deliver IOC capability.

Implementation: All the work which goes into getting the system up and running. It includes data conversion, data loading, and some cut-over period. It includes a period of dual operation before acceptance of the system.

IOC Declaration: The statement that an initial operating capability has been achieved at both sites. It occurs after implementation, data loading, and initial training have been accomplished.

Full Operational Capability (FOC)

FOC will be achieved at the full attainment of the capability to employ effectively the MGS system of approved specific characteristics, and which is manned or operated by trained, equipped, and supported users.

III. Developmental Test and Evaluation Outline

A. Developmental Test and Evaluation Overview

Developmental test and evaluation addresses the system's technical and functional characteristics (hardware, software, communications) and contributes to the acquisition and fielding of an effective, supportable, and safe system. The MGS system developmental test (DT) will be conducted on target hardware using real, supplemental, and user prepared data. The MGS system Developmental test and evaluation is designed to determine whether the MGS system engineering design and development process is complete, the system design risks have been minimized, and the MGS system meets the technical and functional specifications. Developmental test and evaluation is accomplished through formal developmental testing and the continuous evaluation (CE) process conducted to ensure that all capabilities and requirements of the system are exercised and analyzed. This process validates technical and functional design and the system's ability to perform in a simulated operational environment specifically designed to stress the system under normal and peak loading conditions. The results of all supplier DT will be documented by the supplier in a formal report that will be supplied to customer. The analysis of formal test reports and other available data will enable supplier and customer to render a knowledgeable, accurate, and complete evaluation. This information will form the basis for technical recommendations for the MGS system and will be documented for use by the members of the project in the milestone decision process. The recommendations will confirm system readiness for operational test.

Developmental Test and Evaluation

Developmental test and evaluation of the MGS system in support of the deployment decision will be conducted during the development phase. Software development tests (SDT) and software qualification tests (SQT) constitute the developmental test and evaluation for the MGS system.

The MGS system SWP1, SWP2, SWP3, and SWP4 encompass all the requirements previously assigned to all previous levels of a given SWP. Due to the Evaluation Report recommendations, SWP 1 requirements will be re-tested during the SWP1 and 2 developmental test and evaluation process and likewise throughout the development process. A table will identify numerous critical technical parameters which were not successfully demonstrated because the requirements were not coded into the system, failed as coded, or test procedures were not adequately developed to demonstrate the requirement. The program manager has instituted risk analysis and handling measures to ensure these types of problems will be minimized. The first step taken by the program manager will be to establish viable configuration management control (standard procedure at supplier). The next step will be to resolve requirements definition conflicts between the developer, user, and tester. This step also enhances configuration management. The follow-on step will ensure that the test procedures capture all the SWP1, SWP2, SWP3, and SWP4 requirements to be tested. The MGS system metrics will confirm software maturity.

The evaluation of future DT includes, but is not limited to, the following elements:

Performance

1. Determine how well the software supports system performance.
2. Evaluate system response time for conformance to specified time tolerances.
3. Evaluate how well the system performs under load.
4. Evaluate system behavior under abnormal conditions.

Accuracy and Validity

1. Determine the degree of correctness and exactness of data processed by the system.
2. Evaluate system accuracy by the correctness of data and system level decisions and the proximity of computations to expected results.
3. Evaluate conversion processes to ensure that data handling procedures are described and executed correctly. Similarly, the processing that converts the database into the other communications protocol must be evaluated. Recordings resulting from the bridging process must be verified and validated.

Security

Evaluate security issues to ensure the system satisfies the appropriate security requirements and regulations, if any, to support the fielding of a secure, trusted system.

Sustainability and Survivability

Evaluate recovery and restart procedures to ensure that users can overcome potential processing malfunctions.

Interoperability/Communications

Determine the degree to which data is correctly exchanged and interpreted between subsystems.

1. Evaluate the acceptance of legal transmissions and the rejection of illegal transmissions.
2. Evaluate whether prioritization of transmissions is done correctly.
3. Evaluate interface considerations to include inter-system and intra-system data transfer and transmission of data over communication links.

Usability/Manpower and Personnel Integration

Determine the requirements of human interface with the system to prepare input and to interpret output of the system.

1. Evaluate system response to user interaction. The system should accept legal entries and reject illegal entries without any system degradation.

2. Evaluate training to ensure the adequacy of product descriptions. customer will have to negotiate with supplier on this support issue.

3. Evaluate the effort required by the user to access, prepare, and interpret data. The system should demonstrate a relative ease of use through the absence of confusing and complicated procedures and data presentations; i.e., the cluster should meet FMVSS requirements as well as customer ergonomic and styling requirements.

Reliability, Availability, and Maintainability (RAM)

1. Reliability—Evaluate to ensure that an item can perform its intended functions for a specified interval under stated conditions.

2. Availability—Evaluate the degree to which an item is in an operable and committal state at the start of the mission, when the mission is called for at an unknown (random) point in time.

3. Maintainability—Evaluate the ability of an item to be retained in, or restored to, a specified condition when maintenance is performed by personnel having specified skill levels, using prescribed procedures and resources at each prescribed level of maintenance and repair.

Developmental Test Readiness Review (DTRR)

Prior to each developmental software release, the supplier program manager and appropriate staff will conduct a brief DTRR to ensure that equipment, documentation, and personnel needs are being met. Requirements documents will be compared to test results to determine and evaluate the system's ability to meet requirements. The PM and team leaders will ascertain whether appropriate configuration management activities are being followed as well as required reporting.

Software Test and Evaluation Panel Metrics

For this project, the most significant metrics are part of the failure reporting and corrective action system (FRACAS) used in software engineering. The tool currently used by supplier is Track Record®. If desired by customer, supplier will also supply lines of code (LOC) metrics.

Exit Criteria

Developmental testing is complete when the following occurs:

1. All SWPs are approved by customer

2. No problem category 1, 2, or 3 issues remain (mission failure, problem without

workaround, problem with workaround)

3. A "frozen" baseline is available for operational testing

B. Future Developmental Test and Evaluation

The purpose of the software package (SWP) methodology used in this document is to provide customer with usable and measurable results throughout the development life-cycle of this program. SWP1 should provide customer with basic communications functionality and some gauge activity. Subsequent SWP's will build on the capability of the preceding SWP's. The supplier would prefer that customer begin basic operational testing with SWP1 while realizing that SWP1 capabilities will probably not provide a legal set of instrumentation (i.e., use the test track or parking lot to wring out the hardware and software).

Software Package 1 (SWP1)

Configuration description
Undefined should be product of customer/supplier project coordination planning.
Developmental test and evaluation objectives
SWP1 objectives are the following:

- Verify J1939 communications

- Verify J1587 communications

- Verify speedometer and tachometer performance

- Verify stepper motor behavior (environmental & endurance)

Developmental Test and Evaluation Events, Scope of Testing, and Basic Scenarios

MGS SWP1 testing will be conducted at the supplier development facility in Mexico. The SDT will be controlled by the system developer with monitorship by customer (if desired). The system developer evaluation methodology will be both test-analyze-fix-test and activities as specified in the test plan. The SDT will be scheduled for a period of two weeks. The first week is dedicated to test procedure verification, validation, and successful closure. The operator will perform tasks in accordance with the test procedures, record correct performance, and document failures and problems. Subsequently, he will perform regression testing of those test procedures that failed and associated test procedures with interdependencies. Prior to moving into the next phase, a successful DTRR must be documented.
Limitations
Developmental test support consists of live testing of units using the previously designed test bench. supplier will verify that the customer and two supplier test benches are configured identically. Interface testing will occur at every SWP level.

Software Package 2 (SWP2)

Configuration description

Undefined should be product of customer/supplier project coordination planning. Developmental test and evaluation objectives

Undefined should be product of customer/supplier project coordination planning. Developmental test and evaluation events, scope of testing, and basic scenarios

Undefined should be product of customer/supplier project coordination planning. Limitations

Developmental test support consists of live testing of units using the previously designed test bench. supplier will verify that the customer and two supplier test benches are configured identically. Interface testing will occur at every SWP level.

Software Package 3 (SWP3)

Undefined should be product of customer/supplier project coordination planning. Configuration description

Undefined should be product of customer/supplier project coordination planning. Developmental test and evaluation objectives

Undefined should be product of customer/supplier project coordination planning. Developmental test and evaluation events, scope of testing, and basic scenarios

Undefined should be product of customer/supplier project coordination planning. Limitations

Developmental test support consists of live testing of units using the previously designed test bench. supplier will verify that the customer and two supplier test benches are configured identically. Interface testing will occur at every SWP level.

Software Package 4 (SWP4)

Configuration description

Undefined should be product of customer/supplier project coordination planning. Developmental test and evaluation objectives

Undefined should be product of customer/supplier project coordination planning. Developmental test and evaluation events, scope of testing, and basic scenarios

Undefined should be product of customer/supplier project coordination planning. Limitations

Developmental test support consists of live testing of units using the previously designed test bench. supplier will verify that the customer and two supplier test benches are configured identically. Interface testing will occur at every SWP level.

IV. Operational Test and Evaluation Outline

A. Operational Test and Evaluation Overview

MGS is being developed and fielded in four (4) increments; software package (SWP) 1,2, 3, and 4, as shown in the MGS integrated test program schedule. After the PM completes development of SWP4, an operational test and evaluation will be conducted by the operation test groups to support a milestone decision for completing MGS fielding. Testing for operational test and evaluation will be conducted at test sites chosen by customer and using a representative sample of hardware, software, users, and technical manuals.

The TEMP measures of effectiveness and suitability, listed in Paragraph 1.3, and the critical operational issues (COIs) will be addressed as shown in the test objectives for OTE. The total evaluation of MGS will not be completed until the operational test and evaluation for SWP4 is completed.

MGS operational test and evaluation is a multi-divisional effort among the operational test groups.

Prior to start of OTE for SWP4, customer and supplier (divisions) will hold an operational test readiness review (OTRR). The following is to be reported to the OTAs.

1. PM certifies MGS is ready to enter operational test and evaluation, as applicable.

2. PM certifies no software priority 1 and 2 problems remain in the system and workarounds have been developed for Priority 3 problems, with appropriate impact analysis.

3. PM provides test support packages.

4. Site representatives certify sites are ready for operational test and evaluation, as applicable.

5. PM and customer representatives certify SWP4 workarounds are ready for operational test and evaluation.

B. Critical Operational Issues

The critical operational issues listed below apply to the operational test and evaluation for SWP's 1–4:

Operational Effectiveness

COI 1. Performance. Does the MGS system support mission requirements to create, receive, distribute, and use communications as expected in the operational environment?

COI 2. Integration. Does the MGS system architecture handle all communication requirements as well as meet performance requirements?

Operational Suitability

COI 3. Security. Does the MGS system satisfy mission requirements for security by preventing unauthorized access to, disclosure of, damage to, transfer of, or alteration of sensitive information (e.g., upgrade of software in flash), and provide proper security labeling of information?

C. Future Operational Test and Evaluation

Undefined should be product of customer/supplier project coordination planning.

Initial Operational Test and Evaluation for SWP1 (IOTE)

Undefined should be product of customer/supplier project coordination planning.

Configuration description
See previous sections describing the configurations

Operational test and evaluation objectives
Undefined should be product of customer/supplier project coordination planning.
Operational test and evaluation events, scope of testing, and basic scenarios
Undefined should be product of customer/supplier project coordination planning.
Limitations
Undefined should be product of customer/supplier project coordination planning.

Operational Test and Evaluation for SWP2

Configuration description
See package 2 configuration
Operational test and evaluation objectives
Undefined should be product of customer/supplier project coordination planning.
Operational test and evaluation events, scope of testing, and basic scenarios
Undefined should be product of customer/supplier project coordination planning.
Limitations
Undefined should be product of customer/supplier project coordination planning.
Operational test and evaluation for SWP3
Configuration description
See package 3 configuration
Operational test and evaluation objectives
Undefined should be product of customer/supplier project coordination planning.
Operational test and evaluation events, scope of testing, and basic scenarios
Undefined should be product of customer/supplier project coordination planning.
Limitations
Undefined should be product of customer/supplier project coordination planning.

Operational Test and Evaluation for SWP4

Configuration description
See configuration description package 4.
Operational test and evaluation objectives
Undefined should be product of customer/supplier project coordination planning.
Operational test and evaluation events, scope of testing, and basic scenarios
Undefined should be product of customer/supplier project coordination planning.
Limitations
Undefined should be product of customer/supplier project coordination planning.

V.   Test and Evaluation Resource Summary

The following is a summary of key test and evaluation resources, both customer and the supplier, which will be used during the course of the acquisition program.

A. Test Articles

Test articles for the MGS system core test and evaluation (DT and operational test and evaluation) will consist of fully integrated MGS configurations. Each site configuration constitutes a test article. The site configurations will consist of developmental prototype system hardware/software and, ultimately, production representative system hardware and software configuration items (CIs) required to provide the MGS system core capabilities. All test sites will be involved for the entire duration of site SQT, IOTE, and operational test and evaluation test periods.

B. Test Sites and Communications

Customer will specify test sites and communications for operational test and evaluation. The bulk of the developmental test and evaluation activity will occur at the supplier facility in Mexico.

C. Test Support Equipment

Developmental Test (DT)

Common data processing equipment required for DT data collection and reduction may be supplied by typical off-the-shelf equipment. This will include:

- Hardware (1-3 each per test site)
- Work station and/or personal computer
- Printer
- J1939 hardware
- J1708 hardware
- Emulator hardware
- Software
- Microsoft Windows
- Microsoft Word for Windows
- Eaton Jtools
- Parasoft Jpro
- Emulator software

Operational Test (OT)

Operational testing requires installation in a MGS truck.

D. Threat Representation

Not applicable.

E. Test Targets and Expendables

Not applicable.

F. Operational Force Test Support

Not applicable.

G. Simulations, Models, and Testbeds

Simulations:
The supplier may use a "wrapper" around portions of the code before using the code with an emulator or burning it onto a chip.
Models:
None.
Testbeds:
1) The supplier will use two testbeds developed specifically for this project. These testbeds will be updated to reflect modifications from MGS1 to MGS.
2) The supplier will build a test "buck" to more accurately simulate truck conditions.

H. Special Requirements

None.

I. Test and Evaluation Funding Requirements

Developmental test and evaluation internal to supplier.
Operational test and evaluation internal to customer.

J. Manpower/Personnel Training

Test personnel will consist of designated test technicians at the two developmental test sites. These technicians may be engineers or technicians.

APPENDIX 3 – TIEMPO

Product Development Test and Inspection

With good planning, an organization can use test, inspections and evaluation as tools for competitive advantage. We will show how this works in an automotive environment; furthermore, the concepts easily generalize to any industry. A comprehensive approach is required which involves avoiding the need to have the quality function leave the product validation solely to the testing team, and worse still, at late stages in the process.

The test, inspection, and evaluation master plan operations adds an extra wrinkle to the test and evaluation master plan (TEMP). TIEMPO expands the concept of a test and evaluation master plan by focusing on staged deliveries of which each product/process release is a superset of the previous release and the test and inspection iterations are coordinated with releases. Under this plan, we can handle inspections as:

- Code reviews
- Code releases
- Design reviews
- Schematic reviews
- Prototype part reviews
- Production line reviews

A. Philosophy of the Master Plan

TIEMPO helps us reduce risk by developing our superset releases wherein each subset remains relatively untouched and most defects will reside in the new portion (the previously developed part of the product or process is now a subset and should have already proven to be defect-free). We use frequent critical reviews to guide design and to find faults. The frequent testing allows for verification evolution by stimulating quality and reliability growth.

B. Benefits of the Master Plan

Experience suggests that the following benefits arise from this approach:

- Reduced risk
- Identification of early activities to safeguard the quality—even before testing can take place
- Test and design release iterations planned (test tools and test processes developed in time to test)
- Frequent customer access for review of product evolution

C. One Industry Approach: Automotive/Vehicular

The standard approach in the vehicular industries is the advanced product quality planning (APQP) mode of the Automotive Industry Action Group (AIAG). The components of this approach are the concept, product development, process development, verification and validation, and feedback and corrective action—each with its own set of steps and input and outputs.

D. Failure Mode Effects Analysis (FMEA)

Two automotive tools that illustrate the connection between inspection and testing are the design failure mode effects analysis (DFMEA) and the process failure mode effects analysis (PFMEA). The tools facilitate critical reviews of either the design or the processes that produce the designed product (production processes). This tool critiques a particular design or process function using failure modes, causes, effects, and some estimated values. The risk priority number (RPN) is the product of the severity, probability, and detection estimates for a particular failure. The higher the RPN, the greater the risk to the product design or process. Recommended actions are often testing actions to determine if the estimates of severity, probability, and detection are valid or to determine another way to achieve the function. In any case, the results of the DFMEA or PFMEA have an impact on the design verification testing and production validation testing.

E. Design Verification Testing (DVT)

In the automotive world, DVT means we use prototype parts, prototype tooling, an unfinished production process, and maybe even hand-made parts. The purpose of DVT is to test out and verify design ideas before proceeding with development. TQM tools should be applied to the testing results to understand what the testing is telling the testing organization and the project manager—after all, the project manager is responsible for the project and the product quality.

F. Production Validation Testing (PVT)

In the automotive world, PVT means we use production software (if any), production components, production tooling, the final production process, and production information systems. The goal of PVT is to verify that product is manufactured correctly using a real production line.

G. Reliability Testing

We use reliability testing to assess the probable quality behavior of the product or process over some quantum of time. During reliability testing we can use small sample sizes when a baseline exists or larger sample sizes with no baseline. We use physical models for accelerated testing in order to compute probable product life, which can be hampered by lack of good models, especially when a baseline doesn't exist.

H. Inspection Points per APQP

APQP supports multiple inspection points such as bill of materials checks against parts and drawings, appearance approval, and the various review processes.

I. Inspection Caveats

By definition, an inspection is a form of quality containment (trapping the product or process which does not truly break the chain of cause and effect). The function of inspection, then, is to capture bad material and to stimulate meaningful corrective actions. The primary issue with any inspection lies in the length of the human attention span, which ranges from fifteen to twenty minutes, suggesting we have many rest periods or alternative work.

J. The Production Part Approval Process (PPAP) and Inspection

In the automotive approach, we have at least eighteen documents that we must provide to our customer. The list includes the following:

- Warrant (PSW)
- Parts (inspected)
- Drawings (inspected)
- Inspection results
- Lab and functional results (testing)
- Appearance approval report (inspection)
- Measurement system analysis studies (inspection and testing)
- Process capability results (inspection and testing)
- Capability study (inspection and testing)
- Process control plan (inspected and includes inspection in its domain)
- Gage study (inspection)
- FMEA (inspected)
- Flow diagram (inspected)
- Any other customer-specific requirement (inspected

All documents must be inspected before they go out or are reviewed with the supplier quality assurance personnel of the customer organization.

K. Product Development Phases

During product development in many industries, some kind of development (or "launch") process is followed. One hypothetical, generic model for such a launch process might look like the following:

- Concept
- System Level
- Preliminary Design

- Critical Design
- Test Readiness
- Production Readiness
- Launch

The design aspects will apply to process design just as much as to product or service design.

L. So, When Do We Start Testing?

We can do some kind of testing when we have accurate simulators or we have prototype hardware and/or we have prototype software. Testing becomes more formal as we near the launch of the product. We use early testing to verify the state of a design, whether process or product.

M. Types of Tests during Development

We use a variety of approaches to provide reasonable coverage as we attempt to uncover any significant product or process issues. Some of these kinds of testing include compliance testing to specification requirements, extreme testing which is intended to produce product damage as well as characterize the product, combinatorial testing to check all inputs against all outputs, and stochastic (sometimes call "exploratory") testing to randomize test inputs.

N. When Do We Start Inspecting?

One of the nice things about inspection is that it is typically non-destructive. While we often will study a small sample of product under extreme testing, large quantities and samples of product will need to be inspected if we are only inspecting for attributes rather than variables. We can inspect a product or process as soon as we have something at which to look and we can inspect, during development for the following:

- Requirements
- Design (hardware/software) and schematic reviews
- Cad modules
- Models hardware
- Models simulation
- Molds and tools
- Prototype parts
- Review process
- Bill of materials (BOM)
- Pricing

The previous list is not exhaustive, but it is suggestive of the kinds of characteristics we can use during our initial developmental inspections.

Types of inspection during development
We use bill of materials verification to compare the product with the drawings and with the bill itself. This type of inspection is usually tedious; however, we know that a BOM should be better than 98% accurate to support the manufacturing resources planning (MRP) system accurately. Additionally, we can use traceability matrices to verify product/process against the specification. We can use checklists at any phase of the process to assure ourselves that we have completed tasks. We can also inspect our design guidance documents for compliance and perform some level of attribute requirements checking.

O. Inspections—Gauge R&R

In the automotive world we study the accuracy of our machines, processes, and employees with gauge repeatability and reproducibility inspections. We can help ourselves with accurate templates and meaningful measurements.

P. Conclusion

Tests and inspections are critical for the successful launch of a new product or a major modification of a previously released product as well as for a new process. Both testing and inspection provide for verification and validation that the product and the process are functioning as expected. If all goes well, we can expect a successful launch. The automotive approach has been modified and used in the food and drug industry as the hazard analysis and critical control point system. Critical control points are often inspections for temperature, cleanliness, and other industry-specific requirements.
The following is a typical outline for a TIEMPO document:

1.   Systems introduction
    1.1.   Mission description
    1.2.   System threat assessment
    1.3.   Min. Acceptable operational performance requirements
    1.4.   System description
    1.5.   Inspection objectives
    1.6.   Critical technical parameters
2.   Integrated test, inspection evaluation program summary
    2.1.   Inspection areas (documents, code, models, material)
    2.2.   Inspection schedule
    2.3.   Integrated test program schedule
    2.4.   Management
3.   Developmental test and evaluation outline
    3.1.   Simulation
    3.2.   Developmental test and evaluation overview
    3.3.   Component test and evaluation
    3.4.   Subsystem test and evaluation
    3.5.   Developmental test and evaluation to dates

3.6.   Future developmental test and evaluation

3.7.   Live fire test and evaluation

4.   Inspection

4.1.   Inspection of models (model characteristics, model vs. real world)

4.2.   Inspection material (physical) parts

4.3.   Prototype inspections

4.4.   Post test inspections

4.5.   Inspection philosophy

4.6.   Inspection documentation

4.7.   Inspections software

4.8.   Design reviews

5.   Operational test an evaluation outline

5.1.   Operational test and evaluation overview

5.2.   Operational test and evaluation to date

5.3.   Features / function delivery

5.4.   Future operational test and evaluation

6.   Test and evaluation resource summary

6.1.   Test articles

6.2.   Test sites and instrumentation

6.3.   Test support

6.4.   Inspection (requirements and design documentation) resource requirements

6.5.   Inspection (source code) resource requirements

6.6.   Inspection prototype resource requirements

6.7.   Threat systems / simulators

6.8.   Test targets and expendables

6.9.   Operational force test support

6.10.   Simulations, models and test beds

6.11.   Special requirements

6.12.   Test and evaluation funding requirements

6.13.   Manpower/personnel training

APPENDIX 4 – PRODUCT VERIFICATION

I. Product Verification

Why would a project manager need TQM tools for testing? We suggest that the project manager is the person ultimately responsible for the quality, cost, and delivery of the product. He does this, of course, by working with the team. Two of these three areas can be understood relatively immediately. You know the cost of the product once you know what it takes to make the product. Likewise when you deliver the product, you know the delivery date of the product. The product quality does not have such an immediately visible measure. It is possible though, to learn something about the product quality during the testing.

A. Goals of Testing

In our testing book, *Testing of Complex and Embedded Systems*, we discuss the goals and objectives of product testing. The most important aspect is the philosophy of testing: we do not test the product to prove it is good; we test to reveal in what ways the product is not good.

B. Partial Testing

For example, consider a delivery of software for a particular electronic control unit (ECU) for a vehicle. This software is part of a system of a multitude of ECU's for the vehicle. In this case, the software delivery was late and the test department had only had the system in its entirety for a short period. When the systems integration testing was roughly 25% complete (see Figure A4.1), the project manager said, "We need to launch this out to field testing immediately to make the milestone date." A review of the faults found in the software at that 25% mark tells the project manager

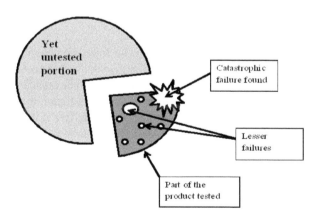

Figure A4.1 Partial testing fault distribution can be used to estimate what other faults may remain.

that there are a number of lesser faults—but one catastrophic failure. It is possible to immediately correct the one catastrophic problem and put out another revision of the software quickly. However, there will be little time to do more than confirm the corrective action solves the original catastrophic problem. Is this really a good idea? The project manager that has an understanding of the proportions and statistics would know that there is considerable risk that other faults remain, and that some of those could be even more catastrophic. It is not possible to say that the software is "good" at this point—it is more probable that there are more failures yet to be discovered within the software.

To completely verify most systems, the number of test cases can get to be more than can be executed expeditiously. In practice, this means that the testing of most products is a subset of the entire set of possible, realistic tests. So we are looking at a fraction of a fraction of the software test cases possible and we have already found significant challenges with product. This situation does not bode well for launching the product at

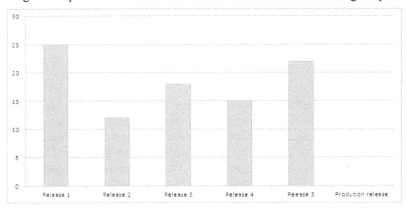

Figure A4.2 Rate of faults found in various releases of software.

the desired release date even for field test customers.

Let us look at the fault reports from a supplier. We have been monitoring the faults reported with each release. We find the distribution to look like Figure A4.2 and we are approaching production release date. Is this product ready to be launched? Maybe—it is difficult to say without knowing the severity of the faults found. It should be clear that there is little or no probability of the product being bug-free if we launch. We do not see any trend in the faults reported that would suggest that we would have a clean launch and a problem free product. In short, we have no statistical basis to inform a relatively risk-free release.

You can tell a great deal about the supplier's process capability by paying attention to the faults. For example, we receive a software release from our supplier. We find a set of problems—we note the symptoms and other fault information for the supplier to use to correct the non-conformance. We get another release of software from the supplier, perform the testing, and find additional problems with the software. We get another build of the software from our supplier with the corrective actions for the previously reported faults. With this build of software, we find non-conformances whose symptoms are identical with the preceding revisions of software. This provides the project manager with the clue that there are most likely issues with the build processes of the supplier. This historical information telegraphs the risks associated with the project. The wise project manager would make sure that all testing of this supplier's software would make extensive use of regression testing and not "bank" on testing only the intentional changes of the software.

- Defect arrival rate
- Defect closure rate
- Criticality of defect
- Frequency of repeat defect from supplier
- Expected or scheduled delivery to actual delivery
- Distribution of defect severity by software build iteration
- Distribution of defect (hardware, software, systems, specification)
- Distribution of defect (manufacturing, assembly, design)
- Distribution of defect severity by project or subassembly
- Distribution of defect by supplier over time
- Total number of test cases executed to test cases planned to be executed
- Defects found per test case executed
- Total costs for testing compared to faults found
- Distribution of faults found during exploratory testing
- Distribution of faults found from requirement based testing by product phase
- Distribution of faults found from requirement based testing by project phase
- Pareto of faults found from exploratory, requirements and stress based testing

The total quality management tools allow the project manager to peer into the testing world to assess how much risk to which the product or project is subjected. Histograms help the project manager understand the defect arrival rate and the severity of those defects. Statistical analysis of the distribution of the faults found will help the project manager assess the state of readiness of the product for the launch date. While it is true these sorts of things could be considered the focus of an organization's line or functional areas, it is also true that the project manager is responsible for the delivery to meet the customers' expectations. The project manager should be aware of the actual state of the product. To do that, the project manager must know what questions to ask and what measurements can help answer those questions.

By way of an example, let us consider a supplier that provides the project manager with software for an embedded product. In the course of a few deliveries we find that this supplier has, on more than one occasion, delivered the software with errors. That is not new. It happens often in product development work. However, what can we say about that supplier, when we see the same faults repeated during different releases? It could be happenstance or it could be that the supplier's configuration management or software build management is less than capable. We discover this information by converting the data we have into meaningful information and by reviewing the measurement that the project or organization accumulates over time. We know then, with this supplier, we must always conduct thorough regression testing and not be content with performing tests on only the changed portions of the software. To do otherwise in the face of the evidence that the supplier is less than capable would be risky. Of course, this evidence can be put to better use, by finding out what part of the supplier's configuration management or software build management systems are less than capable and coach them to improvement. This can be supported also with the use of total quality management tools.

INDEX

A

Activities
  non-essential 12
Activity Sequencing 127
Advanced Product Quality Planning 130
ANSI/ASQ Z1.4-2008 179
Artifacts 39
Attributes data 113
Automotive Industry Action Group 23

B

Buying
  MRO (maintenance, repair, and operations) 3
  MRP (manufacturing resource planning) 3

C

Capability maturity models 201
Change
  Culture 10
Change management 160
Characteristics–process 137
Characteristics–product 137
Checklists 59
Checksheets 59
CMMI 203
Common causes
  Versus special causes 54
Communications basics 82
Communications channels 84
Configuration and verification 170
Configuration auditing 168
Configuration control 166
Configuration identification 166
Configuration management
  Outsourced work 171
  Revision control 171
  Systems development 172
Configuration management 162
Configuration status accounting 167
Contingency budgets 151

Control chart
  Attributes 116
  CuSum 118
  EWMA 119
  Median 117
  Moving average 119
  Selection of variables 55
  Xbar-S 117
Control charts 54
Correlation 46, 48
Cost containment 78
Cost estimating 76
Cost performance index 111
Cost, product 28
Cost, project 32
Critical path 69
CuSum 120

D

Data
  Attributes 113
  Variables 116
Department of Defense
  Systems engineering
    fundamentals 18
Design for manufacturability 24
Duration estimates 127

E

EIA-731 205
Engineering process control 111
Engineering process control
  Box-Luceño 55
EPC 111
Escalation 85
Estimate at completion 111
EWMA 120

F

Failure types 184
  Type 1 failures 184
  Type 2 failures 184

Federal Motor Vehicle Safety Standards 23
Flailing 2
Flow charts 56
Functional decomposition 123

H

HACCP 155
Hazard analysis and critical control point method 155
Histogram 58

I

IEEE Standard
 830-1998 19
Inspection
 Attributes 179
 Continuous sampling plan 182
 First article 183
 Skip lot 182
 Variables 181
ISO 9001 6

L

Lean 4
Lean Six Sigma 4

M

Management by objective 10
Management, program 8
Management system
 Good 27
Maturity models
 CMM 203
 Design maturity model 209
 Education capability maturity model 204
 FAA 211
 ISO 15504/SPICE 219
 Learning management maturity model 219
 Philip Crosby Quality Maturity Grid 202

TMM 213
TMMI 215
Methods–control method 138
Methods–evaluation measurement technique 138
Methods–sample frequency 138
Methods–sample size 138
Methods–specification/ tolerance of product or process 138
Metrics 5
Metrics
 Importance of 16
 Product quality 193
 Project quality 189
 Tracking 189
Metrics, limitations of 36
MRO (maintenance, repair, and operations) buying 3
MRP (manufacturing resource planning) buying, 3

N

Network Diagram 67
Non-conformities 172

O

Organizational attributes 5
Organizational breakdown structure 129

P

Pareto plot 44
 Distortion 44
 Limitations 45
PDCA 6
PDCA—shewhart cycle 6
PERT 66
 Most likely time 68
 Optimistic time 68
 Pessimistic time 69
Process-based 7
Process failure mode and effects analysis 130
Project accuracy funnel 81
Project budgeting 75

Project budgets 77
Project closure 106
Project estimating techniques 66
Project estimation
  historical data 72
Project estimation
  experience / experts 71
Project gates 100
Project management 7
Project metrics and control 85
Project risk 111
Project termination
  techniques 100
Pugh matrix 20

R

Reaction Plan 138
Released products
  Managing 171
Release notes 170
Reliability 195
  Prediction 195
Requirements
  Functional 29
  Internal 34
  Performance 28
  Quality 22
    Internal 23
  Regulatory 34
Requirements and constraints matrix 20
Requirements, derived 34
Requirements, product 17
Requirements, project 31
Risk
  Management 147
  Qualitative 96
  Quantitative 97
  Representation 98
Risk management 96

S

Sarbanes-Oxley 6
Scatter plot
  versus line graph 54

Schedule 33
Schedule performance index 111
Schedule variance 111
Scope 125
Scrum and agile 223
Simulation 20
SIPOC 11
Six Sigma 4
Society of Automotive Engineers 23
Special causes
  versus common causes 54
Specifications 18
Standards 35
Statement of Work 125
Statistical process control 111
  attributes data
    applicability 113
Statistical process control 116
Statistics and Control 110

T

Tagged text 20
Tampering 55
Task Identification 128
Task Sequencing 128
TEMP 142
Test and Evaluation Master Plan 142
Testing
  Exposure time 37
Timeline review 2
Time-phased budget 127
Time phasing 75
To-complete-performance-index 112
Total Quality Management 2, 4
TQM 2
TQM Tools 42

U

UML 57
Understanding, Distortion of 38
United States Department of Transportation 23
U.S. Code 23

V

Variables data 116

W

WBS 65, 124
  Work Packages 129
Whitebook 105
Work breakdown structure 9, 65, 123

X

XML 20

VALUE TRANSFORMATION LLC

Value Transformation LLC provides consulting and training that will heal the wounds of processes gone wild. Value Transformation LLC is founded by Kim H. Pries and Jon M. Quigley. We have extensive knowledge and experience in product development (more than 50 years). This experience is largely focused upon software, specifically embedded products, and the manufacturing of those products. Some of the companies for which the founders have worked are found at our website below. Value Transformation has access to additional and similar talent to meet your needs.

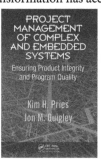
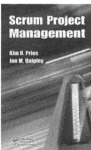
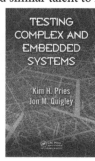

Six Sigma	Software verification and validation
Software quality	Production testing
Intellectual property generation	Lean manufacturing
Quality management	Setting up training programs
Reliability engineering	Formative assessment and summative evaluation
Software development	Project management
Quality/project management	Agile project management
Complex project management	Embedded project management

- Training online
- Training on-site
- Consulting
- Speaking

Visit us on the web at http://www.valuetransform.com or http://valuetransform.com/testimonial. Or you can email us at Jon.Quigley@valuetransform.com

The sooner you call, the sooner you will start to see the changes you need.

Milton Keynes UK
Ingram Content Group UK Ltd.
UKHW031129141024
449569UK00006B/339